Bent Props
and
Blow Pots

Bent Props and Blow Pots

A Pioneer Remembers Northern Bush Flying

Rex Terpening

HARBOUR PUBLISHING

Published by
Harbour Publishing Co. Ltd.,
P.O. Box 219,
Madeira Park, BC
V0N 2H0
www.harbourpublishing.com

Cover, design, typesetting and maps by Nick Murphy.
Photograph on page 1 courtesy of the Canada Aviation Museum, Ottawa. All photographs not otherwise credited are from the collection of the author.

Printed and bound in China through Colorcraft Ltd., Hong Kong

Harbour Publishing acknowledges financial support from the Government of Canada through the Book Publishing Industry Development Program and the Canada Council for the Arts; and from the Province of British Columbia through the British Columbia Arts Council and the Book Publisher's Tax Credit through the Ministry of Provincial Revenue.

National Library of Canada Cataloguing in Publication Data

Terpening, Rex, 1913–
Bent props and blow pots : a pioneer remembers
Northern bush flying / Rex Terpening.

Includes index.

ISBN 1-55017-287-5

1. Terpening, Rex, 1913–. 2. Bush flying—Canada, Northern. 3. Bush pilots—Canada, Northern—Biography. I. Title.
TL540.T476A3 2003 629.13'092 C2003-911081-8

Contents

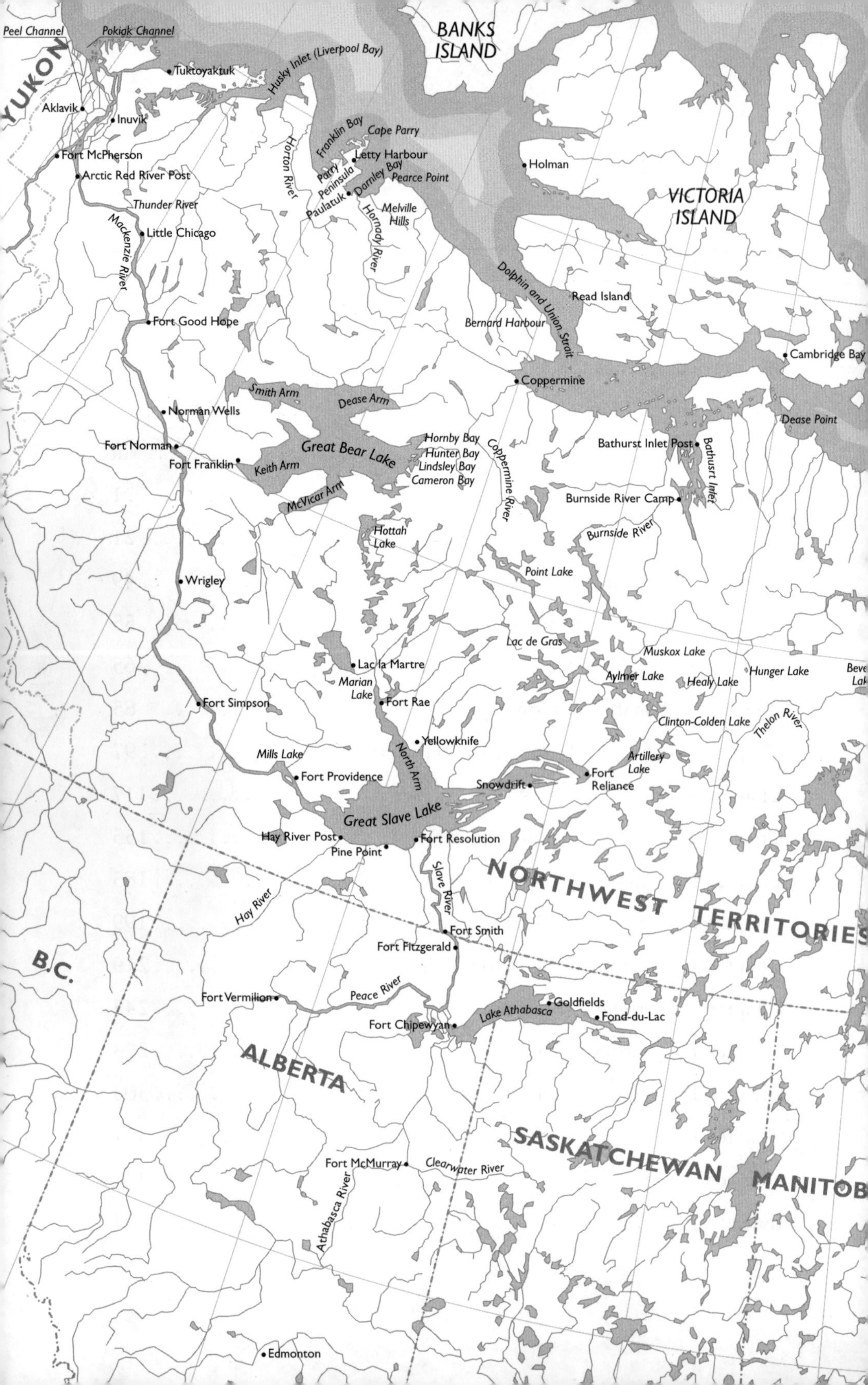

Peel Channel
Pokiak Channel
BANKS ISLAND
YUKON
Husky Inlet (Liverpool Bay)
Tuktoyaktuk
Aklavik
Inuvik
Franklin Bay
Cape Parry
Fort McPherson
Horton River
Letty Harbour
Holman
Arctic Red River Post
Parry Peninsula
Darnley Bay
Pearce Point
Paulatuk
VICTORIA ISLAND
Thunder River
Melville Hills
Little Chicago
Mackenzie River
Hornaday River
Dolphin and Union Strait
Read Island
Fort Good Hope
Bernard Harbour
Cambridge Bay
Coppermine
Smith Arm
Dease Arm
Norman Wells
Dease Point
Hornby Bay
Fort Norman
Great Bear Lake
Hunter Bay
Bathurst Inlet Post
Bathurst Inlet
Fort Franklin
Keith Arm
Lindsley Bay
Cameron Bay
Coppermine River
McVicar Arm
Burnside River Camp
Burnside River
Hottah Lake
Point Lake
Wrigley
Lac de Gras
Muskox Lake
Lac la Martre
Aylmer Lake
Healy Lake
Hunger Lake
Marian Lake
Fort Rae
Fort Simpson
Clinton-Colden Lake
Thelon River
Yellowknife
Mills Lake
North Arm
Artillery Lake
Fort Providence
Fort Reliance
Snowdrift
Great Slave Lake
Hay River Post
Fort Resolution
Pine Point
Slave River
NORTHWEST TERRITORIES
Hay River
Fort Smith
Fort Fitzgerald
B.C.
Peace River
Fort Vermilion
Goldfields
Lake Athabasca
Fond-du-Lac
Fort Chipewyan
ALBERTA
SASKATCHEWAN
Fort McMurray
Clearwater River
MANITOB
Athabasca River
Edmonton

Acknowledgements

The stories that follow owe their existence to many people, some of them busy participants in the events that are described. Others, in more recent times, have contributed photos and shared their memories of events long past. I am indebted to all of them and wish that my personal thanks could reach the many who are no longer with us.

At the end of this section I have listed the names of the Canadian Airways personnel who worked in the Mackenzie District during the 1930s. I knew them all and worked and flew with many of them. I am indebted to each in some way, but time and space will permit special mention of only a few individuals. First, Don Goodwin, our chief mechanic at McMurray, and his wife, Anne, who treated me like family. Don was an unfailing source of encouragement and advice. I'll pass on my thanks to their twin sons, Don and Doug, both retired airline captains. Sure glad you made it, chaps! Punch Dickins and Wop May, two of our early leaders, gave me their invaluable encouragement and friendship. I flew a lot of hours with Matt Berry and was privileged to share his companionship on some difficult flights. His warm smile and gentle humour made the blizzards more bearable and the "white-outs" less ominous. I have dedicated Chapter 14 especially to him. Frank Kelly, the finest of engineers and best of friends—sadly missed by his wife Marion, son Tim, and by Clark Seaborn of Fokker Super Universal CF-AAM fame. Kelly was one of Clark's first assistants when he started the Fokker project—an immense undertaking that has now "taken wing." And lastly, from the old Brandon Avenue shops of Canadian Airways Ltd. in Winnipeg, Tommy Siers and Albert Hutt, pioneers in the field of aircraft maintenance at a time when there was only their personal experience and integrity for guidance. I owe them thanks, as many do.

Among the other fine people who helped me with this book project in many ways are Doug Matheson, retired chief justice of Alberta, and his sister

Jan, both good friends from the 1930s. Doug's support and encouragement were special, and Jan's archival research, coupled with the expert knowledge of early aerial mapping contributed by Ralph McBurney (AVM ret'd), plus his Ottawa Archives research, contributed so much to the story of the search for Coleman and Fortey in Chapter 12. I must also thank Gene Schweitzer of Pratt & Whitney for his detailed explanation of the complexities of cold weather combustion in aircraft engines and for 60 years of friendship, and Greg Lamb of the illustrious Lamb aviation family of The Pas, Manitoba, for his valuable contribution and advice. Greg flew the fatal route that Bill Spence had followed, but Greg survived. Wendy Streit of The Pas Historical Society carried out valuable research and microfilm copying for me. And I want another old friend from Brandon Avenue shops days, Reg Nichols, to know that his photos filled a gap and his recollections were invaluable. Tommy Morimoto, one of Canadian Airways radio operators at McMurray (also a school chum and later a radio operator with the Royal Canadian Corps of Signals) provided some needed background material about early McMurray history.

Among my current and still active group of friends, Ed Young and Jack Rennie recounted some fascinating tales. Bill Hall (an original RCCS operator from the North) and Don Shears helped with photos and recollections. Gordy Beck and Gordy Brown provided some rare information about early and little-known northern episodes. Finally, there is the group with whom I meet every Thursday—the White Rock Coffee Crew—retired aviation people all, both pilots and engineers, many of whom worked together throughout our careers. We gather each week for fellowship and a review of aviation events long past, few of which will ever be recorded or reach the printed page. As we blow the cold ash from the embers of our memories, there is a silent headshake for the tragedies and a chuckle for the oft-told humorous tales. For me these weekly meetings have served as reminders, when my ambition and energy have lagged, of the importance of completing this writing project. Thus will be saved a few more tales from the early days of bush flying. And so, thanks, all of you guys. Your help is appreciated and your friendship valued.

I'll mention only the most senior of this group—friends from the '30s. Don Watson and I shared a workbench at the old Brandon Avenue shops in 1940. As former president of PWA, he is one of the best-known business personalities in Canada. Knowledgeable in all matters relating to aviation and aviation people, he has provided many answers for myself and others, and we look upon him as "The Authority." Captain Craig Stevenson, another veteran from the '30s, was one of those who worked at odd jobs—any job—to pay for his early training as a flyer. Craig has filled me in on many aviation episodes where my knowledge was hazy. Captain Fred Meilecke, an old friend from the McMurray days, has had a thousand adventures, is a consummate storyteller and has a memory that is nothing short of total recall. Fred is another of those who helped to keep my text believable. And Captain Frank Smythe, always happy to talk of the Hornet Moth that he flew in the '30s for Consolidated Mining & Smelting at Yellowknife and of other events of that era. Sad to relate, Frank filed his last flight plan in spring 2003. And finally, Bill Given, old and valued friend from the Edmonton days of the late '30s. We have trodden the same paths together with many of the same people, and I have relied on Bill's advice and his meticulous memory for accurate coverage of many events and people.

Next is a literary group who deserve special mention. First among them is my eldest son, Jon Terpening, MA, educator, writer, inspiration and advisor to a few generations of students and to his old dad. Shirley Render has made a name for herself in several fields of endeavour. She is a pilot, author of two fine books, a director of Canada's Aviation Hall of Fame, one-time president of the Western Canada Aviation Museum and also editor of their quarterly, *The Aviation Review*. My sincere thanks to Shirley for her support and advice and for her encouragement when I first considered writing about early aviation. And thanks to Bev Tallon, also from the Winnipeg museum, archivist and photographer, for her continued help and advice in all matters photographic.

For professional guidance I am deeply indebted to Bill Wheeler, well known within the aviation community in Canada and beyond our shores. A writer, past-president and founding member of the Canadian Aviation Historical Society, and long-time editor of the *Journal of the Canadian Aviation Historical Society*, Bill is one of Canada's foremost aircraft historians and also an accomplished artist. He has, in addition to his *Journal* activities, selected and edited the material for two recent aviation books—*Skippers of the Sky*, an anthology of bush flying stories, and *Flight Through Fire*, and produced an earlier one, *Images of Flight*. Bill volunteered to check my completed chapters but this presented some problems—we live half a continent apart—but he spent endless hours toiling over my manuscript, chapter by chapter, numberless times. After several months of this our mail carrier started to complain! We have persevered, however, and this tale of early bush flying is now before you. If the following chapters are found to have readable qualities, then a large part of the credit must go to Bill Wheeler.

I would like to dedicate this volume to the aviation pioneers who have gone before, and particularly to the comrades and good friends who are listed below. The names have been taken from memory and from the files of Canadian Airways Ltd. and are, I believe, an accurate record of those who worked in the Mackenzie District or were based at McMurray prior to 1937.

Anderson, Andy
Baragar, Frank
Barron, Fred
Benzie, Benny
Berry, Matt
Bowen, Jack
Bowles, Ted
Brindley, Cliff
Bulger, Gordy
Bythell, John
Caddick, Tom
Calder, Paul
Cruikshanks, Andy
Dame, Jack
Davoud, Paul
Dickins, Punch
Farrell, Con
Farrington, Harold
Forrest, Neville
Forrester, Norm
George, Ron
Gilbert, Walter
Goodwin, Don
Cooke, Bill
Hardham, Harry
Hardman, Jack
Hartley, Frank
Hartree, Bill
Haslett, Gordy
Heuss, Rudy
Hollick-Kenyon, Ken
Ingrey, Ron
Jacquot, Bill
Kelly, Frank
King, Harry
Knight, Stan
Lawson, Don
Leigh, Dick
Leigh, Lewie
Little, Fred
Lundy, Fred
Marshall, Bruce
May, Wop
McLaren, Dunc
McLeod, Gord
McMullen, Archie
Meilecke, Fred
McDonough, W.G.
Morimoto, Tom
Morrison, Ron
Nadin, Bill
Parker, Al
Parmenter, Lou
Pearce, Al
Philpot, Al
Piette, Cec
Rankin, Art
Roth, Hank
Sawle, North
Skeel, Jim
Spence, Bill
Stalport, Aimé
Stull, Ted
Sunderland, Bill
Sutherland, Micky
Tall, Bill
Terpening, Rex
Tomlinson, Sammy
Torrie, Horace
Van der Linden, Casey
Winny, Harry

Foreword by William J. (Bill) Wheeler

Rex Terpening has both a fascinating story to tell and a knack for telling it well. A perceptive observer, he writes not only with an insight gained from a lifetime in aviation—much of it at the grassroots level—but with humour and sensitivity. And, as one of the very last of a vanished breed of air engineers who, in the 1920s and '30s, flew with the bush pilots, he shared all of the hazards that they routinely faced. Rex's experiences from that memorable era have themselves become a part of our history.

It was an adventurous time with aerial records being broken regularly. Northern flying was no different; almost every flight could in one way or another be a challenge. By today's standards Rex's wooden-winged and fabric-covered Fairchild aircraft were fragile. (The all-metal Junkers was sturdier.) None of their aircraft were overpowered and their engines, the generally reliable Pratt & Whitney Wasps, were capable of failing. On such occasions the pilots thanked God for air engineers such as Rex Terpening who, until the late '30s, always accompanied them. Radio communications were non-existent because the early aircraft lacked the electrical systems necessary to power radio equipment. With no means of summoning help, it fell to the air engineers to get them back into the air.

Northern weather is notoriously changeable and harsh in the extreme. Forecasting was then in its infancy and for those who flew in the far north, non-existent. The vast, sparsely settled terrain over which they operated was either mountainous or flat and almost featureless. Maps, such as they had, were more a liability than an asset, and since their only navigational aid, the magnetic compass, could not always be trusted, it was not difficult to become lost. As well, they might face whiteouts, drifted snow so hard that it could wipe off an aircraft's skis, wing icing, water levels that changed overnight, ice fog, dangerous cargo, treacherous ice, submerged rocks that could puncture floats, shifting freight, unruly passengers (both animal and human)...the list is endless. But far from being daunted, Rex and his engineer colleagues managed to cope, even to thrive. They were a special breed—tough, resilient and resourceful. His accounts amply bear this out. And they were sustained—as his readers will soon realize—by an unfailing, if irreverent sense of humour.

Rex's narrative is enriched by his knowledge of northern history, his special awareness of Canada's storied past. His meaningful asides acquaint us with local happenings, often centuries earlier, that broaden our understanding by linking the exploits of those early explorers and fur traders with their later counterparts. Even a short roster of those with whom Rex flew and worked reads like a Who's Who of Canadian aviation. Among them are numerous recipients of the prestigious McKee Trans-Canada Trophy. Many others, Rex included, have been inducted into Canada's Aviation Hall of Fame. With *Bent Props and Blow Pots*, Rex Terpening makes a significant contribution to the lore of Canadian northern flying.

Preface

This book began a few years ago as a series of articles for two Canadian aviation historical publications—the Canadian Aviation Historical Society's *Journal* and the Western Canada Aviation Museum's *Aviation Review*. Additional stories have since been added and the original material expanded.

My source materials were my diaries and notes together with recollections, both my own and those of a few close friends. Back in the 1930s while I was actively flying as an air engineer—"on operations" was the common term—there was never a shortage of subjects to write about, but opportunities for thoughtful observation of our day-to-day activities were non-existent. However, I did keep a diary during those often stressful years, and my brief entries—or perhaps just the effort required to put pencil (worn and stubby) to paper—were sufficient to preserve memories of the moment. And I always carried a camera, even though the cameras of the early '30s were only a bare step more advanced than the old box cameras and the slow film scarcely capable of catching an image in the dim light of northern winters. Thus most of the photographs in this book are from my own collection—all elderly, some perhaps historical. Others I obtained in trade from other early camera buffs.

Bush flying is essentially Canadian in origin and is akin to the transportation skills of slightly earlier generations—guiding a birchbark canoe through whitewater or a team of dogs across the tundra. But while the hardware required for those earliest forms of northern travel—the canoe, the *carriole* and the *komatik*—were of local design and manufacture, the equipment needed for our earliest bush flying enterprises required a different approach. Lacking the initial technology, the earliest Canadian operators used aircraft designs from England and from the United States. Among these were the Curtiss and Vickers flying boats used in summer and the Canadian-manufactured Curtiss JN-4C Canucks in winter. Then came various models of single-engined monoplanes—aircraft with float and ski capability, enclosed cabins and cockpits, and reasonably reliable air-cooled engines. Bush flying then began in earnest.

In common use were the Fokker Universals, the Junkers F-13 and W-34, the Fairchild FC2 and FC2W2, and the Bellanca Pacemaker. Then came the Canadian-manufactured Fairchild 71 and 82 and finally the Canadian-designed and -manufactured Norseman, the best of the early bush planes. The first of these improved models became available by the late 1920s. Year-round flying then became a reality and the craft of bush flying was born. Initially this was a struggle for both pilots and engineers, but gradually pilots learned to cope with all manner of problems, winter and summer, and maintenance engineers modified the aircraft and engine systems to keep them operational under the most extreme of northern conditions.

By the early 1930s this native craft of ours—bush flying—had developed into a fairly reliable form of transportation. As Canadian as maple syrup, it has since been exported and used world-wide, and Canadian bush fliers, often using Canadian-designed and -manufactured aircraft and engines, have demonstrated their expertise from pole to pole. From an uncertain beginning three-quarters of a century ago, bush flying has continued to develop and improve. With advances in all phases of the related technology—power plants, aerodynamics, communications—bush flying has achieved an outstanding safety record, despite the risks that are inherent with an operation such as this.

In this book I have related the experiences of a number of aviation people, myself included, in a particular stage of bush flying activity known as The Thirties. Among those of us who grew up in the industry and were privileged to take part in the bush flying of that far-away era, there is common agreement. The bush flying of the '30s was the most exciting and interesting period of our aviation careers. Share with me then some of the experiences that were so much a part of bush flying as it was then.

1 How we got from there to here

First, a word of definition about bush flying. All of the populated areas of Canada were at one time adjacent to forested land known colloquially as "the bush," and this term came into common use to describe any feature or activity that existed or took place in such places. We had bush farms and bush villages linked by bush travel on bush trails. As a natural next step, the flying activities that took place in the 1920s away from the settled areas of northern Quebec, Ontario and Manitoba immediately became known as bush flying. But this being canoe country with no landing fields for wheel-equipped aircraft, the fledgling aviation companies chose flying boats for their aerial mapping, timber survey and forest fire patrol contracts.

The craft in common use in the bush were the Curtiss HS-2L, the Vickers Viking and the Vickers Vedette, all biplanes powered by a single rear-mounted engine driving a pusher propeller. There were two advantages to those rear-mounted propellers: air flow over the cockpits was reduced and mooring/docking operations—hazardous with a front-mounted propeller—were simplified and made safer.

Those early flying boats were graceful in appearance with reasonably good performance, but they had a couple of defects: a lack of cargo/passenger-carrying provision and their biplane wing design. The lower wings interfered with loading activities at crude docks and wooded shorelines. The Curtiss boats were the largest and most numerous of the flock—and also the most unreliable. "H-boats" they were called with the odd hint of

A pilot stands between the wings on the hull of an "H-boat", as the Curtiss HS-2L was called. These flying boats were used for transportation of mail and passengers into isolated areas, despite their inefficient cargo space and frequent engine failures. *Photograph courtesy of the Canada Aviation Museum, Ottawa.*

profanity, their less-than-complimentary reputation being due to frequent failures of their overworked Liberty engines.

The H-boat's pilot and crew—and trusting passengers, if any—occupied open cockpits near the front of the hull. The pilot required this forward location to obtain a measure of visibility; the other crew member (either an engineer or observer) and the passengers just "went along for the ride." These were breezy locations, as they were exposed to the blast of the slipstream with only a small measure of protection provided by little windscreens attached to the forward edge of the cockpit enclosures.

Before long the demand for transportation into roadless areas saw those same flying boats being used for mail and limited passenger-carrying activities

into isolated settlements and prospecting camps. But these were summer operations only. By the mid-1920s, with the proliferation of gold strikes in the Rouyn area of Quebec and the Red Lake district of Ontario, there was a recognized need for a winter flying service, though initially only for passengers and mail. The first aircraft used were two-place, open-cockpit biplanes, Curtiss Model JN-4s, of the same pedigree and from the same American stable as the H-boats. However, because of the demand for training aircraft during World War I, a large number of these JN-4s had also been manufactured in Canada, and while both models carried the same JN-4 designation, the American-made aircraft were known as "Jennies" and their northern cousins became "Canucks." In order to operate the JN-4s on the

CF-ATZ, a Fairchild 71, was ideally suited to bush flying in the North, with its sturdy undercarriage, dependability on skis, floats, and wheels, and a reliable 420 hp Pratt & Whitney Wasp engine. *Photograph courtesy of the Canada Aviation Museum, Ottawa.*

frozen lake surfaces near the mines and settlements, they were fitted with hastily made skis. Like their Canuck steeds, the pilots were mostly the product of the recently concluded hostilities; flying was now in their blood and would become a lifetime occupation. Because of the lack of any form of heating in the JN-4's open cockpits, the pilots wore their conventional wartime flying suits, complete with helmets and goggles, and this garb soon became the badge of their trade. Their unwary passengers, however, were still left to their own devices with the only concern for their comfort being the admonishment to "dress up warm."

The demand for year-round service soon resulted in the development of a more suitable model of aircraft, one that would become the standard for future bush flying activities. These were high-wing monoplanes that could operate on wheels, skis or floats and, with their relatively dependable air-cooled engines, could be operated successfully in sub-zero conditions. These

A Fairchild 71 taxies toward the cameraman amid a cloud of loose snow. Taken in front of the Spence-Mac base on the Clearwater River, March 1932.

aircraft were far more durable than their wooden-hulled ancestors. They had fuselages of welded steel tubing with fabric covering, and wing structures of wood covered with either fabric or thin plywood. The lot of both pilots and passengers was now greatly improved because the design incorporated an enclosed cabin for the passengers and a cockpit for the pilot. This improvement was viewed with mixed feelings by the pilots: while protection from the slipstream was welcome, the need for helmets and goggles was now open to question, and it was with considerable reluctance that they gave up these beloved symbols.

Seating for passengers was an early innovation. Most seats were constructed of welded steel tubing covered with woven wicker and looked like odd-shaped laundry baskets. Some were even equipped with seat belts. The seats for the Fokker Super Universal deserve special mention because they were of all-metal construction and closely resembled an overgrown coal scuttle.

(For those unfamiliar with that antique device, it was a pail with a broad sloping ramp built onto one side; it was used to transfer lumps of coal into the family heater or cookstove.) But it didn't take long for bush operators to realize that seats occupied valuable cargo space, thus reducing their payload and their—always uncertain—margin of profit. From then on passengers sat on their rolled-up sleeping bags if they were fortunate—otherwise their seats might well be kegs of nails, bags of mail or even cases of dynamite.

Ventilation for the new enclosed cabins was provided by air piped in from outside with a valve or valves to regulate the flow. For winter operation this ventilating air was heated by application of hot exhaust gases to the outside of the supply pipe. Though these enclosed and heated cabins and cockpits were a vast improvement over the open cockpits of the earlier aircraft, the interiors would have benefited still further by the application of insulation to the cabin walls. Lightweight insulation, however, had not yet been developed.

The first of this new breed of aircraft, the Fokker Universals and the Fairchild FC-2s, both powered by 225 hp Wright Model J-5 air-cooled, radial engines, had a load capacity of perhaps four or five passengers or an equivalent weight in cargo. Their success and the subsequent availability of the larger 420 hp Pratt & Whitney Wasp engines resulted in the development of larger aircraft—the Fokker Super Universal and the Fairchild 71. Fokker Supers were used extensively in the late 1920s and early '30s in the lake country of northern Ontario and Manitoba, but their first confrontations with the rigid snowdrifts of the Northwest Territories revealed serious weaknesses. Even moderately rough landings caused undercarriage failures and damage to the fragile plywood wing that was difficult and expensive to repair. Consequently, most of the Supers had disappeared from the scene by the early '30s. The Fairchild 71 in its day was probably the most popular and numerous of the bush aircraft. With their sturdy undercarriages, good performance on both skis and floats, and their reliable Wasp engines, they were in general use. (The FC2W2 was a slightly earlier version of the 71 but there was no obvious difference in performance.) Also used, but in lesser quantities, were the Bellanca Pacemaker, powered by a 300 hp Wright J-6 but designed with limited cargo-carrying capacity, and the Wasp-powered Junkers W-34. This latter aircraft, while being similar to the Super and

Fokker Super Universals G-CASK and G-CASL were instrumental in the search for the McAlpine party in November 1929. G-CASK had to be abandoned at Dease Point, and wasn't retrieved till July 1930, while G-CASL, piloted by Herbert Hollick-Kenyon, survived the journey after only one replacement part. This photo was taken at Cameron Bay, Great Bear Lake, summer 1932. *Photograph courtesy of the Canada Aviation Museum, Ottawa.*

the 71 in power and load capacity, was of all-metal construction; the outer covering of both fuselage and wings was corrugated aluminum alloy. They were a fine aircraft in every respect and considered the Cadillac of early bush aircraft by those who had the good fortune to fly them.

All of these aircraft were identified by their three-letter registration—or by the last two letters if the aircraft was well-known. However, the application of names was also popular at one time. Lindbergh's *Spirit of St. Louis* was an early example. And who can forget Wiley Post's round-the-world flight in his beautiful Lockheed Vega, the *Winnie-Mae*?

Mining interests in Canada quickly recognized the potential benefits of aircraft to service mining camps but more importantly to search for minerals. An aircraft could cover more territory in a single day (and in summer, northern days are endless) than could a prospector with his canoe in a full season. To realize these benefits, a number of aerial exploration companies were formed, the two largest being Dominion Explorers Ltd. (DOMEX) and the rather ponderously titled Northern Aerial Mineral Exploration Co. Ltd., which was soon mercifully shortened to NAME. Though both companies were well-organized and financed and staffed with experienced and resourceful pilots and engineers, DOMEX, encouraged by the results of its 1928–29 fieldwork, stole a march on the competition when on February 28, 1930, it imported some of the first Fairchild 71s into Canada. With aircraft just coming into general use, the purchase of even one brand new, late model craft was newsworthy, but DOMEX's purchase of three created national headlines. CF-AKX, CF-AKY and CF-AKZ cost $20,000 each—big money at the time.

By the end of the 1920s, explorations by the mining companies had covered the area west of Hudson Bay from Churchill to Baker Lake. They had traversed the coast of the Western Arctic, flown the length of the Mackenzie River, and begun the exploration of the Barren Lands. In one particularly ambitious undertaking, two NAME aircraft and their crews remained at Coppermine (as the settlement at the mouth of that river was named) over the breakup period, enabling them to conduct an additional six weeks of ski-flying during the spring season. For the summer operation the two aircraft were changed to floats, these having been shipped from Vancouver the previous year on the well-known Hudson's Bay Company supply boat, *Bay Chimo*. According to legend, as ice conditions deteriorated that spring, both aircraft were changed from skis to wheels, and one of them was taxied ashore. Then, just before starting the engine of the second, its pilot, Matt Berry—later to be recognized as one of the deans of northern flying—remarked to his engineer, Jack Humble, "Say, Jack, why don't we do a takeoff and landing? It will be the first-ever wheel-equipped operation on the Arctic Coast!" Jack agreed, and to the delight of the Inuit residents, a bit of little-known northern aviation history was made. The archives of the Northern Heritage Centre at Yellowknife have a photo of this incident, showing Jack standing beside the aircraft and Matt's smiling face visible through the open side-window.

By the fall of 1929, DOMEX had established a chain of bases in northern Alberta/NWT—the first being at Stony Rapids at the east end of Lake Athabasca, a second at the site of old Fort Reliance at the east end of Great Slave Lake, a third at Hunter Bay on Great Bear Lake, and the fourth at the bottom of Bathurst Inlet, where the Burnside River meets the Arctic Ocean. During the summer of 1929 Colonel C.D.H. McAlpine, DOMEX's president, decided on an inspection of his northern empire. The expedition would include four DOMEX employees—Major Robert Baker, mining engineer E.A. Boadway, pilot Stanley McMillan, and engineer Alex Milne—as well as Richard Pearce, the editor of *The Northern Miner*.

The expedition was well planned. They would fly up the west coast of

Western Canada Airlines Fokker Super G-CASQ, flown by Andy Cruikshanks, crashed through the ice at Burnside River on the Arctic Coast in November 1929 while taking part in the search for the lost McAlpine party.

Hudson Bay to Baker Lake, then west to Burnside and Hunter Bay, and south again to Stony Rapids. But well aware of the sometimes questionable reliability of 1929 flying equipment, McAlpine hired an extra aircraft and crew from Western Canada Air Lines (WCAL)—the Fokker Super G-CASP piloted by G.A. Thompson with Donald Goodwin as engineer—to accompany DOMEX's Fairchild FC-2W2 CF-AAO. As an added precaution, two more DOMEX aircraft were positioned at Stony Rapids, ready to start a search expedition if the McAlpine party did not reach Burnside. In spite of all of these elaborate precautions, the two aircraft of the expedition departed Baker Lake on September 8—and then disappeared.

So what went wrong? As in so many similar cases it was a matter of an accumulation of smaller problems. To begin with, the expedition had started out a month too late, considering the weather vagaries on the Arctic Coast, which vary widely from season to season. To compound the late departure date, G-CASP was wrecked during an overnight stop at Churchill, delaying the expedition by an additional week while they waited for a replacement. Finally they were beset with navigation problems, always a problem on the Barrens. After leaving their last overnight stop at Beverly Lake, they should have flown a course of nearly 300 degrees true for about two hours and 45 minutes to reach Burnside. Instead, that elapsed time brought them to the sea coast at Dease Point, 150 miles northeast of Burnside, and by this time they were almost out of fuel.

On the plus side, they had landed beside a small Inuit camp. Learning their whereabouts, they realized that they were in for a long wait before the ice firmed up enough that they could cross Dease Strait to safety at Cambridge Bay on Victoria Island. They planned for their long stay accordingly. Major Baker was appointed group chief and he set them to work constructing a 12x14-foot sod house. At the same time others of the party were engaged in collecting moss and willows for fuel and in hunting for ptarmigan and rabbits to extend their limited food supply. Though they confined themselves to two meals per day, without the Inuit peoples' frequent contributions of fish and game, they would have been on a near-starvation diet. And so they existed under these difficult conditions for 42 days.

Then on October 21, encouraged by a stretch of cold weather, they started for Cambridge Bay, accompanied by Inuit guides with their two dog teams. Sleeping in igloos at nights, and delayed by stretches of warm weather, they reached Trap Point, opposite Cambridge Bay, a week later, but because of their slow progress, the food supply was now exhausted and the Inuit made a trip back to Dease Point for further supplies. Crossing the strait was a two-day ordeal, but they finally reached Cambridge Bay on November 3.

In the meantime the search aircraft, now ski-equipped, had arrived at Burnside. Three of these, G-CASO flown by Roy Brown, G-CASL piloted by Herbert Hollick-Kenyon and CF-ACZ piloted by Bill Spence, landed safely. The fourth, WCAL's Fokker Super G-CASQ, flown by Andy Cruikshanks, went through the ice. This resulted in a long and arduous salvage operation, headed by WCAL's maintenance superintendent, Tommy Siers. The search aircraft now made a series of trips to the Ellice River area but, because of poor visibility, they did not spot the McAlpine planes. Further searching was carried out to the south without success. The next morning as the aircraft were being warmed up to make a search to the west, a dog team with a single occupant, an Inuit named Tommy Goose, was seen approaching from the north. He carried a message from the radio station at Bathhurst, advising that the McAlpine party had reached Cambridge Bay. It was with great jubilation that plans were changed, and on the following day the three search aircraft flew to Cambridge Bay. They received an enthusiastic welcome from the McAlpine party, but as it was already November and the days were growing shorter, there was no time to lose. The planes were quickly loaded and the return flights were made to Burnside. As Andy Cruikshanks' aircraft was now serviceable, the passengers were divided among the four aircraft for the next leg of the trip, and they all departed for Reliance the next day, November 12. The weather was good for the first 150 miles, then they encountered low cloud, and all the aircraft were forced to land on Muskox Lake, remaining weather-bound there for two nights.

Attempting to depart from there on November 14, Bill Spence's aircraft, CF-ACZ, experienced a partial undercarriage failure, and Tommy Siers, convinced that he could make repairs, remained behind with Bill and his engineer at Muskox. The balance of the party reached Reliance without difficulty, although by that time Hollick-Kenyon's aircraft, G-CASL, had developed a cracked cylinder. On November 16, Brown in G-CASO returned to Muskox with further repair parts for Bill Spence's ailing ACZ, while Cruikshanks made a trip to Resolution to advise the location of the parties and beg for a further serviceable aircraft. When neither Brown nor Spence had returned from Muskox by November 23, four dog teams were sent to their aid. The next day when Cruikshanks returned from Resolution, in spite of the doubtful condition of G-CASQ's motor, he decided to make his own search for the missing crews.

Brown, in fact, had never reached Muskox Lake. On his northbound flight,

Fokker Super Universal G-CASO, flown by Roy Brown, was forced down onto Aylmer Lake by a snow storm on November 14, 1929. The aircraft suffered a total undercarriage failure on the rough ice and was subsequently abandoned.

Pilot Jimmy Vance died in the crash of Dominion Explorers brand new Fairchild 71 CF-AKX at the mouth of the Sloan River on Great Bear Lake. July 12, 1930.

he had been forced to land at Aylmer Lake because of weather, and his aircraft, G-CASO, had experienced a total undercarriage failure. This meant that Cruikshanks' G-CASQ was the only remaining serviceable piece of equipment and the only means of final rescue for the marooned parties. Collecting the men from both Muskox and Aylmer, he then returned to Reliance, at the same time bringing along a replacement cylinder from G-CASO to effect repairs to Hollick-Kenyon's G-CASL. On November 30 all of the personnel, both searchers and rescuers, were flown to Stony Rapids and from there in stages back to Winnipeg, arriving there on December 4, 1929.

By good planning and sound judgement no lives were lost during this search but the cost in lost and damaged equipment was high. Fokker Super G-CASP remained a total loss at Churchill. Fokker Super G-CARK, which was damaged at Baker Lake, remained out of service until repairs were effected later in the winter. Fokker Super G-CASK, which was abandoned at Dease Point, was retrieved in July 1930, as was Fairchild FC2W2 CF-AAO. Fokker Super G-CASO was abandoned after being damaged at Aylmer Lake. Fairchild FC2W2 CF-ACZ, damaged at Muskox Lake, was temporarily repaired and flown out to McMurray in March 1930, but never returned to service.

DOMEX, nearing financial collapse after this adventure, nevertheless accomplished a small amount of ski-flying with its new Fairchild 71s in the spring of 1930. Then after changing over to floats, the company's crews followed the ice breakup north, eager to learn what mineral deposits lay beyond that far and fabled horizon. By late June they had reached the sizable exploration camp the company had established the year before at the mouth of the Sloan River on Hunter Bay at the northeast corner of Great Bear Lake. The main point of interest for the company was the Bornite and Dismal lakes area northeast of Hunter Bay where NAME had already staked property.

Spring and early summer is normally a dry period in the north, and summer bush fires were common. Some were caused by prospectors who were less than diligent in extinguishing their campfires; if even a couple of hot coals are overlooked, fire will spread into the dry moss, and the country becomes cloaked in a dense layer of smoke. Such was the case on July 12, 1930. Jimmy Vance, flying AKX, had spent the previous night at Bornite Lake and was returning to base camp at Hunter Bay. The windless day and the existing fires created that most dangerous of summer bush-flying conditions—smoke and glassy water—and indications are that Vance was unfamiliar with this deadly combination. Instead of landing close to a shoreline, he made his approach along the Sloan River, perhaps intending to touch down at the mouth of the river. Watchers at the camp saw the aircraft pass over at close range and disappear into the smoke. Soon they heard a crash—and then silence. They paddled quickly down the bay, but Jimmy Vance was far beyond any assistance they might have provided. The aircraft struck the water at a steep, nose-down angle, then continued over into the inverted position. In a Fairchild 71 the cockpit opening that framed the windshield was a rectangle braced by a steel tube running diagonally across it to create a pair of triangles. The force of the impact had catapulted Vance's body right through the uppermost triangle and through the windshield.

DOMEX maintained a small radio station at Hunter Bay, the only communications source in the entire Bear Lake area, and it was by this means that Colonel McAlpine was advised of the accident. In later years, long after Hunter Bay had been abandoned, a group of Eldorado Mines employees visited the site on a Sunday outing and found the old radio station still intact, although open to the weather. From the debris littering the floor one of them picked up a copy of a poignant reminder of that early tragedy. It read: TORONTO, ONT. JULY 15, 1930. TO ROGERS, HUNTER BAY. PLEASE ADVISE

CHANCES FINDING VANCE'S BODY. MCALPINE. To the best of my knowledge his body was never found. The wreckage of AKX was later dragged ashore at Hunter Bay and may still be there.

Consolidated Mining & Smelting Ltd. (CM&S) was another of the mining companies to realize the advantages of airborne exploration. Their first cautious venture into the NWT was in the spring of 1929 with a couple of float-equipped DH Moths. One of these, CF-AAJ, was lost on August 23 at a site known as Dawson's Landing, west of Fort Resolution. Mining engineer and pilot Bill Jewitt had gone ashore to inspect some of their mining claims, leaving the Moth tied to the dock. But this landing area was exposed to the full force of the waves sweeping in from Great Slave Lake, and during his absence the wind velocity increased, and by the time he returned, little AAJ was no more than matchsticks. In the official shorthand of the day used by the Civil Aviation Branch, it was DBR—damaged beyond repair.

The next year Bill Jewitt returned to the north, this time with an aircraft that was slightly larger and more robust—a Curtiss Robin, CF-ALY. On July 1, 1930, he again paid a visit to Dawson's Landing, by this time known as Pine Point. He must have been confident that the Robin, being a high-wing monoplane and larger than the Moth, would be safe in rough water, but he returned to his docking area to find that the Robin had shared the same fate as the Moth. Bill had another DBR on his hands.

Consolidated Mining & Smelting's Robin CF-ALY, flown by Bill Jewitt, was destroyed by high winds and rough water on July 1, 1930, at Pine Point on Great Slave Lake. His DH-Moth, CF-AAJ, had been lost in the same manner and in the same place a year earlier.

The remaining Moth, CF-AGD, was also lost in July of that unfortunate summer, but under more spectacular circumstances. It crashed out on the Barrens shortly after takeoff. Fortunately, it did not catch fire and the occupants were relatively uninjured. An amazing set of circumstances resulted in their rescue. There were very few aircraft operating in the Territories in those early years, and the only one in the area happened to fly over at low altitude just as the Moth stubbed its toe on a large boulder and did an inverted tail-first landing out on the tundra. The observer was W.J. McDonough, chief pilot for NAME. He landed on the lake immediately and reached shore while the dazed Moth occupants, two brothers by the name of Walton, were still struggling with their safety belts. That these two were doubly fortunate can be well appreciated. Either serious injuries or fire could have taken their lives, and the timely arrival of McDonough saved them a 50-mile walk back to their base camp. After these various mishaps CM&S decided that the north was no place for small aircraft. They then purchased the Fairchild 71s CF-AVY and CF-AWG, with AVY usually being flown by Bill Jewitt.

With the expansion of mineral searches there was a pressing need for maps that showed the lakes and rivers with more detail and accuracy. The large lakes and most important water courses had already been mapped by ground surveys, an immense undertaking carried out by that superb organization, the Geological Survey of Canada. Men such as George Mercer

CM&S's remaining DH Moth, CF-AGD, did an inverted tail-first landing on the Barrens in July 1930. W.J. McDonough, chief pilot for NAME, saw the accident and rescued the crew, two brothers by the name of Walton.

Dawson and Frank Swannell, Richard McConnell and Guy Blanchet had been among those early surveyors and geologists who had traced the major rivers and their drainages, climbed the mountains, herded their pack-trains through the muskegs, and placed much of Canada's northlands on their maps. More was needed, however, in accuracy and detail, and aerial photography was immediately recognized as the solution, particularly for the trackless and remote areas of the NWT. The Geological Survey people then obtained approval from the federal government, and an aerial survey/mapping project was started in the late 1920s. The RCAF provided the crews and aircraft, the Topographical Survey people the controls and mapping expertise. But federal budgetary restraints insured that the program proceeded at a leisurely pace, with the result that maps produced from the first of these photographic surveys were not completed until the early 1930s. As a consequence, the guidance available to those who carried out the early bush flying in the NWT was sketchy in the extreme.

A number of commercial flying companies emerged during this period, the largest being Winnipeg-based Western Canada Airways Ltd. (WCAL). Because of the vision and enterprise of its owner, James Richardson, this company established operating bases wherever there was need or opportunity in Canada. The communities of Quebec's North Shore, normally isolated for much of the year, were the first to receive WCAL's regular flying service. This was then extended to include the mining districts of Quebec, Ontario and Manitoba, then the fishing and timber industries of the Pacific Coast. The far-sighted Richardson also realized that the remote trading posts in the vast Northwest Territories and along the coast of the Western Arctic were completely isolated for much of the year. Up to that time they were serviced in summer only by the sternwheelers of the Hudson's Bay Company on the main rivers and by smaller, gasoline-engine powered craft to the more remote communities. Mail, therefore, for many posts was an annual event, but since service was dependent upon the whims of the Arctic ice pack, a wait of two years was not uncommon. The federal government, frugal as Scrooge in those days, had no interest in the citizens of the NWT, insisting instead that private enterprise (in this case, the Hudson's Bay Company) should bear the responsibility. The government's only gesture of assistance was to provide radio stations at Fort Smith and Aklavik, but these were primarily for communication between government employees.

WCAL's Fokker Super Universal G-CASN in Fort McMurray on January 23, 1929, the day of its flight to Fort Simpson on the first scheduled airmail service to the Northwest Territories. *Photograph courtesy of the Canada Aviation Museum, Ottawa.*

Richardson's first step toward providing service in the north was to base a single aircraft at Fort McMurray as a preliminary to more complete service. As a schoolboy at that little settlement, I have a vivid recollection of watching the takeoff of the first scheduled airmail service to the NWT on January 23, 1929. The aircraft was WCAL's Fokker Super Universal G-CASN, the pilot Punch Dickins and the engineer Lou Parmenter. The post office allowed the company to apply its private airmail stickers to first-class correspondence during that period, thus providing WCAL with a small measure of additional revenue. A strong recommendation for the continuance of this service was provided in a letter to the company, written by Dr. C. Bourget, the Indian agent at Fort Resolution.

> I beg to express my appreciation and feel that in doing so I am the interpreter of the feelings of all residents of the north—missionaries, traders, government officials, trappers—and even natives—for the splendid efforts of your company in establishing a service for this part of the north, so far abandoned to its long winter isolation.

There is no doubt that Dr. Bourget expressed similar thoughts to his masters in Ottawa, but official disinterest in the needs of the north continued. However, WCAL was firmly committed to providing service to the north, winter and summer. Supplies of fuel and oil were shipped to all the northern posts, and accommodation was arranged for flight crews at points where they might overnight. At the same time Richardson approached the government for a more permanent mail-carrying arrangement. An airmail contract was duly drawn up, and Richardson, in view of his company's pioneering efforts, fully expected to receive it. Instead, it was handed to a newly formed company from Edmonton, Commercial Airways Ltd. They had a fleet of good aircraft—one Bellanca CH-300, three Bellanca Pacemakers, and one Lockheed Vega, all powered by Model J-6 300 hp Wright Whirlwinds—but there was shock and disbelief on all sides when they were awarded the contract. But that was only the beginning. As history has amply recorded, the unofficial policy of official Ottawa was to block the expansion of Richardson's company wherever possible, and that injustice has been amply researched and well recorded in Shirley Render's fine book, aptly named *Double Cross*. In the 1929 case, however, nature and circumstances sided with Richardson and leveled the playing field by cutting short the history of Commercial Airways. First, the regular hazards of flying in the north exacted a costly toll in damaged aircraft. Then a glare-ice landing resulted in more aircraft damage coupled with fatalities. Already under-financed and over-extended, the company was absorbed by WCAL, soon to undergo a name change to Canadian Airways Ltd. (CAL). With no other operator on the horizon, the post office was obliged to award the contract to CAL. During the brief Commercial Airways period, Richardson had continued a small scale, money-losing operation into the north, but with the airmail contract at last in hand, he set about improving the handling facilities at Fort McMurray and all of the downriver posts and started year-round service to all points in the NWT and the Western Arctic.

However, year-round operation proved difficult, especially in winter, and CAL's first years in the north were accompanied by myriad problems, many of them caused by the fact that the designers of aircraft and engines in common use at the beginning of the 1930s had only limited knowledge of the conditions under which their products would operate. Engines malfunctioned because of inadequate carburetor heating systems that reduced engine power when most needed. Clogged engine oil filters resulted in low oil pressure and forced landings. (That particular problem turned out to be caribou hair in the oil system, the source of the hair being the caribou-skin parkas worn by some of the early flight crews.) Windshields were always covered with internal frost, especially during the takeoff period when visibility was most needed. This was the situation that resulted in the classic and unforgettable order issued by pioneer pilot Punch Dickins to his engineer, Lou Parmenter: "Stop breathing! You're fogging up the windows!"

The pilot and engineer, as well as the occasional passenger, suffered from the near-constant cold in the poorly heated and uninsulated interiors of those early aircraft. As well, the undercarriages of some aircraft models lacked both strength and shock-absorbing qualities. This meant undercarriage failures that led to structural damage. Also, the pedestals of the early skis were poorly designed. Aircraft broke through the ice, presenting difficult and challenging salvage operations. Most engine changes and repairs were carried out in the open or sometimes under a canvas shelter, if one was obtainable. The resourcefulness and ingenuity of the early maintenance engineers became legendary as they made the best of what was available, modifying and improvising in order to keep the aircraft and engines operating even under the most severe conditions.

Pilots had problems, too. There was no two-way radio equipment on the aircraft and no ground stations to provide either weather status reports or forecasts. Forced landings because of weather conditions or fuel shortages were common. Many a crew spent cold and uncomfortable nights in tents while waiting for the weather to improve enough to take off again. Heavy snowfalls accompanied by gale-force winds produced blizzards, making continued operation both difficult and dangerous. The dim and shadowless light produced a new hazard—"whiteout" conditions that were and are potentially fatal. As far-northern daylight is reduced to a mere glimmer during mid-winter, a flight from Cameron Bay to Coppermine—a mere 165 miles—in December or early January could be a day's journey. Fort McMurray to Aklavik and return in the short days of December could take 10 or 12 days.

Summer, while providing relief from the cold, brought its own problems. Docks, either floating or fixed, were generally non-existent, and riverbank landings were frequently a struggle through mud of various consistencies and depths. Five-hundred-pound drums of fuel had to be rolled through this mud

Northern summers brought as many problems as the winters, with melting snows turning roads to mud, or even flooding them over altogether. Here Bill Cooke, Mickey Sutherland and the author return to their bachelor cabin on the Clearwater River during the spring flood of 1932.

to within a hose-length of the aircraft, and their contents hand-pumped into the tanks. Mosquitoes, black flies and bulldog flies were the standard welcoming committee at every landing. Hotels, showers, and similar amenities of civilization did not exist. Flying personnel spread their sleeping bags on whatever floor welcomed them for the night. With no restaurants at hand, they were dependent upon the hospitality of the local residents, usually a HBC post manager or the local RCMP constable. Forest fires were common, reducing visibility to near-zero. And smoke was a double hazard when coupled with glassy-water landings; the crashes that resulted were invariably fatal. And summers were brief. All too quickly the shortened days and colder nights heralded the end of the float season. Soon it was freeze-up again and time to change the aircraft to skis and prepare them for another winter.

From Herschel Island in the west to Gjoa Haven in the east, those early aviation people ranged the Arctic Coast and the Barren Lands winter and summer and provided service to all of the inland settlements on the length of the Mackenzie River system. Whether radio operators or agents, pilots or engineers, they helped the advancement and safety of early aviation. Sharing in a great experience, each of them made a personal contribution.

2 Beyond the trapline—barely!

By the early 1930s the blight of the Great Depression lay upon the land. At that time my family lived about 16 miles downstream from McMurray where my father was employed at the Hudson's Bay Company's Tar Island Shipyards, so-named because of the numerous bituminous outcroppings in the area. Though born in Illinois farm country, he had been blessed with a wandering spirit that took him first west into Montana as a "rider"—he never used the word "cowboy"—for ranchers Michel Pablo and Charlie Allard, then into Idaho's Snake River country as a packer, taking freight to the small mining operations in the Bitterroot Range. He and a partner later drove their packtrain north into Canada looking for new freighting opportunities, and Dad took a job as a rider on a Calgary ranch. (His partner, Shorty, and their packtrain perished in a forest fire in the foothills.) Dad moved north again, working on ranches in the Camrose and Stettler area, then in 1907 there occurred an event that would eventually move our family into the north. The Canadian government had just purchased a small herd of wild buffalo—the last remnant of the vast herds that had once covered the North American prairies—and had set aside a 200-square-mile tract near the town of Wainwright as a preserve. Riders were needed to care for this herd and Dad was among those hired. In time Dad became a park warden, married an English girl named Ellen Coates and took her to live at the north gate of the park. It was here that my sister Mildred and I were born.

By 1925 the buffalo herd at Wainwright had increased to approximately 10,000 head and had outgrown their grazing area in spite of an annual

The author's parents in front of their home in Wainwright, Alberta, circa 1912.

Fort McMurray in the early 1920s. This stretch of muddy road became Franklin Avenue, the main street of the village. The Franklin Hotel is on the left, Sam Kushner's general store on the right. In the foreground the Snye Road leads off to the right.

slaughter and meat marketing program. It was decided that the surplus animals should be shipped to northern Alberta and released into Wood Buffalo Park in the Fort Fitzgerald area. Dad went along with the first shipment to oversee their transfer from the rail cars of the Alberta and Great Waterways Railroad (A&GWR) onto barges at Waterways, the Fort McMurray rail

Fort McMurray

Peter Pond of the old Northwest Company was the first white man to see the junction of the Clearwater and Athabasca rivers, where the town of McMurray now sits. Paddling westward up the Churchill River system in the summer of 1778, he and his party had crossed Methye Portage from La Loche to the Clearwater River and thus reached the Athabasca River system, unaware that they stood at the gate to the Arctic. Years passed, the Northwest Company and the Hudson's Bay Company amalgamated, and in 1870 Walter Moberly established Fort McMurray as a permanent trading post. Goods for trade were sent north from Edmonton by ox cart and wagon to Athabasca Landing, where they were loaded into scows for the downstream run to McMurray, but in order to move trade goods beyond McMurray and bring back furs the company was forced to develop a marine transportation system. So it was over this same route that they moved the boilers and machinery for the first sternwheelers to ply the Athabasca, the *Grahame* and the *McMurray*. Despite the difficult and rapid-strewn route and its accessibility for only a few months of each year, it was the only route into the north until the railroad was built as far as McMurray in 1925.

terminus. And here again the lure of frontier life overtook my dad with the result that he hired on with Mackenzie River Transport, the transportation division of the Hudson's Bay Company, remaining happily employed there until his retirement in 1953. Because of the rapids on the Mackenzie between Fort Fitzgerald and Fort Smith, the company required two separate fleets of boats and thus also required two separate shipyards. The southern one, where Dad was employed, was 16 miles downstream from McMurray, a distance that translated into three or four hours travelling time by dog team in winter or by small boat in summer.

Our family joined Dad at Tar Island in 1927, then in order to attend school my sister and I moved to a tiny rented cabin in McMurray. But when I wasn't in class, I was down at the Snye, the backwater between the Athabasca and Clearwater rivers, where Commercial Airways operated, or over at the headquarters of Spence-McDonough Air Transport on the

Bill Spence had been chief pilot for Dominion Explorers before joining forces with W.G. "Mac" McDonough to form Spence-McDonough Air Transport in January 1931.

CF-AKZ, Bill Spence's favourite steed, delivering supplies to prospectors camped on the shore of Great Bear Lake. August 1931.

Clearwater River between McMurray and Waterways. There, on evenings and weekends, I helped with a wide variety of aircraft maintenance and repairs. This great though unofficial apprenticeship came to an end in the summer of 1931 when I finished Grade 9, the upper limit available in our two-roomed, multi-grade school. More "book learning" was available in Edmonton, 250 miles to the south, but this was far beyond the financial resources of our family. Gainful employment was the next requirement, but since jobs of any sort were scarce or non-existent, I moved back home to operate Dad's trapline for a couple of winters and cut cordwood for the stern-wheelers. This was long before the advent of the chainsaw, and a neighbouring trapper and I cut the logs with a 6-foot cross-cut saw and split them with steel wedges driven by 10-pound hammers.

My first offer of employment in the aviation industry was an event that I remember as if it was yesterday. One day in early January 1932 I returned from five days in the bush—five cold, hard days on snowshoes—and found a letter awaiting me. This had been delivered by a trapper friend of ours who lived farther downriver, that is, to the north of us. After selling his furs at McMurray, he had stopped in for a meal and a visit. Tired and discouraged after a fruitless—and fur-less—round of the trapline and with aviation far from my thoughts, I opened the letter and found a job offer from Tom Caddick, chief mechanic for Spence-McDonough Air Transport of McMurray. During the course of that long winter evening, I read and reread that letter time and again, savouring the news word by word.

The Spence-McDonough company had a very brief existence—from about January 1931 to early 1933. Bill Spence had been chief pilot for the mining exploration firm DOMEX. His partner, W.G. "Mac" McDonough, had held a similar position with its rival, NAME. When both firms failed at the start of the Depression, Mac and Bill joined forces. Mac, in particular, had close connections with people in the mining industry in Toronto and was able to arrange financing for their new venture, which became generally known as Spence-Mac.

The new company purchased the aircraft that had formed the DOMEX fleet, as they were more up to date and in better condition than those of NAME. These consisted of the two Fairchild 71s, AKY and AKZ, one Fairchild FC-2-W2 (a slightly earlier model of the 71), AAO, and one FC-2 (a forerunner of the 71 series), G-CARH. In addition to the aircraft there were spares of all descriptions—piston and cylinder assemblies, starters, magnetos, exhaust systems and propellers for both the Wasp engines of the Fairchild 71s and the Wright J-5 of the FC-2. Instruments were also there in abundance. The DOMEX people must have had deep pockets, but they had correctly reasoned that they would be operating far from any repair facility and that the short summers were too valuable to risk having an aircraft out of service for lack of spare parts.

Of all the Spence-Mac fleet, AKZ was Bill Spence's favourite mount. During the summer of 1931 he and engineer Tom Caddick had used her to take prospecting parties into the Bear Lake area—the one bright spot in the mining and air transport worlds in those Depression days. They had also ventured to Coppermine and made the first-ever flight into Walker Bay on the west side of Victoria Island. Though this was before my time as a Spence-Mac employee, I was aware of this Walker Bay trip and later became curious about it because I knew how scarce and expensive aircraft fuel had been at that time. I learned that it had been a charter flight for R.H.G. "Bonny" Bonnycastle of the Hudson's Bay Company, and after reading his

Bill Cooke, Tom Caddick and Kel Mews with Spence-McDonough's Fairchild FC2, G-CARH.

Mickey Sutherland and the author at Fort Rae where they were stationed in the spring of 1932 to service company aircraft en route to the mining camps on Great Bear Lake. Here they display the ptarmigan they shot between servicing jobs.

book about his northern experiences, I realized that he had been an early advocate of air transport. In fact, his report on the trip probably played a large part in the HBC's decision to form its own air transport division.

During the winter of 1931–32, with the prospect of a claim-staking rush in the coming spring, Spence-Mac suspended all flying and concentrated on preparing their aircraft. Fortunately for the company, DOMEX had built a small hangar in the 1920s to provide for maintenance and repair. This hangar, facing the Clearwater River about halfway between Fort McMurray and the village of Waterways, became the operating base for Spence-Mac. It was a well-made structure, with sufficient capacity to accommodate a 71 with its wings folded and still have workshop space to spare. It had a graded, unpaved slipway for the pull-out and launching of aircraft and a crane for hoisting them for float installation and removal. Bachelor quarters for the crew were located some 300 feet to the south of the hangar.

When I arrived at Spence-Mac, the staff consisted entirely of ex-NAME people, except for Bill Spence. Bill and Mac were, of course, experienced pilots, and they hired Val Patriarche as the third member of the flying staff. As reserve pilot we had Kel Mews, an air engineer who had also obtained his pilot's licence and flew on a part-time basis. Tom Caddick, our maintenance chief, was also ex-NAME. He was an English gentleman and an aircraft engineer of outstanding ability, one for whom perfection was the minimum goal. As one engineer remarked on one of our less-than-perfect days, "Sometimes we can't even put the wing covers on right." But I had the greatest admiration for Tom and could not have had a better instructor. The rest of our maintenance staff consisted of Bill "Cookie" Cooke,

A Contrast in Prospecting Styles

Only 34 years separated the Bear Lake rush of 1932 from the Klondike gold rush of 1898, but those early prospectors could not have imagined the changes that would take place in the technology of transportation in such a relatively brief span of time. Where they had struggled up the icy slopes of the Chilkoot Pass with their outfits on their backs, these latter-day prospectors flew to their destinations in relative comfort and covered hundreds of miles in a matter of hours.

Mickey Sutherland mans the wobble pump to refuel an aircraft at Fort Rae. The author sits beside the funnel/fuel strainer monitoring the fuel level. March 1932.

Mickey Sutherland and Kel, when he wasn't flying.

We also had a temporary addition to our maintenance staff in the person of Frank Kelly. He hailed from Calgary and had migrated north as engineer for a one-aircraft firm called Airportation. It had been organized by Calgary businessman G.H. Rice, who had hired Harry Hayter and Harold Turner as pilots. (Turner died during that first year of their McMurray operation, while Hayter went on to become a well-known pilot with Mackenzie Air Service and later an executive of that firm.) Airportation's lone aircraft was a Curtiss Robin, one of the post-war ventures of the Curtiss Flying Co. It was a small cabin monoplane with 180 hp and a passenger load of perhaps three. (I have a recollection of another Curtiss product of that era, the Kingbird, a slightly larger version of the Robin but with two motors. Obviously, the single-motored performance of this craft was somewhat less than adequate—on one nacelle some wag had inscribed the word "Nip" and on the other one "Tuck.") Airportation was soon in desperate straits as its owner lacked connections in the mining industry and was unable to attract any shipping contracts. As a result, Frank Kelly, with

Exploring Dease and Hunter Bays

Lindsley Bay is located not far south of Hunter and Dease bays, both of which, though bypassed in the frenzy of the 1932 rush of prospectors, had been briefly touched by earlier history. Off to the east of them, amid the eskers and scanty trees on the threshold of the Barrens, lie lakes whose names provide a permanent record of Sir John Franklin's expedition of 1819–1822. Hepburn Lake is named for his faithful servant, without whom he would surely have perished. Junius and Augustus, the two Inuit interpreters who had travelled with the Franklin party from the Hudson Bay area, are also remembered, along with the voyageurs Vaillant, Belanger, St. Germain and Perrault. The Native people responsible for the ultimate rescue of the party also have their rightful place in the annals—Akaitcho the Chief, Keskarra, Humpy, the alluring Green Stockings, and the rest. Just to the west of the point where longitude 119 degrees touches the mouth of Dease River, members of Franklin's second expedition (1825–1827) erected the dwellings, which they named Fort Confidence. The walls have decayed and collapsed long since, but the chimneys were still standing in the early decades of the 20th century—monuments to the skill of their builders and the fortitude of those early explorers.

Traveller/writer George Douglas and his brother Lionel, who spent the winter of 1911–12 at Dease Bay, were among the first white men to travel overland to the Coppermine River and make contact with the Inuit of that area. This expedition became the basis for Douglas's historic (and now rare) book, *Lands Forlorn*. Oblate priests Rouviére and Le Roux also spent a year at Dease before sacrificing their lives in an attempt to bring a Christian presence to the nomadic Inuit people at the mouth of the Coppermine River on Coronation Gulf. The two young priests, after making some preliminary contact with the Inuit, returned to Coppermine with a group of them in October 1913. Ill-prepared for such a venture and without proper clothing or equipment, they were entirely dependent upon the Inuit for food and shelter. However, the local *angatkok*, or shaman, resented their presence and their influence. Warned of the danger they were in by friendly Inuit, early one morning they attempted the return journey, but they were tracked down and murdered. Some years later a Catholic

The chimneys of Fort Confidence, built by the members of Sir John Franklin's second expedition (1825-1827), were still standing in the early 20th century just west of where longitude 119 touches the mouth of the Dease River.

Oblate Father Jean-Baptiste Rouviere at Hodgson's Point, Great Bear Lake, Summer 1912.

church was established at Coppermine, and in 1933 the resident priests, members of the same religious order, constructed a cross in memory of their lost comrades at the approximate location where Rouviére and Le Roux had met their deaths—"the place being about 15 miles inland from the mouth of the Coppermine and about one hundred yards from the edge of the west bank" (from a 1915 report by RCMP Inspector Denny La Nauze). Today a more permanent memorial exists to the memory of those two dedicated missionaries: some 35 miles northeast of Dease Bay and on the route to the Coppermine, two lakes now bear the names Rouviére and Le Roux.

John Hornby, legendary wilderness traveller, also paused here briefly in his restless wanderings across the vastness of the north in search of some unknown goal—wanderings that would lead him to starvation and death on the upper waters of the Thelon. Hornby Bay, which lies at the point where the Arctic Circle is intersected by longitude 118 degrees, was named in memory of that strange and unusual man.

Lindsley Bay on Great Bear Lake. July 1932

paycheques few and far between—or perhaps non-existent—welcomed the offer of a few days' remuneration from Spence-Mac for aiding in the overhaul of one of our Fairchild 71s, AKY. Frank and I became close friends, a fellowship that lasted through all of our working years. He is still remembered with great affection by all who knew him.

Under Tom's talented hands and direction, in those early months of 1932, AKY became a 71 like no other. We faired the fuselage outwards just forward of the cockpit to achieve more graceful lines and better streamlining—not that streamlining could ever add much to the cruising speed of a 71. We built small storage compartments into the upper side walls of the cabin and added a separate auxiliary door to the left side to facilitate the loading of bulky cargo. And as a final flourish, AKY was fitted with a V-type windshield. This probably did little to improve either streamlining or visibility, but it did give her a rakish appearance, making her the envy of all the 71s in the north. With her overhaul completed, AKY was test flown and joined the rest of our fleet in readiness for the rush of prospectors heading for Bear Lake.

Spring had arrived in the north by then, though not temperature-wise as the overnight lows were in the -20° to -30°F range, but the hours of daylight were long and the strength of the sun intense. With AKY and our

Kel Mews and Vic Stevens with Spence-McDonough's ARH at Lindsley Bay. Spring 1932.

other 71, AKZ, plus our FC-2W-2, AAO, we operated from dawn to dusk—and dusk comes late during spring in those northern latitudes. Fort Rae became the company's transfer point, so Mickey Sutherland and I were based there, servicing the en route aircraft and occasionally making a trip through to Bear Lake with them. The two of us had an enjoyable couple of weeks there, hunting ptarmigan between flights, while the sun and wind turned our skins about the same colour as an old moccasin.

During this freighting operation, Kel Mews was busy on another project back at home base. The FC-2 that we owned, ARH, was a miniature version of our Fairchild 71s. It had the same outward appearance, the same strut-braced wing, and the identical Gottingen 387 airfoil section, but the fuselage and the wing were scaled down dimensionally and the motor was a 225 hp Wright J-5 with only slightly more than half the output of the Pratt & Whitney Wasps in our 71s. However, this FC-2 had a place in the future plans of our company chiefs. Ski-flying in the Fort McMurray area would be over by mid-April, but at rock-ribbed and iron-bound Bear Lake, nestled just south of the Arctic Circle, the ski-flying season would be extended by several weeks. To take advantage of this, Mac and Bill had arranged for

Cameron Bay

After the discovery of Eldorado in early 1932, one of the first among the rush of stakers to arrive on the scene was a well-known northerner, fur trader Jack Cameron, who staked all of the property on both sides of that dark, narrow bay with its steeply sloping sides. Though he abandoned his claims when summer disclosed the lack of any mineral outcrops, his early presence there was initially recognized in the name of the settlement and later by the name of the bay. D'arcy Arden, a long-time resident of the area, was the postmaster during the few years that Cameron Bay prospered. He was of Irish descent, born in Ottawa, well-educated, and had served in the Yukon from 1900 until 1910 as a federal government employee. Later he had spent time at Herschel Island, then made his way to Dease Bay on Great Bear Lake , where he became associated with Hornby around 1912 or 1913.

D'arcy moved to Yellowknife after the settlement of Cameron Bay closed, but he did return a couple of times in later years and provided the following description. "Cameron Bay was once a thriving settlement, you know. There were two radio stations (one government and one airline), a hotel/restaurant, mining recorder's office, RCMP detachment and post office. There were numerous cabins scattered through the trees along the hillside. The war [WWII] was on by then [the time of his first return visit], of course, with all prospecting and mining activity curtailed, except

the floats for ARH to be shipped to Bear Lake the previous summer. These were now at our company base at Lindsley Bay, north-east of Cameron Bay.

Kel's job was to unearth our FC-2, ARH, from her winter snowbank, then assisted by Tom, pack all of the spare parts and materials that might be required to keep her operational in the bush over the spring breakup period. There were spares for the Wright J-5 engine—a cylinder/piston assembly, a magneto, a starter, engine gaskets and spare exhaust sections. For the airframe there were spare screws and bolts, needles, thread, dope and fabric, together with a float repair kit for the upcoming summer season. With these preparations completed he and Tom said their farewells, and Kel and ARH were on their way to Bear Lake and Lindsley Bay.

Eldorado, and the settlement lay silent and deserted. The only visitors were the occasional ravens and whisky-jacks and the only permanent residents were the squirrels. In summer it was a peaceful little village but with no sign of activity, as though all the residents were having a siesta. But it was an unnatural silence. The chimneys produced no smoke, the normal sounds of woodpile activities were missing. Saw and axe lay silent and no dog barked. The dock had fallen into disrepair, emphasized by the half-submerged skiff moored beside it. It was a far different place from what it had been in '35.

"I came back once in winter—in December. What a gloomy place it was, especially in the dark confines of that narrow bay. Nothing is more forlorn than an abandoned village with the deserted cabins standing lifeless in the half-light of a winter afternoon, some of them barely visible under the shadows of the surrounding trees. No warm and friendly light glowed from a cabin window, there was no sound to break the silence. Heavy snow, unmarked by footprints, covered the path to the restaurant. The door was closed but not locked as though Jerry Murphy had only stepped out for a moment. Within, the benches were neatly drawn up to the rough-hewn table, complete with its oil-cloth covering. The dishes and cutlery were assembled in their proper places. But the customers who once enjoyed the cheer and hospitality of that frontier inn were now far away. Few would ever return. Some were bearing arms on distant shores, some had already died in action. It was a most depressing place, I tell you. I never wanted to go back, especially in winter."

When the first big uranium strike had been made in 1930 at Labine Point (later to become Eldorado Mines), it was anticipated that a large mining community would develop, and Lindsley Bay, to the north of Labine Point, was selected as the townsite. The choice of location was, I believe, largely on the recommendation of Major "Lockie" Burwash, a mining engineer who had held a number of high level positions with the federal government. It was a beautiful spot and would have made an ideal townsite. The bottom end of the bay was somewhat over a quarter mile in width with a gradually sloping beach of fine gravel extending across it. Back from the lake the terrain levelled out with a good covering of timber, through which ran a small and boisterous creek. This area, together with the level and well-timbered northeast side, would have easily accommodated a town of several thousand people. Although ultimately Cameron Bay was chosen for the townsite because it was closer to the Eldorado mines, in 1931 the federal government, anticipating Lindsley's future development, had ordered the army to station a unit of the Royal Canadian Corps of Signals (RCCS) there. There were two operators and the station was equipped with a small, low-powered transmitter, but it had sufficient strength to contact the larger and more powerful RCCS stations at Fort Norman, Fort Resolution and Fort Smith. Around the same time Spence-Mac constructed a sizeable log building at Lindsley to serve as both restaurant and sleeping quarters for our own people, the area prospectors and the RCCS operators.

That spring of '32 Lindsley Bay was probably the most important location on Bear Lake—and certainly the busiest. As the snow began to disappear from the hills, the prospectors became anxious for transportation, convinced that each hill and headland contained another Eldorado. Kel and ARH were in great demand and flew long hours each day. With ideal landing and takeoff conditions on the frozen surfaces of the lakes, now clear of snowdrifts, prospecting parties could be ferried to their selected areas and their canoes and supplies delivered to distant lakes.

Unfortunately, the story had a less than happy ending. When breakup finally arrived, ARH and Kel again became waterborne. Eager to start the summer season, and with customers clamouring for transportation, Kel made a rush trip to deliver prospector Vic Stevens to a staking area. During an onshore landing on a lake (later named Jory) near the headwaters of the Coppermine River, the wind suddenly tricked him. Touching down too close to shore, ARH displayed surprising agility. Though failing in her attempt to go cross-country, she performed some neat, low-level aerobatics, climaxed by a somersault onto the lakeshore. The damage was of a repairable nature, but because of the remote location, salvage was too difficult and costly. There she lay for more than 50 years, mouldering on the moss of the Barrens, a landmark to the few fliers who passed that way and a constant reminder to pilots of the need for everlasting caution. It was only when it was finally realized that ARH was an endangered species and that even in her tattered condition she was of value to posterity that she was salvaged by a party from the Western Canada Aviation Museum with much help from the operator of a local tourist lodge. She will now have a new and well-deserved home as part of our aviation heritage.

Bill Spence with the wreckage of G-CARH on Jory Lake near the headwaters of the Coppermine River. After mouldering there for 50 years, ARH was salvaged by the Western Canada Aviation Museum. (The tail of Spence's CF-AKZ is in the foreground.)

After breakup at McMurray I spent a couple of weeks back at Bear Lake with Bill Spence on AKZ, servicing prospectors' camps, but it was Bill's intention at the conclusion of this project to spend the winter at The Pas in northern Manitoba. On our way south we stopped briefly at Cameron Bay, and there learned that Andy Cruikshanks, a pilot for Canadian Airways, southbound from Bear Lake two or three days earlier, had not arrived at Rae. The weather had been clear and warm so the consensus was that Andy, with his two companions, engineers Horace Torrie and Harry King, had experienced an engine malfunction of some type, resulting in a forced landing. No one felt any cause for alarm.

We flew along the route that was generally followed, watching carefully and fully expecting to see Andy's Super Fokker moored on a lakeshore with the crew sitting in the shade and fighting the mosquitoes. But not far north of Rae we spotted the crumpled remains of the Fokker in a stretch of muskeg between two lakes. We circled at low altitude, looking for signs of life. There were none. We then searched the adjacent lakeshores on the off-chance that some of them had survived and reached the shore but without success. We flew on to Rae, where we met a Canadian Airways crew who told us that the accident had been sighted on the previous day. They were on their way to the crash site to recover the bodies.

Andy, Horace and Harry were well-known and popular in the industry, highly regarded by all who knew them, and each of them in his own way had made a contribution to the advancement of aviation in Canada. Harry King had been based at various airports across the prairies to service the aircraft of the first Prairie Air Mail operated by Western Canada Airways. Horace Torrie, as a sergeant in the RCAF, had been one of the members of the Hudson's Straits Expedition of 1927, carrying out ice patrols to determine seasonal limits for grain-carrying freighters. And Andy Cruikshanks with his Ryan aircraft, *Queen of the Yukon*, a sister ship to Lindbergh's *Spirit of St. Louis*, had carried out some of the earliest flying in the Yukon. Following this he had been employed by Western Canada Airways, and in 1929 he had been the pilot of that company's Fokker Super Universal G-CASQ when it broke through the ice at Burnside River, south of Bathurst Inlet Post. The aircraft had been recovered by heroic efforts on the part of the engineers of the party and made serviceable again just in time to assist in the rescue of the lost McAlpine party from Cambridge Bay. But his role in that adventure was not over. After reaching Reliance with some of the rescued McAlpine people on board, his aircraft developed mechanical problems that left it underpowered. However, since it was the only serviceable aircraft remaining in the area, he flew one group of the rescued men to Resolution before returning to Reliance to find Bill Spence and Roy Brown, both down in the Aylmer/Muskox lakes area and missing by that time for two weeks. He located first one, then the other, loaded both crews into his aircraft, and flew them out to Reliance. Had it not been for his determined efforts, those men may not have survived.

In those days there were so few people in the flying business in Canada that all these men were known to one another, either personally or by name, so the deaths of the three men shocked everyone in the north. But this was only the start of a sad period in northern flying. Paul Calder and Bill Nadin

Bill Spence and Bill Cooke taxi out into the Clearwater River in Fairchild AKZ for the last time, October 17, 1932. Spence died when the aircraft crashed near The Pas, Manitoba. Cooke survived the crash, but his frozen hands had to be amputated.

were the next to go. In January 1933 they were flying from Rae to Bear Lake in a Fairchild FC-2W-2, G-CATL, bucking a blizzard, when they reached their trail end. As the flying time between those points was close to three hours with our old aircraft and as the accident site was only 30-odd miles south of Cameron Bay, the crash must have occurred late in the day. With only a short distance to go, they must have pressed on in the failing light of the winter afternoon. Crossing one of the bays in Grouard Lake in what would have been whiteout conditions, Calder had obviously lost contact with the surface and they crashed. The shoreline for which he searched would be found only in eternity.

And then it was Spence-Mac's turn. Following our return to McMurray after our Bear Lake stint, Bill Spence had continued with his plans to spend freeze-up and part of the following winter at The Pas, taking Bill "Cookie" Cooke with him as engineer. We overhauled the skis, repaired the winter engine cover, and assembled the equipment that would be needed for the winter months ahead. With the equipment loaded and after a general round of handshakes, they were on their way. My diary entry for that day reads:

> **October 17, 1932.** Freezing hard last night. Bill Spence and Bill Cooke left this morning with Fairchild AKZ, going to The Pas where they will spend freeze-up.

After the departure of our companions we continued our normal routines as I noted in my diary the next day.

> **October 18, 1932.** Ice is running in the Clearwater today. AKZ got away just in time. We pulled out AAO today, removed the floats and changed her to wheels.

There is an unfortunate gap in my records at this point. But the headlines of The Pas' newspaper, *The Northern Mail*, on December 22, 1932, state "W.A. Spence of Spence-McDonough Airways was expected here from Waterways, Alberta, today." (This is an error: they did not return to McMurray—Waterways—after leaving there in mid-October.) In later issues of the paper there is mention of a freighting contract awarded to Spence-Mac but no details. It is probable that after leaving McMurray they had worked in the Norway House area until freeze-up and changed from floats to skis at that point. Their base of operations was then moved to The Pas in early January 1933, where on January 11, the local weather was recorded as "Blizzard, temperature -23°F." The following day it was "Blowing snow, temperature -30°F."

On the evening of the 11th, Bill Spence received a message from the RCMP at Norway House advising that they needed transportation for two passengers to The Pas. Norway House is located on the Nelson River, slightly downstream from its source in Lake Winnipeg. It is almost due east of The Pas, the distance being about 135 miles, as the whisky-jack flies, but considerably longer if the weather was "down." In such cases our airborne people would fly at a lower altitude from lake to lake with the ever-present threat of a whiteout if they lost contact with the surface.

When morning came on January 12, the weather at The Pas was -30°F with blowing snow—in other words, a blizzard, but these conditions seem to have been variable. Generally the snowfall would have been of such intensity that flying was impossible, but there would also be the odd brief period of limited visibility, so Bill's flight to Norway House apparently didn't raise serious concerns. But that was early in the day when the light was better. It is also possible that Norway House was near the edge of the weather disturbance—one that was perhaps centred in the area of The Pas.

After Bill and Cookie arrived, they learned that their passengers were Corporal P. Greaves of the RCMP and a prisoner by the name of Buster Whiteway of Berens River, a young Native wanted by the Saskatchewan RCMP for some misdemeanor. A third passenger had also appeared—Ernest Robinson, a well-known prospector who had completed his season's work in the Norway House area and was taking advantage of this flight to return to The Pas. It was nearly mid-afternoon and the light was already beginning to fade as they loaded up and prepared for departure. Cookie removed and stowed the engine cover, then inserted the crank into the starter opening. Four turns of the crank brought the inertia flywheel up to speed, Bill engaged the starter, and the Wasp roared to life. With Cookie now on board, Bill taxied down the river along their inbound ski tracks, then turned to take off on their fateful last journey.

There is no doubt that Bill would have considered the advisability of remaining overnight at Norway House. It is difficult to know what factors he would have weighed in making his final decision, but having just traversed the route from The Pas, all of the landmarks would be fresh in his mind. If he'd had no difficulty with the eastbound flight weather-wise, he would probably feel it would be no worse during the return. These were all conditions that he had experienced before in his thousands of hours of bush flying. The only real variable, therefore, was probably the amount—and the quality—of the remaining daylight. If he had been queried on this point, he would probably have said, "Well, yes, it is getting late, but it's only an hour-and-a-half flight. We'll just have time to make it."

His route would have taken AKZ across the north end of Lake Winnipeg, then into the chain of lakes to the west—Limestone, William and Davidson—and finally into the numerous bays that form South Moose Lake. The safe route would have been to go southeast and then along the south shore of the lake, which would have taken them over Tom Lamb's trading post at the south end. Here they might have landed for the night. Daylight and weather permitting, they could then follow a chain of small lakes leading to The Pas. This route would have allowed them to remain in touch with the timbered shorelines of the lakes, any one

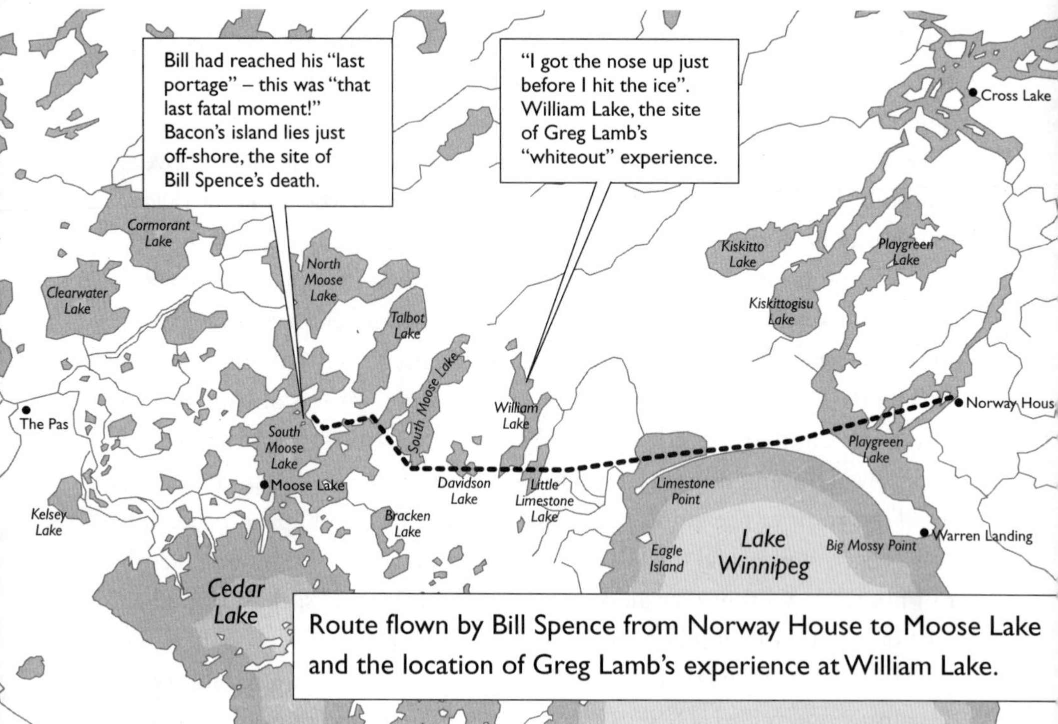

Route flown by Bill Spence from Norway House to Moose Lake and the location of Greg Lamb's experience at William Lake.

of which would provide a safe landing area. But there are other elements that could have influenced his decision, one of these being the almost total lack of accurate maps. The main watercourses had been surveyed quite accurately by the early water-borne travellers, but coverage of the general area was sketchy. Another consideration was the extent of Bill's knowledge of the rather intricate drainage of the area. He was far more at home in the western Hudson Bay area or the Northwest Territories than in Manitoba.

I can only assume that the weather was down after he left Davidson Lake and picked up the south end of South Moose Lake. It is only a four-mile hop across the base of this peninsula into the southeast corner of Moose Lake, and with bush under him, he could have made this crossing even with poor visibility, but it would seem that Bill was not aware of this proximity. Instead, he followed the shoreline, turning to the northwest. About six miles farther on he reached the northeast extension of Moose Lake. Here again he had the option of turning to the southwest, toward the Moose Lake Post, but once again his lack of detailed knowledge of the area robbed him of this opportunity. The south-bearing shoreline seemed to veer in the wrong direction, so he maintained his course, crossed over the northeast arm of Moose Lake and then made a fateful turn to the west. Even this route might have saved them if he had realized that the relative safety of the main northwest shore of Moose Lake lay just beyond. Instead, he turned to the left, toward Bacon's Island.

There is no doubt that the blizzard was at its worst at that time, with visibility close to zero. As the main northwest shore—a bare three miles away—was invisible to him, he certainly could not have seen the south shoreline, some eight miles distant. To fly across a lake of any size in winter in fading light and with visibility further reduced by heavy snow is more than hazardous—it is suicidal. As an experienced northern pilot Bill Spence would have been well aware of the risks involved. Given the circumstances, it is quite unbelievable that he would have attempted such a lake crossing.

As he had been flying adjacent to wooded shorelines almost since his departure from Norway House, a relatively safe landing could have been made anywhere. Why then did he attempt such a hazardous one at this particular time and place? I can only assume that he had spotted some sign of the existing fish camp or that one of his passengers had advised him of the location. As it was, he turned to the left and attempted a landing beside Bacon's Island.

Bacon's Island was named after Louis Bacon, an early resident who had used it as a base for his commercial fishing activities. It is barely a mile in length but Bill would have been unaware of this. Part of this distance would have been consumed in the execution of the turn toward the island and the initial preparation for the landing. Feeling his way down toward the ice surface—below him but invisible—and maintaining visual contact with the adjacent trees on the shoreline, he suddenly shot past the end of the island and into the shadowless void beyond. It is possible that he might have reduced power and made a blind landing at this point—hazardous though this would have been. Bill's instincts probably took over, and his reactions became automatic—he kicked on left rudder and swung the aircraft into a steep turn. With the benefit of a few more feet of altitude this might have been successful, but the ice was too close.

The headlines of the January 13 issue of *The Northern Mail* read: "Pilot

Wm. Spence Killed. Crash at Moose Lake Kills Famous Airman, Three Others Injured."

The story that followed said in part:

> A MAN OF THE NORTH, KNOWN AS THE SMILING AVIATOR TO TRAPPERS, HUNTERS, MINING MEN, INDIANS AND ESKIMOS, PILOT W.A. (BILL) SPENCE, ACE OF BARREN LAND FLIERS, IS DEAD TODAY.
>
> Swirling snow, mist and early twilight brought death to Pilot Spence and injury to four other men, one a prisoner of a Royal Canadian Mounted police officer, at Moose Lake, near Bacon's Island, 45 miles northeast of The Pas, Manitoba. Forced to land, a wing was torn off the plane and the machine sped on to destruction, tearing itself into a mass of debris on the northern lake.
>
> Pilot Wm. Spence, chief of Spence-McDonough Air Transport Ltd., was killed yesterday afternoon at Moose Lake when his plane crashed on the ice, 10 miles from the Lake settlement. Spence was instantly killed and his mechanic, W.L. Cooke, and three passengers seriously injured. The others were: John Robinson, pioneer north country prospector; Corporal P. Greaves, R.C.M.P.; and Buster Whiteway, a Beren's River youth wanted by Saskatchewan authorities. The injured were brought to The Pas by a relief plane are now in hospital and are still expected to recover.
>
> Spence, 41 years old, had been flying for more than 15 years. He was a Royal Air Force pilot during the War. His wife and two children were visiting in Toronto when news of the crash was received. Spence was born at Oshawa, Ont., although he had made the northland his home for the past 10 years.
>
> How an Indian prisoner, his ankle broken in the crash, crawled through a sub-Arctic blizzard to bring help to his captors was told in The Pas as an aftermath to the death of Pilot Spence. The Indian, Buster Whiteway, was being returned to civilization by an officer of the Royal Canadian Mounted Police to face the white man's laws. The Indian prisoner, his ankle swollen to twice its normal size, crawled away from the wreckage to get help.

Whiteway had been hurled through the roof of the cabin when the plane struck the ice and knocked out by the impact, but he was the first to regain consciousness after the crash. In the debris that had been the aircraft cabin, he found Robinson lying on top of Greaves and dragged the two men from the wreck. A few yards away he discovered the body of Spence thrown across that of his mechanic. Cooke, regaining consciousness, was digging at the snow with his bare hands, trying to free himself. Whiteway's first impulse was to get to the shoreline and build a fire where he could bring the injured men, but as he started for the shore of Bacon's Island, dragging his fractured ankle, he saw a fish caboose returning with a last load of fish for the day. His shouts went unheard, and when he finally rounded the point of the island the caboose had disappeared. Then he heard dogs howling and knew that the camp was nearby. Half walking, half crawling along the shoreline, he finally came close enough for his voice to be heard. When the fishermen came to his aid and learned of the accident, they immediately went to the wreckage and brought the injured men to the warmth of their bunkhouse. Two Native runners left almost immediately for Cormorant Lake, a RCAF summer base located adjacent to the Hudson Bay Railroad (the CNR), where a caretaker had phone communications with The Pas. On their way the two runners met fire ranger Rod McKenzie and his brother, and one of the McKenzies returned with the two runners to Cormorant and telephoned the news to the RCMP headquarters in The Pas.

There were still traces of the blizzard blowing when pilot S.J. McRory of Canadian Airways took off for Moose Lake with Dr. N.G. Trimble and RCMP Sgt. Perry Rose on board. Less than 25 miles from The Pas they met a blinding snowstorm and were forced to return. When the storm abated an hour later, they tried again. This time they got as far as Tom Lamb's trading post at Moose Lake settlement, 10 miles from the crash site, before the growing darkness overtook them. They made one attempt to taxi across to Bacon's Island but it was now snowing heavily and visibility was impossible. Finally a local Native fisherman volunteered to take them with his pony and sleigh, and they reached their goal at 11:00 that night. McRory arrived at the fish camp at 10:30 the next morning and the survivors, plus the body of Bill Spence, were then ferried to The Pas.

Both of Greaves' collar bones had been broken as well as five ribs on

Local Knowledge Pays Off for Pilot

While researching this story, I had some correspondence with Greg Lamb of the illustrious Lamb family, bush fliers of The Pas. After we discussed Bill's flight and the route that he might have followed between Norway House and The Pas, Greg mentioned that he'd had a very similar experience in the same area. "On one trip just after freeze-up, I went to Norway House with BHS, a Mark V Norseman, to pick up a Father LeMay and another passenger. The weather was terrible and I wanted to stay at Norway House until it improved. This other passenger was anxious to reach The Pas, and because of his constant urging I finally decided to try it. I was following the 'cut line' from Playgreen Lake to William Lake. The visibility was nil in heavy snow. When I got to William Lake I was all of a sudden over the open lake [ice] with no shoreline or black bush under me. I had been hoping to pick up the small island in the middle for reference but couldn't locate it. I remember seeing the opaque snow drifts going by the small corner window—vertically! I wrenched the left wing up and pulled back on the stick, and I got the nose up just before we hit the ice! Being familiar with the lake I taxied through the narrows and stopped at George Campbell's cabin, spending the night with him. The next day we got to the post at Moose Lake, spent the night there and finally got into The Pas the following day. I'm relating this, Rex, just to show how easy it is to get into jackpots—some of us survived them and some didn't." In retrospect, it is obvious that Greg, because of his detailed knowledge of the area, knew the safe route to follow (the south shore to the trading post) while Bill, lacking this critical knowledge, had no other option than to follow the shoreline that was before him.

his left side. Ernest Robinson suffered muscle injuries to his head and neck. Bill Cooke had both hands frozen from digging in the snow to free himself, lacerations to his mouth, both eyelids, forehead and scalp.

The doctors were unable to save Bill Cooke's frozen hands. Crippled and unable to follow his profession, he returned to England. His countryman Tom Caddick kept in touch with him, and I later learned that Bill was operating a hardware store, a far cry from his life of adventure on the Canadian frontier.

And what of our fine 71, AKZ? I can only quote the melancholy words from the DoT report: "13/1/33: DBR (damaged beyond repair) at Moose Lake, Man. Wingtip hit ground during landing in whiteout."

The question of why AKZ crashed still remains. Bill Spence was an excellent pilot with years of accident-free northern flying behind him. During the McAlpine search he had carried out some of the most extensive and difficult of the search flights. On his last flight, there is nothing to indicate that there was any mechanical problem with the aircraft or the power plant; they were relatively new and in excellent condition and the motor was functioning normally until the final moment of the flight. The weather was most certainly a factor but who can say whether it was beyond limits. As in most cases of VFR operations, limits depend upon a pilot's judgement and his personal experience, meaning his experience in that particular type of operation, including the variables of daylight, location, type of terrain, and rate of snowfall. There is no doubt that Bill had flown in similar difficult situations in the past. After all, if pilots landed whenever snowfall started, very little northern flying would have been done. Of course, a pilot who was both wise and experienced would certainly not initiate a flight under heavy snowfall/failing light conditions, nor did Bill. The snow conditions at Norway House had undoubtedly been much better than at The Pas, creating the belief that the storm had ended. Finally, it is a matter of the pilot recognizing the point where he is beyond his personal limits; this is always difficult—he's had it this tough before and got through, so he presses on. He is also influenced by the remaining time and distance to his destination. If he is down on the deck and still 100 miles from home, then the decision to pack it in for the night will be easier to make than if the home corral is only 25 miles away. And if he carries only a minimum of emergency gear—barely enough for pilot and engineer, say—but he has three extra passengers on board, how will he provide for them during an overnight stop? Reaching home base becomes a more urgent matter.

I can only assume that the weather and the visibility were not worse than Bill had encountered in the past. In his judgement, measured against his considerable experience, conditions were "flyable." But there are certain risks inherent to bush flying—risks that are part of the game. Without warning Bill reached the end of the island, and as a natural reaction he made a desperate attempt to turn back. With a few more feet of altitude he might have executed the turn safely, but Bill had reached his last portage.

This tragedy caused the failure of Spence-McDonough Air Transport. The remaining partner, Mac McDonough, did not have the will to continue after Bill's death and the company was absorbed by Canadian Airways Ltd., which obtained our remaining two aircraft together with all of the spares and equipment. Tom Caddick was also included in this deal and later in the year, Val Patriarche, Micky Sutherland and Frank Kelly were hired. While I had gained an additional year of experience, a job was still beyond my reach because I lacked my air engineer's licence. As the local economic picture was still bleak for employment of any kind, I regretfully said farewell to my friends and returned to the trapline. There was one bright spot, however—I was just in time for the spring muskrat hunt.

3 And then there was one

By the beginning of 1933, of the three Fairchild 71s bought new by DOMEX two years earlier, only one remained—AKY—and on March 4 she gained a new owner, Canadian Airways Ltd. She operated in the Mackenzie District for part of that year, then was transferred to the company's base in Vancouver. This was a peaceful sort of an existence for AKY but there were hazards to contend with, even along the Pacific Coast. One day she was landing in the harbour and the pilot made a slight error, landing between a tug and a barge without noticing that the barge was under tow. AKY had just touched down and was still on the step when the cable tightened and emerged from the water. The pilot and passengers survived this mishap but AKY was out of service for some time.

As the company did not have repair facilities at Vancouver, AKY was turned over to the Boeing plant for overhaul. Upon inspection, she was found to have such extensive damage to her fuselage due to the accident and to the effects of saltwater corrosion that it was beyond economical repair. A new fuselage was obtained and the aircraft given a complete overhaul, including modification to 71C category. But the new fuselage made it necessary to re-register her, and she emerged from the shops as CF-AOP to resume her West Coast duties, keeping a wary eye on barges and tugs.

After breakup in the spring of 1936 she was transferred to the company base at Prince Albert, remaining there until the end of the summer season of 1938. According to all reports—and partly because of a lack of same—it must be assumed that AOP led an exemplary life during her residence there. In the late summer of 1938 she was transferred to the Mackenzie District, with headquarters at Edmonton. Then in October of that year AOP and her crew were sent to spend freeze-up at Yellowknife in order to continue with a freight-hauling contract. Now the resident aircraft at Yellowknife, she became familiar to the locals, both within the settlement and at the various camps she visited. One group, intrigued by the fact that AOP had been rebuilt using a fuselage from a different aircraft, decided that AOP stood for All Old Parts, and that's the name she became known by.

AOP continued with her camp servicing routine until mid-December when an incident occurred that again changed her title. She was returning from a trip to Gordon Lake in the limited visibility of early twilight on an overcast day when, during a landing at a prospector's camp on Prosperous Lake, she struck some exposed rocks. These inflicted considerable damage and AOP was out of service for some time while repairs were carried out. When she returned to her camp servicing routine, however, the same group who had conceived the idea of hanging the All Old Parts title upon their faithful servant held further discussions and all agreed that a new title was required, something that would bear witness to this latest chapter in her career. Consensus was finally reached; instead of All Old Parts, she would henceforth be known as All Over Prosperous.

No records exist of AOP's adventures and location between late 1938 and 1941, when she was transferred to the mining district of Beauchesne in northern Quebec and encountered a motor boat during takeoff. (Boats were apparently her nemesis!) By a stroke of great good fortune I happened to be discussing this illustrious aircraft with an old friend, Reg Nichols, and asked him if he had any knowledge of this accident. His reply was the kind that anyone with an interest in aircraft research dreams of. "Oh, yes," he said. "I was there and saw the whole thing."

Beauchesne was the supply centre for the huge Manuan power development, and Canadian Airways Ltd. had a contract to deliver the thousands of tons of machinery and supplies that were needed for it. On the day in question AOP was making her first trip of the day with a load of cargo but no passengers. The rising sun was low on the eastern horizon and she was taking off in that direction. Unknown to the pilot, a small, double-decked passenger craft was off to the right and steering a collision course with the aircraft. If the boat operator had been even semi-observant

The remains of Fairchild CF-AOP (also pictured on page 49) were hauled ashore after a collision with a power boat at Beauchesne, PQ, on May 20, 1941. The DoT inspector's assessment of AOP after the collision was DBR—damaged beyond repair.

he could have avoided the aircraft, but because of the sun, the pilot was using the left front window for visibility and had no hope of spotting the boat.

The aircraft had just become airborne when it intercepted the boat, the floats striking the boat's front superstructure just above the hull line. (Had the boat been just a few feet farther along its course, the daydreaming helmsman would have received a sharp reminder of his duties!) Meanwhile, the aircraft had bounced straight up, turned in the air, and nosed straight down into the water. As the aircraft was reversing direction after the impact, the pilot had the time and foresight to switch off the engine. The propeller blades were, therefore, stationary when they contacted the water, and as the photos show, they received no damage.

As the floats had taken the brunt of the impact they were completely demolished. Fortunately the air trapped inside the wings created sufficient flotation to keep the aircraft from sinking. Had the pilot been seriously

III-3 Wartime scarcity of new aircraft for bush flying duties made the damaged AOP, bought in 1930 for $20,000, virtually priceless. Her remains were bought up and she was rebuilt to fly again.

injured or even just stunned, there is no doubt that he would have drowned. Good fortune was with him, however. He released his safety belt, opened the cockpit door, and abandoned ship. The boat people were luckier than they deserved to be. Shaken up and bruised, they were able to assist the rather waterlogged pilot to come aboard.

Those on shore immediately started up a small work boat that Reg referred to as an "alligator" (apparently the local name for that model of work boat). Proceeding to the wreck site, they picked up the survivors and ferried them to shore. Cuts and bruises were the only reported injuries. The passenger boat was still afloat so ropes were secured around its propeller hub and the wreckage towed into shallow water. A tractor dragged the remains of poor old AOP out of the water and onto the shore. If her Yellowknife supporters could have seen her they would doubtless have had some difficulty in creating a title to properly describe her condition. The local CAL maintenance staff certainly considered her a write-off and the DoT inspector had a similar view. His official report states: "20/5/41—DBR (damaged beyond repair) at Lake Onatchiway, hit motorboat on takeoff from Beauchesne Depot."

However, the date that this incident occurred is important to this story. In more peaceful and prosperous times it is probable that the fate of AOP would have been sealed by the DoT's verdict, but once again AOP's lucky star was not to be extinguished. By 1941 virtually all aircraft manufacturing facilities in Canada—Noordyun, Fairchild, Vickers, de Havilland—were concentrating on military production, and replacement bush aircraft were becoming increasingly scarce. Thus, the well-bent remains of AOP became an object of increasing value, and before long some bush operator in the area—long on contracts but short on equipment—purchased the remains from the insurance company and arranged for the overhaul.

At this point there is another gap in my information. AOP's next appearance was in the service of Parsons Flying Service of Kenora, Ontario. Keith Parsons remembers that "We operated Fairchild 71 CF-AOP during the winter of 1948. It was a former Ontario Department of Lands and Forests aircraft, purchased by Andy Madore of Twin City Industrial Equipment, Port Arthur, Ontario. They leased it to us and we were prepared to purchase it in the spring of 1948 but a C of A [Certificate of Airworthiness] inspection found dry rot in the wing spars so we returned it to Twin Cities."

Fairchild CF-AKY, alias CF-AOP, had a service life of almost 18 years, far exceeding the life span of her sister ships AKX and AKZ, and certainly better than the average for the bush aircraft of the 1930s. During her working life she seems to have had only two serious mishaps—the Vancouver harbour incident and the one at Beauchesne. Neither resulted in loss of life, though her passengers and crew were shaken up, and all of them had exciting moments. Other than that, AKY/AOP led an almost trouble-free existence. She might have died with her boots on in the same manner as her sister ships and so many other bush aircraft, a crumpled, fiery wreckage on some northern hillside or an oil slick on a smoke-shrouded lake. Instead, she reached the end of her days peacefully, and I would hope that some aviation historians have appreciated her value as one of the last of her type and that somewhere she is being preserved and restored. When one considers the myriad of potential disasters that existed, summer and winter, her excellent record is a tribute to a fine aircraft and to those who flew and maintained her.

4 Workin' on the river

In March 1933, with Spence-Mac gone, I had returned to live with my parents at the HBC shipyards, downriver from McMurray, hoping that some kind of employment would come along. One sunny morning in late June our normal activities were interrupted by the sound of the approaching steamer, the *Northland Echo*, southbound toward McMurray. As the twice-weekly passing of the steamer (a northbound trip followed by the southbound one) was about the only break in our routine, we always watched with interest. Normally it would pass by with a friendly toot of the whistle. On this occasion the boat slowed, coasted to a stop at the shoreline, and the gangplank was extended. Dad was there to meet them, expecting that they were in need of some repair parts from the stock at the shipyards—a spare valve, perhaps, or a steam pressure gauge. Instead, John Sutherland, the chief engineer, told Dad that one of the firemen was quitting at the end of that trip, and the job was mine if I wanted it. I had just ambled up and my reply was, of course, a delighted affirmative. It was arranged that they would pull in the following day on the northbound trip to pick me up.

The operating crew of the boat worked shift-on-shift, that is, two six-hour shifts on and two six-hour shifts off—a twelve-hour working day. The crew on the two 6:00 to 12:00 shifts consisted of the captain, the chief engineer and the first fireman. The other two shifts were taken by the first mate (or sometimes by the pilot), the second engineer and the second fireman. Being the junior slave, these were the shifts I drew—from midnight until 6:00 a.m. and from noon until 6:00 p.m. My opposite in the stokehold was "Duke" Downing, a fine man well known to my family, one of the many Englishmen who had migrated to the Canadian north at the end of the World War I. Because of his accent, his fellow workmen had referred to him—initially behind his back or beyond his hearing—as "The Duke," and the sobriquet became permanent.

On the day of my embarkation, the *Echo* had departed McMurray in the early afternoon, so by the time they stopped to pick me up, Duke had worked part of my noon to 6:00 p.m. shift. Because of working around the shipyards and visiting with Duke on my odd short trip on the *Echo*, I already had some knowledge of the job requirements. These were simple enough: short on skill, long on muscle. Duke worked with me for part of that first afternoon—until about 4:00 as I recall—then took a nap. I worked a couple of hours into his shift—until about 8:00—then had a brief nap before returning at midnight to do my graveyard shift.

The stokehold on the *Echo* was the area immediately in front of the boiler, about four feet below the level of the surrounding main deck. It was in this depression that Duke and I spent our days and nights feeding the fire, one stick at a time. The main cordwood supply was stored amidships, so it was therefore necessary to maintain a small supply of cordwood within reach on each side of the stokehold. These stacks were replenished every half-hour or so by the "wood-passers"—Native deckhands who took turns at this duty. A couple of these fellows were not overly keen—the task interfered with their sleep or card games—and sometimes Duke or I would be down to our last sticks of wood before our helpers appeared. Being junior in years and experience and knowing all of the deckhands personally from winter trips along the river, I suffered rather less from these minor neglects than did Duke. He became somewhat indignant—vocally so—if his woodpile was less than adequate, and his objections always carried a veiled—at times unveiled—threat of physical violence. Needless to say, Duke was not overly popular with the deckhands.

Besides the considerable physical labour of firing the boilers—some of those cordwood sticks, especially the wet ones from the bottom of the pile, were very heavy—a certain technique was required. This was learned only through experience. There were a few occasions when I was unable to maintain the required steam pressure of 160 psi (pounds per square inch), due to the nature of the wood, to the great displeasure of the second engineer,

George King. It had been George's misfortune to lose both an eye and an arm at some point in his career, perhaps during a naval experience, which also might have accounted for his attitude. To him, engineers were officers and were to be addressed as "sir" by all of lower rank. Fortunately for the firemen, rank did not sit heavily with our chief, Old John, who had spent a lifetime in the service of the Hudson's Bay Company and was on a first-name basis with everyone, including the deckhands. George, however, while realizing that he had no support from John, still believed that the firemen would benefit from the application of basic discipline, and he had intimated as much to Duke during their first season together. Duke's reply, I understand, had been negative and profane, and George had to admit defeat, though his feelings on the subject remained unchanged and occasionally these came to the surface in future dealings with Duke. One such exchange had taken place just prior to the evening shift-change a few years before my time on the *Echo*. Still smarting from some remark by George, Duke had relieved the afternoon shift fireman with the remark, "That old b——d! Just because he's lost an arm and an eye, he needn't think he's Lord Nelson!" And so it was that George earned his nickname, one that was so little-known outside of the small group of Hudson's Bay Transport people that I doubt even George himself ever became aware of it. However, the story was often told in his absence, rough humour being a reflection of the frontier environment in which we worked.

Besides the almost continuous task of firing the boiler to maintain steam pressure, there were a number of other concerns for the firemen. As the quality of our cordwood often varied considerably from one batch to the next, we would have to make a joint decision with the shift engineer on the amount of cordwood we should load at each particular woodpile. The engineer would arrive for these discussions with a couple of cups of coffee in hand, so they were a pleasant diversion for both parties. We burned roughly 36 cords of wood in a five- or six-day round trip. To put that figure into recognizable terms, 36 cords is a stack of wood four feet wide, four feet high and 288 feet long. Each fireman would handle half this amount during the trip. Great stuff for muscle-building.

The water level in the boilers had to be constantly checked and replenished every half hour or so. Hull leakage was also the firemen's concern; the hull had to be checked perhaps once per shift and the bilges drained by the use of steam syphons. Operating the steam engine that powered the capstan was another of our regular duties. We were also expected to have a general knowledge of the maintenance and operation of the auxiliary equipment in the engine room—high and low pressure water pumps, turbine electrical generators and gasoline-powered auxiliaries. With this array of jobs at his disposal the duty engineer had no difficulty in keeping his firemen safely out of mischief during layover periods.

Rest days occurred only when we were in port at either Fort Fitzgerald at the north end of our journey or as close to McMurray as we could get on the south end. From midsummer on, the water level was usually too low to reach McMurray and we would tie up about four miles downriver. The freight would then be yarded the rest of the way on shallow-draft barges that were handled by power boats. But our layovers there, usually of up to two days' duration, were never idle times, since our chief engineer, Old John, was of the opinion that there was virtue in gainful employment and that it was his duty to instill such moral rectitude in others. He always had a long list of tasks for his two firemen, the worst being to wash down the boiler—a job we performed reluctantly two or three times that summer. These periods of boiler torment were always at the south (McMurray) end of our voyages, and for Duke and

A steam boiler of the kind on the Northland Echo. The valves and gauges have been stripped away; the draft control is at the bottom below the ash clean-out door.

myself this was akin to placing a choice fish just slightly beyond the reach of a chained husky dog. On the way upriver when we met at shift change, we would discuss the possibility of one of us enjoying a visit to whatever the McMurray of the '30s had to offer while the other remained with the *Echo* to maintain minor steam requirements. All of this, of course, hinged on whether or not boiler-washing was in the cards—a decision always cloaked in suspense. As McMurray drew closer with still no hint from Old John, our optimism would mount—only to be quenched by the dreaded verdict from our chief: "Boys! I think we'd better wash down the boiler."

There was a reason for this boiler washing. Our sternwheelers, the *Northland Echo*, and her sister ship, the *Northland Call*, had horizontal water tube boilers in which the hot gases from the firebox passed through the tubes, heating the water that surrounded them. Forced draft was supplied by the exhaust from the main drive engines directed up the smokestack or funnel. (In a fire tube boiler the situation is reversed, with the water filling the tubes and the hot gases on the outside.) We drew our boiler water directly from the river, unfiltered and usually muddy. This mud, plus the minerals in the water, formed scale in the 2½-inch spaces between the boiler tubes, which were also of the same diameter, and the accumulated scale impeded water circulation around the tubes, reducing our steam output. The scale could only be removed by forcing iron rods of varying lengths down between the stacks of tubing until each channel was cleared to the bottom. Then hook-shaped rods were used to clear the scale from between the vertical stacks of tubing.

To begin this task we first "blew" the steam, drained the hot water, and finally hosed down the interior of the boiler with cold water. This boiler, though, was a pretty massive chunk of cast iron, rolled steel plate and steel tubing, and its normal working temperature was about 250°F. The cold water that we applied probably did reduce the temperature by a few degrees—although this we doubted. In fact, when we first made our entry at the continued urging of Old John—"Come on, boys! She's nice and cool now!"—I'm sure that the temperature was still in the 120°F range.

The entire washing operation was then carried out from above, with Duke and me lying in the area between the tube stacks and the curved top of the boiler. But for the heat, this would have been nothing more than a difficult task in close quarters. We wore gloves to avoid burning our hands and lay on thick pads that only marginally insulated us from the hot tubes.

Working in this confined space, gasping for air and drenched with sweat, we chipped away at the scale hour after hour.

On one particular boiler-washing occasion, after the cleaning was completed to our satisfaction (though never to John's), Duke and I went out onto the adjoining barge to get some much needed fresh air while our exacting task-master entered the space as usual, extension light in hand, to inspect the job from end to end, top to bottom. The high pressure water hose, previously used for cooling the boiler interior, just happened to be still lying on top of the tubes. John was down at the far end of the boiler, carrying out his inspection, when someone—by accident or design (we suspected the latter)—opened the valve that supplied the hose—a valve that was in the engine room at the aft end of the boat. Now, an unrestrained high-pressure hose thrashing around from side to side can be safely approached only from the rear. John, unfortunately, was in front of it, receiving constant blasts of high pressure water. When Duke and I heard the commotion coming from the open manhole on the top of the boiler, we rushed back. The brass nozzle was striking the tubes and the boiler top, kicking up a fearful din, and John was yelling at the top of his lungs—between water blasts, that is. He was in no danger, just wet and angry, otherwise we might have reached the shut-off valve a bit sooner.

When order was restored and Old John had resurfaced, we had some difficulty exhibiting the proper degree of concern for the mishap and for his damp and bedraggled condition. Fortunately Duke and I, the obvious suspects, had been out on the barge and were therefore innocent beyond doubt. Suspicion then fell upon the half-dozen Native deckhands, but they stoutly defended their innocence, each one alibiing his mate. Duke and I had our own theory, however: we suspected that he and I had been the intended victims of a plan that had backfired beautifully. Seeing Duke and me out on the deck of the barge, prime targets for a hose attack, they had concocted a scheme where one of them would open the supply valve while the other gave us the full benefit of water at 125 psi. Fortunately—or otherwise, depending upon the point of view—they had failed to notice that the hose nozzle was still inside the boiler and that the victim would be Old John, Lord of the Lower Deck.

But John had his own means of evening the score. In his position of authority he could (and did) assign any number of extra duties to the deck-

Because jobs in aviation were scarce during the Depression, CAL's McMurray base was staffed with some of the best engineers in the industry. L to R: Sammy Tomlinson, Lou Parmenter, Bill Tall, Don Goodwin, Frank Kelly, Al Parker, Tom Caddick, Rudy Heuss at the Snye in McMurray. Summer 1933. (Parker and Heuss later obtained their pilots licences.)

hands, the innocent as well as the guilty. The innocent then administered physical retribution to the guilty—and so Old John had his revenge. And Duke and I, innocent in deed and pious in thought, chuckled quietly in the background, remembering always to maintain a sober countenance when in John's presence. Planned or otherwise, it was truly an incident to remember—a bit of humour that was told and retold for many a season. That was my only summer of work on the *Echo*, but Duke told me later that this incident did have some lasting benefits. After that, during boiler cleaning, the cooling water was applied for much longer periods and the cleaning operation, while no less difficult, was not so unpleasant.

My pay as a fireman on the *Echo* was good for the north (or for that matter, anywhere else during the '30s): $60 a month with meals included—and we ate well. So by the conclusion of my sternwheeler summer I had a few months wages saved up. These, together with the revenue from the sale of my muskrat pelts, enabled me to return to McMurray. Thanks to the help of some good friends who provided low-cost room and board, I was able to close in on my goal—my air engineer's licence. For the next year I spent most of my waking hours at Canadian Airways Ltd. (CAL) in close company with

Junkers W-34 CF-ARI moored at the CAL dock on the Snye, Fort McMurray, 1935.

their fleet of fine old bush aircraft—Fokker Super Universals, Bellanca Pacemakers, Junkers W-34s and Fairchild 71s. Occasionally I was allowed to stroke the sleek flanks of CF-AAL, the one and only Lockheed Vega. There were Fairchild 82s and the Norseman on CAL's horizon, but we had to wait a few more years for the arrival of the first of those improved models.

Though considered a regular member of CAL's crew and working the same hours, often long and always unscheduled, I worked without pay. Two years of practical experience were needed before one could write the exams for an air engineer's licence, and I had only completed one year with Spence-Mac. This was a well-travelled apprenticeship path that I followed; for both pilots and mechanics there was no other way to obtain the necessary experience. However, at McMurray in the early '30s there were some distinct advantages to the system. Because of the Depression and the scarcity of jobs in the industry, CAL's McMurray base was staffed with some of the most experienced air engineers in the business. Encouragement and advice was always there, and the opportunities for practical experience were endless.

All early aviation from McMurray into the Territories took place from the surface of the Snye, the backwater channel that joined the Clearwater and Athabasca rivers. This waterway was connected to the town by a narrow trail through the surrounding bush—the Snye Road. It was along this trail

After freeze-up, dog teams again became the general mode of travel. These six heavily laden teams head north from Fort McMurray on the Athabasca River in the late 1920s. There has been fresh snow and one man on snowshoes is out in front breaking trail.

Six of Canadian Airways Fort McMurray maintenance staff , February, 1935. (L-R) Don Goodwin, Frank Hartley, Art Rankin, Dick Leigh, Casey van der Linden, and Bill Jacquot. The Junkers behind them is CF-AMZ, and beyond it is the CAL nose hangar.

that we hastened in the darkness and cold of early winter mornings or cursed the sticky, slippery mud of summer. Along the south bank of the Snye were seven buildings—two nose hangars, two offices, and two oil heating sheds, one of each owned by CAL and the other by our competitors, Mackenzie Air Service. CAL's hangar had been constructed by Commercial Airways Ltd. during the two years or so that they operated from McMurray before being taken over by Canadian Airways. In addition, CAL owned a small workshop.

From this base on the Snye we provided service to the settlements and the trading posts, the prospectors and the trappers, the RCMP detachments and the missions throughout the Northwest Territories and along the Arctic Coast. These were the beginning years for aviation in the north and we were trailblazers in a sense—a fact we would not appreciate until viewed in the retrospect of the years. The equipment was untried, the facilities primitive, the terrain unmapped and largely uninhabited.

We had snow conditions to contend with—granular snow that stalled our skis, snowdrifts so hard that undercarriages failed, damaging the wings and bending the props in the process. Sometimes the snow covered a layer of slush—even at -50°F!—and our skis sank through it and became immovable, and our moccasin-clad feet were soaked in icy water. Some of the ice on which we landed was of marginal thickness, and we were submerged, along with our cargos and passengers. Dense smoke and winter blizzards also took their toll on aircraft and people. Our few maps covered only the rivers and large lakes; we had no guidance for the balance of the Territories nor for the Barren Lands, vast and featureless. We groped our way to trading posts and missions on the Arctic Coast in winter, faced with the ever-present threat of whiteouts. If we were forced down because of fog, smoke, blizzards or any combination of these, we erected our tents and waited for conditions to improve. We seldom had enough daylight or fuel supply to turn back and await better conditions. Getting lost was a common hazard and not everyone lived through such experiences. Radios would have been a great asset, but they didn't arrive until a later date. We had engine failures—total and in part. Valve failures and the inevitable cylinder changes were not uncommon. One January we had three cylinder changes on the same aircraft. A valve or piston failure could usually be repaired in the field (which might be 1,500 miles from main base) but our spares kits rarely included major replacement parts. Total engine failures could have more serious consequences—crews did not always walk away from them. And if a forced landing was successful, and the aircraft was still right side up and undamaged, the resultant bush engine change was a problem in itself. Clean wings were also recognized as a necessity, though not until some aircraft and a few lives had been lost. The survivors of white-knuckle takeoffs became firm converts.

Most of our flights were more routine in nature, however. It was a case of beating the averages and managing to stay upright and in one piece.

5 They'll lie through their teeth

The early winter—when many of the lakes were barely frozen, ice-laden clouds hung low, daylight was brief and visibility limited—was the most dangerous flying period of the year. No one, regardless of his knowledge and experience, could be sure of a safe landing in these conditions, especially if he was unsure of his location and/or low on fuel. And one of the most common aviation experiences on these occasions was "going through the ice," an unpopular activity and one that we tried hard to avoid.

In the case of a forced landing in early winter, if the chosen place was an unknown lake, a quick survey was necessary to check for rivers running in or out, for narrow channels, and for the dark patches in the snow that might indicate thin ice. A sheltered bay was always a better bet than an open lake. Failing this, the landing would preferably be made close to a straight shoreline. There, the water would probably be shallower and the ice more substantial than out in the middle of the lake, and with trees close at hand there would be shelter and firewood—assuming, of course, that the ice did not give way and that the crew survived to make use of those essentials. The unknown factors would be the average temperatures during the previous couple of weeks and the amount of snow on the ice.

After the post-freeze-up period, with better flying weather and lower temperatures, ice problems would be behind us for the balance of the winter. We would be calling at settlements, bush cabins or mining camps where safe ice existed and where the landing strips had been checked and marked with spruce boughs. Most pilots, after a few winters of bush flying, learned where

Canadian Airways Ltd. Junkers CF-AMZ ready for takeoff from the frozen Snye, bound for Yellowknife with an external load consisting of two prospector's canoes. April 1936.

the pitfalls were and how to avoid them. I say "most" because even those who were old and grey in northern experience sometimes came to grief either by taking a chance or by encountering an unfamiliar situation. All, however, knew the one rule to be followed: never taxi through a narrow channel between an island and the lakeshore, no matter how low the temperature because there was often a flow of water through such channels, even on landlocked lakes with no obvious inlet or outlet. Even a slow movement of water can nibble away at the ice and reduce its thickness, especially if abetted by a cozy layer of snow. The Inuit people were well aware of the insulating qualities of snow—a fact that is amply demonstrated by the internal comfort of an igloo. They also realized that the temperature of the water below ice was in the 33°F range while the soil or rock underlying the snow onshore might bear a temperature of -40°F. Unless they were travelling overland, therefore, their igloos were always constructed over ice.

We considered six inches of ice as the minimum for our ski-equipped aircraft as most of them had a gross weight of some 6,000 pounds. These included the Fokker Super Universal, the Fairchild 71, the Junkers W-34, and later the Norseman. A six-inch layer of ice could develop in a few days of weather in the -10 to -15°F range. If this freezing period was followed by a snowfall, however, and a few days of moderate temperatures of perhaps 10°F, then our safe six inches of ice could become a very unsafe four inches. One would think it a simple matter to cut a hole in the ice to measure the thickness, but there were human elements to confound this logic.

Thirst—a subject seemingly far removed from winter flying—was the first of these human elements. The hard-rock miners and the prospectors of the north had a great fondness for alcoholic beverages, particularly overproof rum, but in the '30s there were no liquor stores in the mining settlements of Yellowknife, Cameron Bay or Goldfields. Alcohol had to be ordered by mail and flown in as express shipments. Freeze-up, however, would temporarily cut off this flow, the last mail of the season probably being received from McMurray (or from Prince Albert in the case of Goldfields) by mid-October. Thus, by late November when the collective thirst of the populace assumed immense proportions, when housewives had become anxious for the arrival of winter clothes ordered from Eaton's catalogue (Eaton's being the one and only mail order outfit serving the north at that time), and when all of the magazines had been read and re-read time and again, an increasing clamour would arise for resumption of mail services. (Of course, by far the most important of these items were the gurgling parcels from the Liquor Control Board.) Flying weather and ice conditions were a matter of indifference to these citizens; those were problems for the pilots to solve.

The agent for the company holding the airmail contract would be under enormous local pressure to advise his company headquarters that the ice was, indeed, of the required thickness and safe for landing. Numerous locals were prepared to guarantee this. ("I'll put it in writing, Harry, if you don't believe me.") If the agent delegated the ice measuring—and such was often the case—then, like a fish story, the thickness of the ice would magically increase. A meagre five inches of ice might be reported as, "Okay, plenty of ice now, Harry—there's better than six inches. And Pete here was with me, isn't that right, Pete? The weather's clear and it's freezing hard tonight—it'll probably be eight inches by tomorrow." This report would be verified by numerous volunteer ice scientists, and pressure on the poor agent would become overwhelming.

Competition between the flying companies was also a very real and serious concern. If company A had the mail contract for a particular year, then company B would be almost certain to make the first flight after freeze-up, probably with a near-empty aircraft to guard against ice failure. Company B would then let this be known up and down the rivers and among the mining camps, intimating that, if they were the holders of the contract, the mail and express would arrive on schedule. This fact would also be emphasized to the postal authorities, particularly when the mail contracts were next reviewed. The luckless agent was therefore caught in a squeeze-play. If local pressure overcame his better judgement, resulting in an aircraft through the ice, then he was partially blamed for the mishap. If his report was negative, but company B made a successful flight, he was still in disfavour with his own company and jeered at by the local Ice Advisory Committee.

Even in winter a steady current flowed through the channel at Fort Rae. Bill Jewitt's Fairchild CF-AVY, here seen after it was raised from the ice, had the distinction of going through the ice there twice.

When one of these ice break-throughs happened at a settlement, it was not particularly dangerous to those on board. Although cold and wet, they could usually scramble out onto the ice with no great difficulty. Our Junkers aircraft were ideal in this respect as the low wing supported the fuselage, keeping it above water. Both passengers and crew could usually escape dry-shod, while the aircraft, being of all-metal, low-wing construction, would seldom be damaged. The fabric-covered, high-winged aircraft—the Fokker, the Fairchild—and later the Norseman—were a different kettle of fish. With the fuselage, including engines and instruments, fully submerged, they were difficult to recover and often out of service for the balance of the season.

For all of these reasons, Fort Rae was one of our least favourite stopping places. It occupied a strategic location, however, being at about the mid-point between Bear Lake to the north and Smith to the south, and thus it became the most frequently used overnight stopping place on the Bear Lake run. One of the oldest settlements of the north, it had been named after Chief Factor John Rae of the Hudson's Bay Company, a prodigious traveller who had explored and mapped much of the Arctic Coast. He was also the man who, in 1854–55, obtained the first definite proof of the fate of the Franklin party. The site chosen for Rae was treeless, barren and inhospitable, winter and summer. The village was partially on a point of land that jutted out from the east shore of Great Slave Lake and partially on a small island off the point, with a narrow channel separating the two. For the local Natives, the original founders of the village, this was an ideal location, especially in summer as the channel provided a snug harbour for their canoes, regardless of wind directions, while lack of vegetation discouraged the mosquitoes.

Landings by CAL aircraft were made, winter and summer, in the bay to the south, and we would tie up along the shore to the east of the channel because at any time of the year Rae's channel was especially dangerous; even in winter a steady current flowed through it. That it was a place to be avoided at all times had been proven one winter by Bill Jewitt of CM&S in Trail, BC, flying Fairchild 71 CF-AVY. Bill was the company's field manager (and later its president). A mining engineer who had been a fighter pilot in World War I, he also had considerable flying experience in the north. His engineer was big Dave Bishop, a genial gentleman who was universally popular. It is possible that Bill had never overnighted at Rae in winter and was therefore unaware of the channel's hazards. The particular spot Bill was aiming for was only about 50 yards from the residence of Bob Dodman, the Northern Traders post manager, where we usually hung our hats or unrolled our sleeping bags. By comparison, the parking area normally used was perhaps ten times more distant. It is possible that Bill was emboldened by a long stretch of extremely cold weather—thin ice is hard to visualize with the temperature at -55°F. In any event, Bill did taxi into the channel and almost got away with it. He arrived at what he considered the most suitable location, then applied power to make his turn. This concentrated the weight on the outboard ski, and the ice—of marginal thickness—gave way. The entire party—Bill, Dave, and AVY—took a cold bath. After the usual wet and weary, freezing struggle, they finally raised AVY clear of the ice, only to have the tackle break, giving them the questionable distinction of going through the ice at this same location a second time. As this was the first such mishap for CM&S, Dave claimed the first dunking had been just a practice run. I believe that this was Bill's final aviation misadventure.

The thin-ice season of early winter was also the season of low clouds and fog from some of the still unfrozen lakes. Under such circumstances a forced landing on an isolated lake and a break-through with a high-winged monoplane had the potential for serious or fatal consequences. Even if the crew and passengers escaped drowning, their outlook was grim. Soaked in icy water, with their tent, stove, matches, and emergency rations submerged in the aircraft, survival would be doubtful. In my own case, as a result of being dunked once, I was particularly twitchy on this subject. I never worried when aboard the Junkers, but with a Fairchild or Norseman I always secured the tent, the axe and ration kit in the upper part of the rear cabin where it could be retrieved by cutting open the top of the fuselage. Happily, I never had to field-test this precaution.

My experience of being dunked occurred during freeze-up at Fort McMurray in late November 1934 while I was still serving my unpaid apprenticeship. Our maintenance staff was temporarily short-handed because of the expected transfer of another air engineer into the district, the transferee in this case coming from the Evergreen Playground on the West Coast. We strongly suspected that, being faced with a winter of below-zero weather, he was dragging his feet.

Our company had a sizeable operation on the West Coast, with fisheries patrols, traffic to fish canneries and logging camps, and passenger traffic between Vancouver and Victoria keeping aircraft and personnel fully occupied during the summer months. With the advent of the slack winter season, however, there was always a surplus of staff, though mostly in the maintenance department; the resident pilots were generally prepared to tough out the winter after a busy summer earning monthly base pay plus a bonus of three cents per mile. Our company owner (and patron saint), James Richardson, having a keen interest in the welfare of all of his employees, had an unwritten policy that layoffs were to be avoided if at all possible. As a result, it was usual for one or more of the Vancouver maintenance staff, usually the most junior member, to be transferred to McMurray for the winter. But it became a standing joke among the McMurray staff that these "West Coast Salmon Poachers" were almost impossible to lure east of the Rockies. The names of the transferees would be posted, but they would never materialize on the appointed date. Sometimes weeks would go by with a litany of excuses. But later in the winter, let there be the faintest rumour that business had started to pick up at the coast and staff was needed at Vancouver, and they would "fold their tents like the Arabs and as silently steal away." They were fine fellows, all of them, and we did enjoy their visits, reluctant though they were.

A blow pot misadventure, January 3, 1936.

And so they headed back to the coast and their Boeing Totems and their crab traps, their Rapides and their geoducks. "We'll see you again next fall, chaps," we'd say, "but try to be on time, eh?"

In this case, I was highly pleased with the delay as it meant that I would be temporarily placed on the payroll and have the opportunity of flying as crew on a couple of interesting trips. Don Goodwin, our chief mechanic, loaned me a few essential tools and located a spare sleeping bag. I was to go north with Rudy Heuss as soon as the ice in the Snye was of sufficient strength. Our aerial steed would be Fairchild CF-AAO, an aircraft I had worked on and flown with during my Spence-McDonough period.

I spent the following day in close communion with AAO and her power plant, a Pratt & Whitney Model C Wasp. I checked the engine tool kit (the special tools provided by the manufacturer) to ensure that all of the essentials were there. The ration kit was next on my checklist and this was an important item. During the early '30s before detailed maps became available, with no radio facilities or weather reports, a night out in the bush was a fairly common event. The emergency equipment—the ration kit, tent, stove—had to be complete and serviceable as one never knew when the need might arise. The balance of the equipment was then called up for inspection—axe, shovel, broom, ropes, jack, blow pots and spare fuel for the blow

Blow Pots: Noisy, Smelly and Dangerous

Blow pots, the gasoline-burning devices that we used for heating the engines of our aircraft, had been used by plumbers long before bush flying was invented. They were simply constructed. A half-gallon can held the fuel. It was topped by a filler cap, a pump to pressurize the gas, a shut-off valve, a jet to atomize the fuel, and a generator to vaporize it, all of which was protected by a metal framework supporting a perforated plate or rack. Though highly effective as heating devices and easy to operate, they were noisy, smelly and extremely dangerous.

To light it, the tank was pressurized, the valve opened to allow a few drops of gas to flow into a small pan under the generator, the gas ignited, and the valve reopened to permit a steady supply of gas to escape. With his two gasoline-burning blow pots roaring in unison, the air engineer would retire under the engine cover with a cushion and a fire extinguisher to alternately freeze and roast for an hour or so. These pots, while raising the temperature to about 150°F in the vicinity of the engine, filled the entire space down to within six inches of snow level with acrid fumes that burned the eyes and were totally unbreathable. At ground level, however, where the engineer crouched or knelt (I took along a felt pad for this purpose), it was only a little warmer than the air outside. Different methods were devised to make the situation more bearable: one was to stand bent over at the waist so that the head was down in the breathable air at moccasin level. This placed the derriere and other assorted organs in the heat zone and was great as long as the doubled-over position could be maintained. The feet, however, were always at the bottom and always cold.

Blow pots required constant attention because of the danger of setting the fabric of the wings and fuselage on fire. Hence, the engineer's fire extinguisher. However, a few aircraft were incinerated through blow pot misadventures.

pots, and, of course, window scrapers. I then cleaned the jets of both blow pots, gave them a short test flight, and was ready for morning.

During the afternoon two of our staff had checked ice thicknesses in various parts of the Snye, and it had been decided that there was just sufficient for departures the following morning. When the next day dawned the Snye was a scene of great activity. As these flights would be the first ones since freeze-up, we had our entire fleet of four or five aircraft ready for departure. All of them were in the process of being loaded with the usual mix of mail and express. I completed the engine heating on AAO, refilled the blow pots, added the oil, and then gave our senior agent, Fred Lundy, a hand with the final loading. The cabin of a Fairchild 71 was high and narrow, and Fred claimed priority over the use of any and all of it. He even looked upon engineers as necessary evils because of the cargo that they might displace. In the case of AAO on this particular morning the load was stacked nearly to the roof. However, we did have one passenger, and I'm sure that Fred had personally applied the tape measure to him beforehand. He was a young French priest making his inaugural trip into the north. Since he was slight in stature, I think Fred must have assessed our combined volume at something like one-and-a-half people because that was the amount of space he left for us.

Thanks to Fred, our loading was a bit of a shoehorn operation. My cabin companion, who spoke no English, stared at me in disbelief when I indicated the space allotment that was his. I gave him a hand to climb in, at the same time mentally shivering at the sight of his thick, leather boots. Even mukluk-clad, my own feet were frequently cool, and I could not imagine how this poor chap would be able to endure two or three hours with leather boots in an unheated cabin. Some readers may challenge me and state that the 71 cabins were heated. Well, they were—and they weren't. With the cabin fully loaded, we had to keep the cabin heaters closed to avoid scorching His Majesty's Mail. The engineer and the odd unfortunate passenger would then lie on top of the load, wedged between the cargo and the cabin roof. (Comfort can never be fully appreciated until one has spent a couple of hours lying upon a sack of cold-soaked Newhouse steel traps.) Any heat that reached our elevation was overflow from the cockpit heater, therefore second-hand and minimal. On this occasion our load was piled well above the cabin door handles and closing these from the inside an impossibility. Casey Van der Linden helped me to wedge my way in and did the honours with the hand crank. (Casey's real name was Cornelius but Casey had more of a transportation ring to it.)

As an ice break-through with a Junkers was not nearly the disaster that would be created with a high-winged aircraft, our first departure aircraft would be one of our Junkers, AMZ, with Con Farrell and Frank Hartley on board. We were scheduled to be number two and were ready, with our engine running. AMZ roared past, just visible through the light fog. Knowing that our ice thickness was marginal, Con in his Junkers had made a wide and gradual turn at the end of the Snye, then taken off without stopping. Rudy, perhaps emboldened by Con's success—or lack of failure—executed a fairly short turn at slow speed. With my head wedged between the cabin roof and a case of Trumilk, I recall trying to project my eyeball downwards to get a glimpse out of the top of the cabin window. Then I realized that AAO seemed to be sitting in a depression in the ice. I contemplated this phenomenon for a matter of perhaps two seconds, then the answer came to me: we were going through the ice.

I do not remember whether or not we were moving at the time but we were submerged in a matter of seconds. Rudy was both busy and profane. With the water level rapidly approaching my bent eyeball, I realized that haste might be in order. Sliding my right foot between the mail sacks and the right-hand door, I located the handle and kicked it downwards. At the same time I applied pressure to the door to displace the icebergs on the outside. Reaching backwards and getting a grip on my ecclesiastical friend, I launched myself in the direction of the solid ice. This, fortunately, was not far away and was solid enough for us to scramble onto. I never did learn whether or not my companion had taken time to square himself with the High Command before the abandon ship order was given. If so, there was certainly no impediment in his speech. He was hot on my heels—if this can properly describe a hasty trip through ice-cold water.

By this time Rudy was also up on solid ice and came around AAO in a wary circle to see how we were faring. We looked at one another in shared disgust and for similar reasons. "What a helluva way to start the winter season," remarked Rudy. His thoughts, no doubt, were on the three-cents-per-mile flight pay that his enforced idleness would cost him. My own monetary situation was also adversely affected to the tune of about $3 per day, a fat salary in those days. It is also my recollection that I was not paid for the activities of that day, but then—those were the '30s. I was working for experience, and getting dunked was part of the curriculum.

McMurray being our home base, we had plenty of equipment and sufficient manpower for a salvage operation. As the water was relatively shallow,

Cutting away the fabric covering of the AAO's fuselage to extract the cargo and bags of mail. A view to the east with the Clearwater River beyond.

erecting a tripod was a straightforward operation and was completed on the day of the mishap. The following day AAO was pulled from the water with the chain hoist that was attached to the tripod and hung out to dry, the accumulated water being drained from the fuselage by cutting holes in the fabric. The mail bags and express shipments were removed, and some attempts were made to drain these and ensure that the labels were still legible. I never did learn what procedure was used for the first-class mail, though I suspect the letters were drained of surplus water, separated and re-frozen. They would then be placed in dry bags and stored in an unheated place to keep them in a frozen state until the next northbound flight. Maintaining the letters in a frozen condition until they could be delivered would minimize the action of the water upon the writing, giving the recipient a fighting chance at receiving something legible.

The aircraft could not be lowered until sufficient ice had formed, so planks were laid down around the front of it. This provided a relatively safe platform for those working around it while the cabin load and the accumulated ice were removed, all of this through the cockpit door. We then had a most fortunate break in the weather—the temperature suddenly dropped into the -30°F range, ideal for making ice. To accelerate the freezing process, the snow was cleared from the ice in the vicinity of the aircraft and along a strip leading from the aircraft to the shore. We borrowed several hundred feet of heavy rope from the transport division of the HBC, sufficient to reach from the aircraft to a point near shore where the ice was thick. Our venerable tractor had been laid up for the winter, but as Ryan Brothers Transport was well equipped with good horses, Don Goodwin decided that a pair of hay burners would be a good substitute.

We only had to wait about three days for a sufficient depth of ice to form. A layer of planks was then laid under the skis to reinforce the ice where it was thinnest, and AAO was gently lowered onto this frozen pad. We removed the chain hoist and sawed off our tripod components as close to surface level as possible. A rope bridle was attached to the skis and extended to the shore where there was good footing for the horses. One of the Ryans' best teams was hitched to the tow rope and, with teamster Sammy Delorme in charge, they were ready for action. Normally a couple of us would have walked beside the rear fuselage, holding onto the lifting handles and pushing or pulling as necessary to maintain our course. In this case our path was bare, slippery ice, so instead we tied two ropes to the lifting handles, allowing the steersmen to walk to the sides where there was good footing in the snow. "Go ahead, Sammy!" called Don after a final check. The horses surged forward, and AAO shot toward shore at a brisk pace. We removed the tow rope, hitched the horses to the bridle, and before long AAO arrived at our hangar on the Snye Road.

Here the fuel was drained from the wing tanks, the wings removed, and the skis replaced by wheels. Because our workshop was heated by a woodburning stove and gasoline fumes would create a distinct fire hazard, some of the fuel was also drained from the fuselage-mounted centre tank to avoid an overflow when the fuel expanded in the warmth of the hangar. The engine and the fuselage were covered with canvas tarps and heat was applied from a couple of blow pots to melt the remaining ice from around the engine, in the cabin and fuselage. Following this the fuselage was moved into the shop for final repairs.

Our first and most important job was to check the fuselage tubing to ensure that no water had penetrated because it would later freeze and split

On Thin Ice

Recovery of some aircraft the size of a Fairchild or a Norseman required weeks and months of work. In 1935 our Junkers ARI went through the ice at Fort Chipewyan about November 20 and limped home to McMurray, still in a slightly damaged condition, on December 24. This recovery was unusually long because the break-through had occurred at a point where a steady current flowed westward out of Lake Athabasca and moderate weather meant that the ice remained in a treacherous state for a couple of weeks. The salvage crew had some troublesome and at times dangerous moments.

But the most difficult and lengthy salvage jobs that I'm aware of involved a pair of Bellanca Aircruisers, one on Lake Athabasca and the other on Kingsmere Lake, north of Prince Albert. These were both expensive operations, each requiring most of a winter, with the aircraft out of service for the entire season. In each case, a complete overhaul of the airframe, engine, accessories and instruments was required.

the tubing. The most time-consuming job was the extensive sewing and patching of damaged belly fabric, which required about four days and evenings of work. A replacement set of instruments had already been ordered from our main base at Winnipeg, and these were all installed. The total lay-up time for AAO was relatively brief—only about 12 days.

While AAO was under repair, I headed for Coppermine with Matt Berry. At that time of year daylight appears with reluctance along the Arctic Coast, and when we began the return trip on November 30, our departure was late. At Cameron Bay we picked up southbound mail and made a fuel stop. Hottah Lake was next, a mining camp noted for its hospitality and good food. Though it was almost dark by the time we landed to pick up mail there, Matt declined a warm invitation to spend the night because the moon had made its appearance far off to the southeast and he felt we could use its light to push on to Rae. There is a vast assortment of lakes south of where that Hottah Lake mining settlement stood in those days. Hottah itself is the largest of these and well defined, but the others—Hardisty, Rae, Faber, St. Croix—are irregular in shape with numerous channels and islands that extend far

Don Goodwin looks on while Frank Kelly works beneath the fuselage of CF-ARI. Note the lifeline tied around Kelly's waist. Fort Chipewyan, November 1935.

to the east, a labyrinth of water that was virtually unmapped in the '30s. Consequently, between Bear Lake and Rae we followed the large lakes along a strip about 20 miles in width. In clear weather we could fly this route at greater altitude, considerably off to the east, and still be in sight of them. In overcast conditions and poor visibility we stayed close to the normal track.

On this night we flew for an hour or so in the general direction of south with the dim and hazy moon as our directional beacon. On the move since early morning, with breakfast—our last meal—hours behind us, we were tired and hungry. And at the end of a day of sitting in the uninsulated and poorly heated cabin of that old 71, we were also chilled to the bone. Our main thoughts centred on the warmth and food ahead of us at Rae, and we were paying little attention to our course, other than keeping our lunar beacon in plain sight. But as time passed, we became aware that a circle had formed around the moon. The light was fading and an overcast was developing. Matt reduced altitude and began to search for a landmark among the hundreds of lakes that extended on all sides. As we had very little in the way of cabin load, I had been kneeling on our rolled-up sleeping bags just behind Matt's seat. This allowed me a measure of forward visibility together with the opportunity for conversation. Matt called back, "I'm not too sure of our location. We must be off to the east, so I think we'd better sit down for the night."

We were now flying in an area of small lakes—actually little more than muskeg potholes—and it was another 20 minutes in dim and failing light before we found a good lake. This had a ridge along one side—the side that we believed to be the east—with a good stand of spruce between the ridge and the lakeshore. Wise in the ways of water-courses, Matt was always wary of any shoreline that might harbour a creek, and he very carefully avoided narrow spots in lakes or channels between an island and the main shore. The lake below us appeared to have the proper credentials—there would be no creeks flowing out from this ridge to create thin ice or overflow. Matt landed parallel to the shore and continued to taxi while I checked behind the skis for signs of overflow. "Looks okay, Matt," I called, and he taxied in closer to the trees, keeping the motor running while I jumped down, donned my snowshoes, and cut a couple of small poles to place under the skis. While I was busy draining the oil and installing the engine cover, Matt packed down a small patch of snow in readiness for our tent. I drained the oil and hung the pails on the exhaust collector ring, using the two steel hooks that I carried for just such a purpose. In the morning the oil would then be heated by the blow pots along with the engine.

Our tent was one of the eight-foot-square, umbrella kind supported by a single, telescoping steel pole. As tents go, it was not a bad device and had the advantage of quick and easy erection. Using the last of the moonlight, we quickly transferred our sleeping bags, the ration kit and the stove into it just as the first flakes of snow began to fall. Then we had a close look at the contents of our ration kit. We had both checked this individually and carefully at the start of the winter season, so we knew that there were no shortages. Matt deliberated for some time over a can of bully beef, and then remarked, "We don't really know how long we might be here, so perhaps we should go a bit easy on the grub. This can of bully beef should do us for tonight and for breakfast. We've got plenty of hardtack and cheese to fill the empty corners, and honey for dessert." With that, he searched around for the frying pan and started to wind the little key that opened the

The Hudson's Bay post at Coppermine, which was originally named Fort Hearne. 1935

The Catholic church and residence at Coppermine. The snow-block wall was standard winter insulation for all buildings on the Arctic Coast as none of them had insulation in their walls.

Matt Berry at Coppermine examining the address on a parcel. December 1935.

can. I always enjoyed Matt's little soliloquies, steeped with the wisdom of years of northern flying and tempered with good humour and common sense.

We soon had the Coleman stove in operation and started the slow job of melting snow for tea—the entire operation illuminated by the tiny, cheerful glow of a single candle. The temperature was somewhat better than outside—thanks to the Coleman—and we would have been fairly comfortable except that the upper layer of warm air was also well-laced with fumes from the stove. We used our rolled-up sleeping bags for seats, rising and moving around occasionally to promote circulation in our feet and legs. This allowed us to absorb some of the warmth, but the stove's fumes soon chased us back to lower altitudes. With supper behind us and another mug of tea at hand, a review of our situation was in order.

"I'm a bit concerned about our fuel supply," said Matt. "We were flying for quite a while and I'm not real sure how far we are from Rae. How much fuel did you add at Cameron Bay?"

"I filled both of the wing tanks, which is about what we normally do. That should be enough to get us to Rae," I replied.

"How about the centre tank?" Matt queried.

"Not much there, I'm afraid. There was a bit left in the last barrel—maybe ten gallons—so I added that to the centre tank. I think it had been nearly empty before that, though."

Other than concerns about our fuel supply, we spent a fairly comfortable night with a temperature of -30°F and no wind. Alternately during the evening we reminded ourselves of the good meals we had turned down at Hottah Lake, and the promise of one of Bob Dodman's caribou steaks at Rae. But sleeping in a tent at temperatures of -30°F and lower, one only sleeps for short periods. As sleep comes on, the metabolism slows down, the body engine drops to idle speed, and soon you are awakened again by the cold. This is followed by a period of active shivering to consume a few calories and generate a bit of body heat, then it's off again to the land of nod. During one of these periods I heard Matt at the tent door, just returning from a call of nature, and I sat up to check the time.

"May as well stay in bed for awhile," he said. "It's been snowing all night by the looks of things, and it's still at it." But as the temperature had warmed up considerably, we enjoyed another couple of hours of comfortable sleep, finally scrambling out about 9:00 a.m. We were pleased to note that the snow had stopped although the ceiling was low and there was no break in the clouds. With breakfast over (hardtack with the rest of our bully beef), we packed the stove and the ration kit, and rolled up our sleeping bags, but left the tent standing in case of further snow.

"I think we'll wait for a better ceiling," said Matt. "We haven't enough gas to go exploring, and I'd like to get up high enough to pick out a landmark."

I didn't want to waste torch gas (the unleaded gasoline used in the blow pots) with unnecessary heating, so I joined Matt in clearing off the accumulated six inches of snow from the aircraft. We tossed a rope over each wing in turn, and with one of us on each end we worked this back and forth to dislodge the snow. By this time the ceiling had improved, so Matt said, "How about packing up the tent now? Then you can start heating. I'm going to climb up that ridge to see if I can get our bearings. I'd hoped to see something of the sun by now—I'd like to be sure of where south is." Although there was a compass in the aircraft, it was mounted in close proximity to a cluster of steel tubing, and the readings were always viewed with suspicion. Neither of us carried a pocket compass at that time, an omission that we corrected soon after that trip. By the time the heating was completed, there was a further improvement in the ceiling. Anticipating Matt's return, I added the oil, checked that all of our gear was on board, and loosened the fasteners of the engine cover.

In a short time he appeared, breathing hard from his trek up to the top of the ridge and back. "I see some hills that I think I recognize," he said, pointing. "That's south, I'm sure. From the top of that ridge I could see a bright line on the horizon."

With that, I removed and stowed the engine cover, cranked the engine and we were soon airborne. We climbed up to the base of the cloud cover at about 800 feet, fully expecting that the North Arm of Great Slave Lake would be visible, but this landmark—our destination—still eluded us. We could see nothing except timber, small lakes and patches of muskeg. Fuel, of course, was our primary concern. "We've a fair idea of what's left in the wing tanks," said Matt, "so I'll run out the gas in the centre tank first. You keep a close eye on the fuel pressure gauge."

We had flown for perhaps 30 minutes when the fuel pressure became nervous. "Fuel pressure!" I called, and Matt switched to one of the wing tanks. At about this time far off to the south we could just make out the long reach of the North Arm, and Matt headed directly for the north end of this, where Rae was located. We were feeling quite comfortable by now and I had renewed my thoughts about Bob Dodman's caribou steak. Suddenly the fuel pressure gauge took a dive. "Damn," said Matt "I wasn't expecting that. I don't know whether we're going to make it."

The lakes below us were numerous, of course, so a forced landing would not be a problem, undesirable though that might be. The end of the lake and Rae drew slowly closer—15 miles, 10 miles—and finally Matt dropped the nose for a straight-in landing. It was fortunate that he did not make a circuit. We taxied up to the gas cache, I got out and put the poles under the skis, Matt opened the throttle—and the engine quit! He started to laugh, probably at the startled expression on my face, then called out, "I always did want to know exactly how much gas a 71 would hold—and now we've found out."

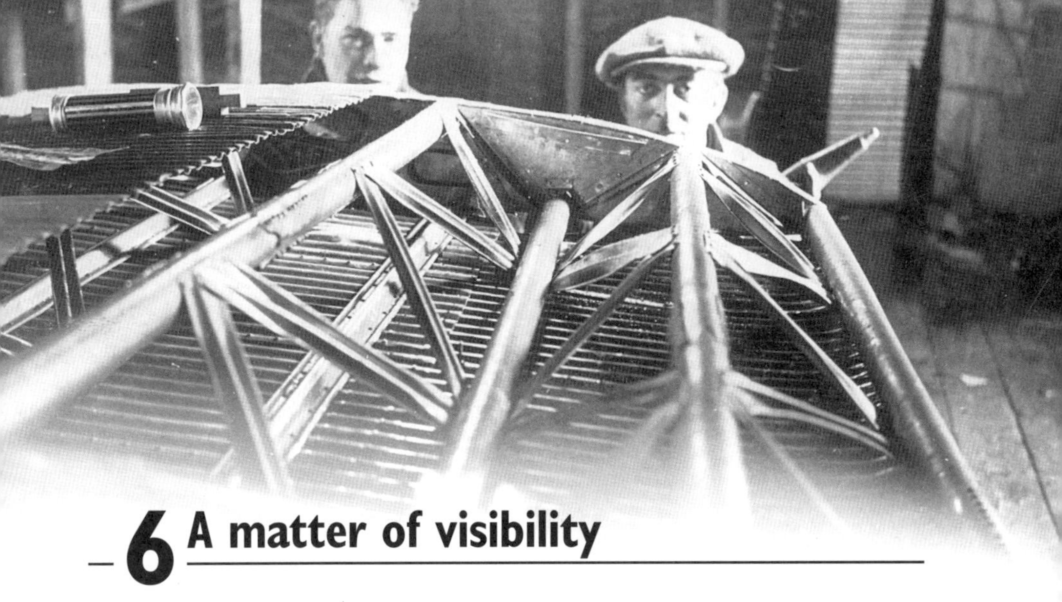

6 A matter of visibility

McMurray's Snye was quite narrow and the opposite shore—the north side—was a cutbank about 15 feet in height, topped by a substantial growth of timber. In winter this narrow corridor became a tunnel, trapping fog and ice crystals to the point of zero visibility. The ideal situation for intense fog generation was a clear morning in early January, with the sun still hidden below the eastern horizon, the temperature at -50°F or lower, and no wind to disturb the fog.

To add to this scene, smoke and warm air poured forth from the chimneys of each of the seven buildings facing the Snye, instantly condensing into fog which accumulated in layers along its length. And since at that time the combined fleets of the two companies, CAL and MAS, probably amounted to a dozen aircraft, while CM&S was operating a couple of 71s, on many mornings there were as many as five or six aircraft there preparing for takeoff. Each would be heated by a pair of blow pots, all of them producing fog in prodigious quantities. The combined vapour output was more than sufficient to fill the Snye completely, restricting visibility to two or three plane lengths.

Our normal takeoffs were toward the west so that we would have the wide valley of the Athabasca in front of us. When we taxied to the east end of the Snye, we would leave the worst of the fog behind, but when we turned for takeoff, there it would be again, stacked up in a solid wall with only a few ski tracks as navigational aids. The hazards could have been easily reduced or even eliminated by positioning a single row of small spruce trees

A typical winter morning on the Snye at Fort McMurray. March 1936. The combined fleets of Canadian Airways and Mackenzie Air Service amounted to a dozen aircraft while Consolidated Mining & Smelting operated a couple of Fairchild 71s. On the morning of January 21, 1935, CF-ATZ was positioned approximately where CF-AXE (furthest right) is in this picture, except that it was facing east (toward the camera).

on the left side of the takeoff path to help pilots stay between the ditches. Oddly enough, such an obvious solution was never considered.

It was always a race to see who would be first away in the morning. The lead aircraft would stir up a dense cloud of snow and frost crystals as the pilot taxied into position, then his takeoff would stir up a healthy cloud of fine snow to mix with the fog. When number two arrived at the takeoff point he would have even less in the way of visibility. But business competition required that if a Canadian Airways aircraft took off first then a Mackenzie Air Service machine would most certainly be number two, whether he had visibility or not. I can recall waiting there for endless minutes, staring into the dense cloud of fog and ice crystals. The cockpit would be only marginally warmer than outside, and we would be fighting a constant battle with windshield frost. We knew that somewhere out there were obstacles to be avoided—a line of parked aircraft to the left, a tree-crowned cutbank to the right. I could only hope that my pilot would remain patient and not lose his cool. This nail-biting situation became even less attractive if our steed was a 71 with its single-place cockpit. Because our northbound loads from McMurray were usually heavy, the engineer was left with just the morsel of space the agent hadn't been able to fill. Invariably I would be wedged between the load and the roof (did someone mention safety belts?)

Three of CAL's maintenance crew completing cylinder changes on CF-ATZ's engine on January 20, 1935. (L-R) Frank Hartley, Casey van der Linden and Don Goodwin.

without visibility and wondering what the escape possibilities might be if our luck ran out. I have another recollection of waiting beside our parked and heated aircraft when we were going to be perhaps the number three aircraft. Number one had taken off; we had a brief glimpse of him through the fog. Then we heard number two open the throttle and the engine noise increase in volume, and we tried to guess whether or not he was on course as the sound came closer and closer.

These somewhat dicey takeoffs had become fairly routine over the years (a familiarity-breeds-contempt situation) until in January 1935 we had a close call, and a degree of sanity returned to the operation. A contributing

Con Farrell was at the controls of Junkers CF-AMZ on January 21, 1935, when she collided with ATZ.

Engineer Frank Hartley was occupying the right-hand seat of AMZ at the time of the accident.

factor to this particular incident centred upon some work that was required on one of our Fairchild 71s, CF-ATZ. Her motor had low compression on a number of cylinders, accompanied by the inevitable high oil consumption.

In winter, as we didn't have tractors to move our aircraft into the nose hangar when it was necessary to service them, we would scrape the approach to the hangar down to bare ice, and the aircraft would be taxied on its skis to the end of this path, then pushed into the hangar by hand. Removal would be by the same method but in reverse. To move the aircraft either in or out, it was necessary to rock it by pushing up and down on the wing struts, while all available manpower (including our two agents) applied their utmost muscle to the pushing operation.

On the night of January 20, 1935, after working all day and most of the evening on ATZ's cylinder changes, we were cold, tired and hungry—and

CAL senior agent Fred Lundy was loading mail into CF-ATZ when it was struck by AMZ.

Engineer Bill Jacquot, who usually flew in CF-ATZ, was the first to realize that the aircraft had been damaged in the collision.

lacking in manpower. But, since the aircraft was due out the next morning, Don Goodwin made the only reasonable decision. "All right, fellows, at least we have the job completed in time for the trip tomorrow. We'll push it back until it's clear of the hangar, then push the tail around until it's facing east and we can heat it up there in the morning." Now, our standard procedure when returning from a trip was to taxi the aircraft toward the south bank, then execute a 180-degree turn to face out toward the centre of the Snye, in order to allow departing aircraft to taxi out without blasting their neighbours with their slipstream. In the case of ATZ, however, though we left it some 200 to 300 feet from the centre of the Snye, it was 50 feet closer to the takeoff path than usual, and it had one wing projecting out toward the Snye's centre.

I do not recall who was first away the next morning—it could have been one of the Mackenzie machines or a CM&S 71, but the number two machine was our Junkers AMZ with Con Farrell at the controls and engineer Frank Hartley in the right seat. The fog was particularly dense that morning, and there was a long wait after the first takeoff. Finally, impatience overcame Con's caution, and even though the fog seemed as thick as ever, we heard AMZ's Wasp accelerate. The noise grew louder and we realized that he was too close to our side of the channel. As we had two other aircraft there in addition to ATZ, Don shouted, "Jeez! Clear out of there, you guys! Sounds like he's coming right at us!"

Needless to say, there was a hasty exodus from the vicinity of the parked aircraft. Our senior agent, Fred Lundy, who was loading mail into ATZ at the time, was a gentleman of ample proportions who was never known to hurry—until this particular morning. He shot out of ATZ and reached the bank in seconds. Moments later we had a glimpse of AMZ, seriously off-course and just beyond the line of parked aircraft. Then it disappeared from view into the thick layers of fog just beyond ATZ and our nose hangar. When the engine noise died away, for a moment we thought he was airborne. Then we realized he was taxiing back and had pulled to a stop in the vicinity of ATZ. As we converged around AMZ, Con opened the side cockpit window and poked his head out. Don called, "What are you trying to do, Con—make sure that we're awake?"

"Damn it all," replied Con, "as if I didn't have enough trouble fighting this damned fog without you guys leaving that damned 71 in my path." All of this banter was in good spirits as no one yet realized that there had been contact between the two aircraft. Meanwhile, Bill Jacquot, usually the engineer on ATZ, returned from a quick inspection of that aircraft with a concerned look on his face. "Say, Don, there's a bit of damage to ATZ. The wing tips must have connected." We all trooped over for a look but, other than torn fabric and minor damage to a couple of wing ribs, ATZ seemed intact. We then returned to AMZ, reasoning that, as ATZ had fared so well in the encounter, our sturdy Junkers would surely be undamaged. Our reasoning was flawed. AMZ had actually been airborne, or nearly so, at the time of passing, and the left wing of the westbound AMZ had passed beneath the left wing of the east-facing ATZ, striking the Fairchild's wing from below. Checking the Junkers, we found a couple of diagonal wrinkles in the upper wing skin, indicating a displacement of the internal structure. It was a situation that could only be corrected by drilling out countless rivets and removing wing structural panels to gain access to the spar tubes. Although the damage was slight, we were now faced with a repair of unknown dimensions.

In thinking back on this incident, I must give credit to the design and integrity of the Junkers wing structure. Though damaged, the wing was still structurally sound. If the damage had occurred downriver, the aircraft could certainly have been ferried back to McMurray for repairs. And later, after I became much more familiar with Junkers wing construction, I realized that the aircraft could have been easily and safely ferried as far as our Winnipeg shops for repair.

Since ATZ had the least damage, we rigged a temporary tarpaulin shelter around its wing, and used blow pots inside it for heat. The wing was opened at each bay so that the internal diagonal tie-rods could be checked for tension. A variation in tension would indicate internal damage and the need for a more extensive inspection, but as all of these were found to be satisfactory, the rib damage and fabric were repaired, and in a couple of days ATZ was on her way again, as sound as ever.

Meanwhile, Don sent a wire to our main shops in Winnipeg, outlining the visible, external damage to AMZ. From this information our shop manager there, Albert Hutt, who was knowledgeable about all things mechanical, assembled and shipped all of the material that was needed, complete to the last rivet and spar splice. In the Junkers there were no main spars, as in a conventional aircraft. Instead, the wing structure consisted of eight aluminum-alloy tubes, four at the top and four at the bottom, each being riveted to the corrugated wing skin. A ninth tube formed the wing's leading edge. The corrugated skin provided the chord-wise stiffness while the spar tubes were joined together internally by light-gauge, Z-section diagonals. The spar tubes decreased in diameter and gauge as they approached the wing tip, while the Z-sections became progressively shorter, thus creating the taper in thickness and in plain view.

The wing attachments were a piece of typical German ingenuity: instead of bolts with all of their myriad problems, they consisted of nine ball-and-socket joints. Attaching a wing to a fuselage was simplicity itself. With the wing offered up to the centre section, all of the ball sections would automatically fit into the sockets, and the joints were then secured by circular, threaded rings, similar to a plumber's pipe union.

With its wings removed, Junkers CF-AMZ has been backed into CAL's hangar at McMurray for major repairs.

In the Junkers there were no main spars. Instead the wing structure consisted of eight aluminum-alloy tubes, four at the top and four at the bottom. A ninth formed the wing's leading edge. Here CF-AMZ's repaired spar tubes await a skin.

Once we had ATZ out of the way, we were able to concentrate on AMZ. First we taxied it up the slipway from the Snye, and then about 200 yards along the Snye Road to our hangar. We drained the fuel from the three wing tanks, removed the wing, and put it in the shop. Five days after the accident, maintenance manager Tommy Siers arrived from Winnipeg on the weekly train, bringing with him the repair kit and the special tools needed for the blind riveting inside of the spar tubes. McMurray was not electrified in those days nor did we have air compressors with which to operate pneumatic rivet guns or drills. All of the rivets had to be removed by drilling off the heads with a hand drill. The riveting followed the same hand-hewn path, with each rivet being driven—that is, "headed over"—by means of an eight-ounce hammer and a rivet snap. This latter item was formed from a piece of half-inch steel bar stock, about six inches in length, with one end slightly contoured to fit the head on the size of rivet that we were using.

The actual riveting was carried out one blow at a time, with the snap placed on the rivet head and a bucking bar held against its opposite end. On fuselage structures where the bucker had the rivet end in plain view, his bucking bar would be a solid block of steel about the size of his fist. Riveting the wing panels to the spar tubes, however, was quite another matter. The original Junkers tool provided for this purpose consisted of an anvil made of a short block of steel, flattened on its upper surface and welded to the end of a length of steel tubing. By means of a separate control rod—an expander—on the inside of this tube, the anvil could be raised or lowered. To form a rivet on the inside of a spar tube, the bucker (the man controlling the handles of both rod and tube) would insert the tube/rod assembly into the spar tube, moving it inward until the centre line of the anvil was directly below the rivet hole. A rivet would then be placed in the hole, with the snap placed on the rivet head. The bucker would slowly rotate the expander until the anvil just started to lift the rivet from the hole. The driver would then strike the snap a series of light blows while the bucker made minute adjustments after each blow of the hammer. This operation required the most delicate touch on the part of the bucker because too much pressure would cause the rivet to bend rather than forming into the correct mushroom shape.

After about a dozen rivets had been driven, the assembly was removed from the spar tube and replaced by a beautifully made micro-telescope, another Junkers development. This was made in sections so that, when fully

The wing skin sections have been rejoined and are ready to be riveted onto the structure.

assembled, it could reach the full length of a spar tube. At the tip of this probe was a tiny mirror, set at a 45-degree angle. Illumination was provided by a small, high-intensity, battery-powered light. By positioning the mirror directly below the rivet and adjusting the lens to bring the rivet into sharp focus, we could see if it required additional driving. Unfortunately, there was always the odd one that had bent over instead of forming a mushroom head, and it would have to be drilled out and replaced.

The rivets we used were also German-made. They were "heat-treatable" and, in their as-received condition, flint-hard. To anneal or soften them so that they could be formed, it was necessary to immerse them in a liquid bath of 50/50 sodium nitrate and potassium nitrate at 500°C. These "cooked" rivets were then quenched in cold water to alter the grain structure so that they became soft and easily worked. The shelf life of a batch of annealed rivets was about four hours, after which re-annealing would be required.

Our repairs to AMZ's wing began with drilling out the rivets and removing about seven feet of the upper wing skin to expose the inner wing structure. This revealed that the leading edge spar tube was kinked in one place, as was the number one upper tube. We cut out the damaged sections and replaced them with new material. As the Z-section members were undamaged, we re-riveted them to the new spar tubes. We were then ready to replace the skin, but it was at that point that we realized the difficulty of rejoining the skin sections while they were on the aircraft. The first section we had removed extended about four feet aft of the leading edge; now we had to remove the remaining portion of skin right back to the trailing edge, rivet the two sections together to form a complete assembly, then reattach them to the wing by picking up the original holes in the number three and four upper spars and drilling new rivet holes in the new spars. Fortunately, Frank Hartley, the engineer who regularly flew with AMZ, had considerable Junkers repair experience at our Winnipeg shops, and he was well versed in the operation of the eccentric bucking bar—expertise that we greatly needed. As usual I kept careful track of our progress in my diary.

> **February 3, 1935:** *We finished the wing today and Don and I painted it—looks good. We didn't work tonight though I went down to check the stoves.* [Our shop, as well as all of the homes and buildings in the village, were heated by wood-burning stoves of various sizes and some of very uncertain vintage. House fires due to over-heated stoves or stovepipes were not uncommon, and constant vigilance was needed.] *Howard Ingram* [DoT Inspector] *came in today from Edmonton in his Puss Moth. He is going to inspect the wing, although he admits he is not a technical man and will accept the statements and signature of Tommy Siers. The log book will state that the repairs have been carried out in accordance with the Junkers Repair Manual. Believe he is also here to have a word with Con regarding the takeoff incident.*
>
> **February 4:** *Replaced the wing this a.m. and test flight was planned for p.m. but held up due to twisted gas line.*
>
> **February 5:** *Made up and installed new gas line. Aircraft taxied back to Snye, refuelled and test flown by Con. Due out on regular trip in a.m. Howard Ingram left for Edmonton today.*

And so, with Ingram's Puss Moth disappearing over the horizon to the south, another little saga of McMurray in the early days of aviation was concluded. Though there had been only minor damage to two aircraft, the incident had held the potential for serious damage, loss of aircraft, and loss of life. It was a forcible reminder to everyone that our day-to-day activities contained enough unavoidable risks without compounding them with unnecessary ones.

7 Eye to the keyhole, ear to the ground

For an air engineer's licence, besides the minimum two years of "hands-on" aircraft experience verified in writing by two licensed engineers, there were government exams to write. The catch was that they had to be written in the presence of a government airworthiness inspector and there was only one for western Saskatchewan and Alberta. In my day this individual—a stern Scotsman named Jock Currie—was based in Edmonton, and you had to forward an application and references, then wait for months until he might arrange a visit to your particular base. By the fall of 1935 I had completed all of the requirements, Jock managed to schedule a trip to McMurray, and the coveted licence was in my hands at last. By a further stroke of fortune CAL had a job vacancy at that particular time and I gained immediate employment.

In December 1935 pilot Matt Berry and I, northbound in Fairchild CF-AAO to Aklavik with a load of winter mail, set down at Resolution. At that time the only lodging place in the settlement was operated by well-known northerner Bobby Porritt. Besides serving as postmaster, local agent for Canadian Airways, innkeeper and cook, Bob operated a trading enterprise, dealing in raw furs. His quarters, roomy though somewhat Spartan, consisted of one large, square room that functioned as kitchen, dining room, trading room and washroom, as well as accommodation for the overflow from the one-room post office. His trade goods were stacked in various parts of the room, together with the products he had taken in trade. To the uninitiated it was a scene of hopeless confusion, but in his mind Bob kept a running inventory of all items and their

Fort Resolution

The present settlement of Resolution is on the south shore of Great Slave Lake, just west of the Slave River delta. Moose Deer Island, just to the north, was the original site, having been selected by both the Hudson's Bay and the North West companies for forts, those pioneer fur traders always having been careful to choose sheltered landing places for their fragile canoes. Regardless of wind direction, there is always a lee shore and protection on an island. Sir John Franklin and his party stopped here on their first expedition, which took them to Coppermine and the Barrens. "We pursued our voyage on the following morning," he wrote on July 24, 1820, "and by eight a.m. reached the establishment of the North West Company on Moose Deer Island. Soon after landing I visited the Hudson's Bay post on the same island." And in 1822, after their near miraculous rescue from the Barren Lands ordeal, he and the remnants of his party regained their strength there while waiting for the spring breakup and the start of canoe navigation. Again, to quote Sir John, "We quitted Moose Deer Island at five p.m. on the 26th [May 26, 1822], having resided there for about five months."

locations. As his stock of food stuffs served his kitchen as well as his trade customers, the ingredients for the next meal were always in sight—partially emptied cases of canned goods, slabs of bacon, rounds of cheese, containers of Trumilk and dried fruits and vegetables. Sacks of flour, sugar, oatmeal, potatoes, carrots, turnips and cabbages also filled his larder. The combination of odours defied description—essence of abandoned root cellar combined with that of a zoo on a hot day!—though sometimes we could appreciate the dominant pungent scent of weasel and wolverine pelts because they helped to mask the smell of cabbage that was beyond retirement age.

Smoked moose hides were there as well, redolent with an aroma no northerner can forget—a smell that carried with it the memories of a hundred campfires. I can recall Native elders picking up a new moccasin or a piece of freshly smoked leather, pressing it to their noses, and inhaling deeply. Their eyes would be half-closed, their thoughts focussed upon some half-remembered event from the past—that smoky aroma brushing away the

CF-AAO at Fort Resolution, the first overnight stop on a mail run to Aklavik by pilot Matt Berry and engineer Rex Terpening. December 1935.

Bobby Porritt, Fort Resolution's postmaster, agent for Canadian Airways, innkeeper, cook, fur trader and local historian.

grey ash from the embers of their memories. Once again they were enjoying some triumphant moment from their youth. On a couple of occasions I asked them what memories that fragrant smell recalled. The reply was the same—"the old days."

Bob's stock included cigarette lighters, snowshoes, bolts of gaudy cloth and fancy garters for the village belles, ice chisels, Stanfields one-piece woollies, and the heavy wool knee-length socks that were worn by both sexes. Mixed with these were combs, beads, dog harnesses, and bales of oakum to caulk the seams of the locally-made scows and that finest of northern craft, the Chipewyan skiff. The upstairs room, where guests were accommodated, was finished—or unfinished—with rough lumber, a product of

Bob's part-time sawmill endeavour. The unfinished cubicles might have given a sense of privacy had the carpenter (Bob himself) not been called away on other business and failed to return to the task. The saw and hammer, plus assorted spikes, were still lying on the floor—a constant reminder of the need for caution while on late-night journeys to the outdoors.

Of beds there were none, but to us even a mattress on the floor smacked of luxury. There were four or five of these available, but as Bob's service did not include reservations, he assigned them on a first-come, first-served basis. Unfortunately, air engineers were always the last ones to finish their day, and we would have slept on the floor but for the soft spot in Bob's heart. He always managed to find an extra mattress for us latecomers. None of this was that unusual for the north. In fact, the standards for overnight accommodation for that era in the NWT are described to perfection by my long-time friend, Charley Reiach, who was post manager for the HBC at Coppermine when I met him. "I remember coming out from Coppermine with Rudy Heuss in 1937," he said. "We overnighted at Yellowknife and we were charged $1 per night to sleep on the floor with our own bedrolls."

In spite of Bobby Porritt's small stature, he was "a man of the north" at a time when that term indicated bulk and muscle. He qualified as an entrepreneur long before the term became common, and he had a sincere concern for the future of the Natives. He was also an amateur historian, with a keen interest in events and people, and would probably have expanded into the newspaper business had there been such an opportunity. However, he did make some attempt to record the passing scene with cards and notes and with an occasional publication entitled *The Northern Scrapbook of Bobby Porritt*. I treasure a very early issue and I wish I had more. As Bobby did such an excellent job of illustrating the experiences of some of our aviation pioneers, I still prize a copy of a page from his *Scrapbook* in its original form. I'm unable to thank him in person for the pleasure of this material as he is no longer with us, having gone to join Punch Dickins and Lou Parmenter. Perhaps they can get together and enjoy a chuckle about the events of January 1929, when Punch's Fokker Super shed its undercarriage at Resolution while they were on their pioneering first trip into the area, and he and Lou became Bob's guests. Their Fokker Super, G-CASN, lay spread-eagled on the snow, the first of many aircraft to lose the contest with Resolution's mighty snowdrifts. There was urgent need for a message to be sent to Edmonton, advising Western Canada Airways of their problem, but at that time there was no Royal Canadian Corps of Signals (RCCS) station at Resolution. The nearest wireless was at Fort Smith, some 180 miles away, through bush, muskeg and untravelled wilderness. But Jim Balsillie, a young northerner, took the message, travelling through heavy snows in temperatures of -40 F. He did those 180 miles in 50 hours, a record that still stands. The reply came that night over Edmonton's CJCA radio broadcast: RELIEF PLANE EN ROUTE THURSDAY. (signed) WESTERN CANADA AIRWAYS.

What nobody bothered to mention in the newspaper reports of the day was that the tools and talented hands that repaired the undercarriage of Punch's Fokker and straightened the propeller blades to a usable condition belonged to a young man named Joe Durocher, one of Resolution's local craftsmen.

Fortunately, by the time Matt and I were on our flight to Aklavik in December 1935 RCCS stations had been constructed at McMurray, Resolution, Simpson, Rae and Norman. As a result, before we took off from Resolution the next morning the radio operator was able to provide us with the weather reports for both Simpson and Norman: Simpson WX low, solid overcast, temp. -10°F, calm; Norman WX clear, calm, temp. -35°F.

My preparations that morning were typical of any day in the life of an air engineer. Bob called me at 5:30. I dressed, washed, and made a quick trip to the one-holer out back. (I wished Bob would replace the door; the snowdrift was nearly up to seat height.) It was the usual Resolution January morning—temperature -20°F and wind about the same, 20 mph. I could see stars so I figured visibility would be okay except for ground drift. Bob made me his usual good breakfast—eggs, bacon, strawberry jam on toasted homemade bread. (Bob cooked a good loaf.) Some of the eggs were getting a bit ripe; that batch wouldn't last the winter. While I was eating, the RCCS radio operator brought the weather reports and left a parcel for "Beep" Palmer at Simpson.

I went to the aircraft at 6:30—that biting wind sure pierced you, especially early in the morning when blood circulation was not too brisk—stowed my sleeping bag and gear, and took a quick look around. Because of the wind there was no frost on the aircraft. I lit a fire in the tent stove to heat the oil then did three fast circuits around the aircraft to get my blood flowing. By this time the weather was getting dirty with the wind around 30 mph, and I placed two empty barrels on the upwind

Imperial Oil Aircraft Establish Northern Flying Record

Hay River Post, situated where the brown, muskeg-stained waters of the Hay empty into Great Slave Lake, had seen the first ski-equipped aircraft landing in the Northwest Territories on March 27, 1921, when the two Imperial Oil Company Junkers aircraft, *Rene*, G-CADQ, and *Vic*, G-CADP (appropriately named after the early voyageurs), had overnighted there while en route to their planned destination—the site of Imperial Oil's successful well-drilling undertaking, later known as Norman Wells. Their story, told by Ken Molson in "The Rene and the Vic: Early Flying Along the Mackenzie," (*CAHS Journal*, Summer 1982) tells how the party flew north from Edmonton with overnight stays at both Peace River Town and Fort Vermillion. From this point they had abandoned the river routes and boldly struck off to the north, their destination being Hay River Post, some 200 miles distant over completely unmapped and untravelled country. With no knowledge of what lay between and probably with little in the way of emergency provisions and equipment, they faced serious hazards, though perhaps they considered a second aircraft to be a sufficient safety factor. In any event, they flew the approximate 200 miles straight across country and landed without mishap at the post after 2 hours and 40 minutes of flying. They refuelled and stayed at the post overnight, taking off the next morning for Fort Providence.

At Providence the snow on the field where they landed next to the HBC post was over three feet deep, the deepest so far encountered, and when they attempted to take off after refuelling, the machines could only accelerate to about 20 miles an hour, and the attempt had to be abandoned. That night the Imperial Oil crews and a number of the Native people donned snowshoes and walked abreast up and down the takeoff area to compact the snow, but a broken ski prevented them leaving until March 30, when they headed directly for Fort Simpson.

Another source, the NWT Northern Heritage Centre video "Wings of Change" provides a different perspective on the Fort Providence part of the story. Cecile Tourangeau, a young student at the mission at that time, clearly recalled the events. "In 1921 during benediction in church—in March

Two Imperial Oil Ltd. Junkers Model F-13 aircraft, G-CADP and G-CADQ, christened the "Rene" and the "Vic", on the waterfront at Fort Simpson, in the summer of 1921. Earlier in the same year these two planes had carried out the first ski-equipped landings in the Northwest Territories, at Hay River Post. *Photograph courtesy of the Canada Aviation Museum, Ottawa.*

at 6 o'clock there's still daylight, it doesn't get dark—during the Rosary—well, suddenly, just noise, just like thunder, and you never hear thunder in March. It was just above the church. Everybody got all excited and thought, Was the roof falling in or what? Then it passed. It was quiet. Everybody ran out and we were not supposed to leave the church without permission from the nuns who were supervising us, but they all ran out so we all ran out to see what it was. So we put on our coats—our warm coats on—to see the plane. The pilot was sitting in the plane, chatting with the priest, so he had to stay. All the men—the Bouviers and the Laffertys—they were all there so there was lots of people to help him cover his plane. Anybody who came always went to the mission to stay. They gave him a room and he had his meals there. When he was ready to go they had to go see when he was ready to take off. The first thing then, you know, they told everybody if anybody had snowshoes to take their snowshoes back to the plane. We didn't know what was going on. In those days they didn't have anything to clear snow so planes could fly, so they used the snowshoes to trample the snow. All the people in town who had snowshoes trampled all the snow. Three or four days after that, I guess, they tried the plane and it worked so he took off and went to Fort Simpson."

As a personal observation, comparing the snowshoeing abilities of the two groups, I would guess that most of the trampling was carried out by the Bouviers and the Laffertys. However, by the time we appeared on the scene the novelty had worn off, and we had to do our own trampling.

side of the engine cover to act as a windbreak, got the blow pots going and started heating, knowing it would be a slow job with that wind. When checking the tent stove, I found one torch was acting up and I had to remove it. About 7:15 I heard Matt in the cabin and he stuck his mitt through the cover and waved at me—no use talking with the blow pots so noisy—before taking care of the oil heating in the tent. When Bob brought down the northbound mail, he and Matt rearranged the load. By 7:45 the engine was hot, but the light was still dim due to blowing snow. I added the oil, refilled the torches, stowed both pails and torches, then as soon as the light brightened, I removed the cover, started the engine, stowed the cover and climbed aboard. Finally around 8:30 it was light enough for takeoff, and we were bound for Hay River.

Matt's route to Hay River lay along the south shore of Great Slave Lake. He was far too wise to risk taking a shortcut across the lake and getting caught in a whiteout. This was a dull and monotonous stretch of country with little of interest and even less in the way of shelter if one had a forced landing. The shoreline was totally exposed to the sweep of the winds, which arranged and rearranged the serried drifts of snow with every change of direction. We knew that every drift was tightly packed and iron-hard with the potential for breaking a ski or damaging an undercarriage.

Though we had clear weather when leaving Resolution, a heavy overcast developed, and we completed the balance of the trip at 500 feet. We landed on the smooth surface of the river, then taxied down to the vicinity of the Northern Traders post. The post manager, who was now our agent, was the same Jack Cameron after whom Cameron Bay on Bear Lake had been named. After Matt shut down the engine, he sat for a moment squinting up at the leaden sky. With the Simpson weather report in mind, he remarked, "Sky doesn't look too good, does it? Wonder if the snow will hold off until we get to Simpson?"

As ours was the first mail flight since freeze-up, there were several people down to meet us, with hand-shaking and health enquiries all around. A number of Native children, in residence at the large Anglican mission there, stood discreetly in the background, apparently excused from classes for the occasion. Soon the little crowd dispersed to the post office with letters and parcels uppermost in their minds, while Matt and Jack made their way to the Northern Traders post.

Though on this occasion it was not essential to refuel as we had plenty of gas to reach Simpson, as a matter of routine most of us refuelled at nearly every post when northbound in order to conserve the more expensive fuel at the northerly posts. The odd crew would find some excuse to sidestep this practice, with the result that fuel caches at places like Camsell River on Great Bear Lake were seldom tapped because they were bypassed by so many of our stablemates. So at Hay River I covered the engine and prepared to refuel. Three or four barrels of gasoline had been positioned on the ice near the shoreline, but our approach to them was blocked by intervening driftwood frozen into the ice, and I had to roll one barrel closer to the aircraft. This was not usually a problem—moving those 500-pound barrels was a daily exercise that kept us in top condition—but some overflow had occurred so ice-chopping was required. Then I attacked the barrel with a heavy log from Jack's cordwood pile, eventually jarring it loose. Jack had promised to help with the fuelling, so I positioned the pump, hose and funnel in readiness.

It was at this point that I discovered that water had entered the pump during the freeze-up season, our pumps being sometimes too handy when a skiff needed pumping out. Now the mechanism was frozen solid and the handle was absolutely immoveable. This was not a difficult problem to correct but it meant lost time—so precious during the short daylight hours of winter. I removed the handle from the pump and the cap screws from the face plate. This came off after some judicious hammering, exposing the rotor and its coating of ice. I soaked a small rag in gasoline and placed this inside the pump cavity, carried the pump some distance from AAO, and touched a match to the rag. By the time my bonfire had died away the pump body was warm, and the water—there was no more than a tablespoonful—could be wiped up.

I had reassembled the pump when Jack appeared, most apologetic about the pump and the frozen-in barrels, but he had prepared some en route sandwiches for us of homemade bread and roasted caribou, so his misdemeanors were forgiven. With refuelling completed, we were soon on our way to Fort Providence and munching on Jack's excellent sandwiches. These Hay River problems were typical of those we encountered on the first trips after freeze-up; they were expected and taken in stride. That day, though, we were unhappy over the wasted time and the lost daylight. It had taken us nearly an hour to reach Hay River, and we had lost another 45 minutes there, and since the quality of the light was further reduced by the heavy overcast, our day would be that much shorter.

West of Hay River, where Great Slave Lake begins to narrow, the far-off north shore became visible to us. On our right were Big Island and the start of Alexander Mackenzie's stream. Over the next 50 miles the Mackenzie gradually narrows to the point where Fort Providence sits on a high bank on the north side of the channel. The small cluster of buildings that comprised the settlement in those days were located on good, level ground, and the industrious Catholic church people had cleared a sizeable area for gardens and crops, providing us with an excellent landing field. We made one pass to check the field. It was level with no obstacles, and since there were no spruce tree runway markers, we assumed that the selection of a landing area was not critical. The snow cover was obviously light as the odd clump of dirt was visible, though toward the north side, closer to the trees, it appeared to be deeper. Consequently, Matt selected that side instead of the middle where we would normally land.

The landing was routine enough until near the end of our run when the aircraft lurched, swung to the left and then slowed. To maintain our direction, Matt had to apply power and right rudder, then further power in order to maintain a moderate taxiing speed. After getting the aircraft back on course and again headed for the Hudson's Bay post buildings, Matt called back to me, "Something's wrong here. She wants to swing to the left. We must have hit something back there and damaged a ski."

I had been lying on top of the load during the trip so that Matt and I could talk. Now I moved back to observe the left ski through the side window. The track emerging under both its left and right runners showed a normal, smooth pattern. The centre runner, however, showed a pattern of roughened snow, a sure sign that its brass coating had been damaged. I moved back to be within earshot of Matt to tell him the news, adding, "We must have run over a sharp stone." We pulled up adjacent to the Hudson's Bay post buildings and the manager, Fred McLeod, was there to welcome us. As he was also our agent, he had the gas barrels and refuelling equipment in readiness. As at Hay River, most of the small population, junior and adult, Native and white, two-legged and four-legged, were there to share in the excitement.

Fort Providence, showing the Catholic church and the mission buildings behind it. The cleared land in the foreground grew vegetables and field crops in summer and became a landing field in winter.

Matt told Fred about our damaged runner. "We ran over something out there while we were landing," he said. "Rex figures it could have been a sharp stone."

"We cleared all the loose ones from the centre of the field where you guys usually land," replied Fred, "but I don't know about that area over on the north side. Could be there's a big one there the brothers couldn't uproot. Maybe just the tip of it sticking up. What are you going to do now?"

Matt turned to me. "What do you think?"

"Well," I replied, "I've got a spare piece of brass with me and I'm sure I can patch up the ski. It'll take time, though. If you think you can take off with it in this condition, then I'll repair it tonight at Simpson. That way we won't lose any time."

"Okay then," said Matt, "we'll give it a try. If we can't get off, we'll have to fix it here. If we can get an early start from Simpson in the morning, we might still make Norman by tomorrow night."

The unloading was quickly carried out, and then we were handed a few pieces of loose mail for delivery to individuals at Simpson and Norman. The post office tried to discourage this practice, insisting that all mail be posted and thus carried officially. Invariably, however, our agent would have a few loose letters entrusted to him. These would be carried by our pilots as a matter of courtesy and passed along to our agent at the next post—a carryover from the days of the Moccasin Telegraph and dogsled communications.

We had a final word with Fred, who agreed to check the field thoroughly for stones, particularly in view of the light snow cover, and to mark a safe strip with spruce trees. We were particularly interested in the rock that had caused our ski damage and Fred promised to locate the offender by following our ski track and let us know when we passed through on our southbound trip.

We had been so engrossed in our ski problem that we had paid no attention to the weather. It was different with Fred. Having spent a lifetime in the north with so many of his activities dictated by the weather, he was constantly aware of changes in wind direction and velocity, light conditions and cloud cover. With his next observation we realized that we would do well to show the same interest.

"You guys sure you don't want to spend the night here?" he asked, pointing to the lowering sky. "Looks like it could start snowing any minute."

Matt paused for a moment to stare at the sky. "It doesn't look too good, does it? On the other hand, it's been much the same since about ten this morning. Anyway, it's only about an hour and a half to Simpson. If we overnight here we might be snowed in for a couple of days!" With that he climbed into the cockpit, I cranked the engine, and we taxied out to our starting point.

I should point out that, as all NWT rivers flow to the Arctic, it is the custom in the north whenever you are heading downstream to refer to your direction of travel as north. Matt and I were definitely heading downstream to get to Simpson, but the McKenzie actually flows west and then northwest from Providence until it joins the Liard, which flows in from the southwest. From that point on they get their acts together and resume their ordained course, heading once more for the Arctic. For this reason a few of the statements in the following paragraphs will seem to be twisted about 90 degrees from what one would expect.

We had landed on the north side adjacent to the timber, and this presented no problems for a landing. For a takeoff, however, with the constant drag of our damaged ski, this would be a quite different matter. The snow was soft—almost sticky, in fact—and, unlike the crews of *Rene* and *Vic*, we did not have the Bouviers and the Laffertys to trample it for us. Whichever direction we selected for takeoff could get us into the glue unless Matt's judgement was exactly right, the urgency and necessity of becoming airborne being balanced precariously against the need to cut the throttle at the last moment to avoid obstacles. Going east we might end up among some Native cabins or in the stump field. Going west we might ruin the good brothers' fences and end up with our prop festooned with barbed wire.

Matt had undoubtedly given considerable thought to this matter because he taxied to the northwest corner of the field using plenty of power and a considerable amount of right rudder in the process. I assumed that he was going to say, "Stumps be damned," and take off toward the east. Instead, he turned the aircraft toward the southeast, throttled back the motor, and sat there looking through the left side window toward the corner of the field where a couple of cabins crouched behind a fence near the top of the riverbank. This side-window view was the normal routine in a 71. More visual reference was obtained through them than through the windshield, Fairchild's designers having had little interest in the pilot's need for forward visibility when airborne and even less for when the aircraft was in the tail-down position on the ground.

Half turning his head, Matt said (as much to himself as to me), "This diagonal run will give us the most distance, and there are no obstacles. If I have to cut the throttle, I'll give her full left rudder. She'll want to ground-loop to the left anyway. And if we have to do a ski-jump off the riverbank, well, that bank must be thirty feet above river level so we can afford to lose a bit of altitude." After a final glance down the field, he remarked, "I wouldn't mind a capful of that Resolution wind right now." With that he opened the throttle and urged AAO in a southeasterly direction.

During a normal takeoff our speed would have increased rapidly, but with the drag from the damaged ski and the considerable amount of right rudder required, we seemed to be glued to the ground. From my horizontal perch on top of the load I probably had better forward visibility than did Matt, and I watched with little confidence as the corner of the field quickly approached. Then suddenly the riverbank disappeared from my view below the top of the engine, and I realized we were airborne. We shot off the top of the bank, climbed and turned to the right and were westbound again.

Simpson was only 150 miles to the west so we could expect to land there by 2:30 p.m. and service the aircraft in daylight. With luck I could make a good start on the ski repairs before supper. Our immediate concern, however, was weather. Our ceiling had been considerably less than 1,000 feet before reaching Providence and there had been no improvement. As we headed west we climbed—but not for long. We had barely topped 500 feet when we were into the lower fringe of the clouds, and an ice layer started to form on the leading edge of the wing. Matt eased the nose downwards until we were again in the clear.

From Providence the river widens out into Mills Lake. We kept to the left, following the south shore of the Mackenzie. Much of the river surface below us had frozen into a mass of rough and tumbled ice that would, at a minimum, demolish an undercarriage if we were forced down. It also had the potential for writing off the entire aircraft. Smooth ice did exist but good light was needed to pick out a section reasonably free of obstacles and of sufficient length for a landing—and good light we did not have. It had instead become dim and shadowless. If the snow came—heavy snow with reduced visibility—then we had three choices. We could try for a landing while there was still enough light, retrace our route and try to reach Providence ahead of the storm, or if beyond the halfway point we could try to reach Simpson.

The river gradually unwound below us. Here and there we spotted sheltered places where the ice appeared to be smooth, but we both noted them without comment. The difficulty would be in trying to relocate them in poor light when running before a blizzard. Slowly the time added up. With an hour behind us, we reached the point on the river that the voyageurs knew as "The Head of the Line." Here its nature changes as increasingly it is confined by high banks that accelerate the current flow. The sheltered stretches of river and patches of smooth ice disappeared; there would be nothing but rough ice from here to Simpson. But passing Jean Marie River we relaxed slightly. Simpson was less than 50 miles away and there were lakes on the south side of the river where the ice would be smooth—though the thin ice of early winter was still a concern.

And then the first snowflakes appeared. We had been anticipating their arrival for over an hour—or perhaps half a day—but had convinced ourselves that they would hold off. I had been immersed in thought, mentally repairing the ski, so Matt's comment, "Snow!" came as a shock. The horizon, which had been several miles ahead, suddenly disappeared. The light, such as it was, began to fade. We seemed to be immobilized, as though anchored up there in the overcast with the snowflakes racing toward us. Far ahead we could see the big flakes surging toward us faster and faster until finally they flashed up and over the cockpit or off to one side. None of them actually appeared to contact us, but with the passing minutes their ranks closed in. Matt applied some carburetor heat and grudgingly gave up some of our altitude. We were soon down to near tree-top level, the trees and the riverbank just below our left wing. Off to the right the river was a mass of upturned, broken ice. It had not appeared attractive from 500 feet; it was even less so from 50. A river landing was out of the question. And our limited forward visibility and minimum altitude were a poor combination for a cross-country jaunt in search of a lake. The minutes crept by with no change in our situation. It was bad but at least it was flyable. And every minute was bringing us closer to Simpson.

Our thoughts then centred on the difficulty of landing in Simpson in such a dense snowstorm. This settlement is on an island on the north side of the Liard just above the point where it joins the Mackenzie, but it is a big river at this point, and crossing it in heavy snow without a guiding shoreline would be risky in the extreme. We would have to execute a smart left turn and follow the Liard upstream until the visibility improved or until the river narrowed enough for a safe crossing, then follow the north bank downstream again until we reached Simpson.

Then suddenly, while we were both pondering the difficulties ahead, the visibility improved. Almost as quickly as they had appeared, the snowflakes vanished. Within a minute or so we were able to climb back to a more comfortable altitude where we could see the river swinging off to the west. Before us was the last straight stretch of 25 miles or so, with Simpson, perched on its island, dead ahead.

There was a narrow channel—a snye—between the island and the mainland, and this was always used for our winter landings. Because of its sheltered location and the slow current behind the island, it froze in advance of the main river and the ice was always smooth. Sheltered from the worst of the winds, close to the settlement, and with uniformly smooth ice, this was one of our favourite destinations. It had the added advantage of a sizeable Signal Corps station with steel cots, mattresses, and a good cook. As at all of these stations, we were welcome visitors—a couple of fresh faces with a bit of first-hand news from outside and local gossip from the other posts along the rivers.

Sleigh Boards and Moose-Hoof Glue Make History

Fort Simpson with the Liard River in the background and Hudson's Bay buildings in the foreground. The junction of the Liard with the Mackenzie River is just out of sight to the left.

The channel behind the island at Fort Simpson had been the scene of the landing of Imperial Oil's Junkers G-CADP, piloted by Elmer Fullerton, on March 31, 1921. The previous day, this machine, along with its sister ship G-CADQ, had made the first-ever landings on the island, but the latter's propeller had been damaged in the process. The serviceable aircraft, CADP, was then ferried to the safety of the snye, its propeller removed and transferred to CADQ in order to ferry it to the snye, too. However, a second accident resulted in the loss of that propeller as well, and the stage was set for a history-making and much publicized event—the local manufacture of two replacement propellers. The components of these were oak sleigh boards, glue made from boiled moose hooves, and a liberal application of ingenuity and determination on the part of those early bush engineers, Bill Hill and Pete Derbyshire. But the ultimate suc-

Imperial Oil's Junkers CADQ sits wingless at Fort Simpson in the summer of 1921 awaiting the arrival of repair parts on the Hudson's Bay sternwheeler.

Imperial Oil's Junkers G-CADP provisions the company's station at Fort Norman in the summer of 1921.

cess of this enterprise was only made possible by the skilled hands of Walter Johnson, one of those who had been lured into the north by the appeal of the frontier and the fur trade, a man who had exchanged his cabinet maker's trade for a life with the Hudson's Bay Company. It is a fitting tribute to all of these people that the two propellers have been preserved and are now on display at the Science Museum in Ottawa.

We made a quick pass over the channel, thinking of obstructions rather than rough ice, then returned for a smooth landing. As we turned and taxied back toward the gas cache and the tent where our pails of oil would spend the night, Matt turned to grin over his shoulder. "I suppose you're disappointed that we're not moonlighting under the spruce trees up north of Rae?" He was referring to one of our first winter flights together a year earlier. Although neither of us had mentioned this incident on the flight up from Providence, it had crossed my mind a couple of times, and obviously the thought of another night in the bush had brought it back to Matt's mind. As we taxied up toward the small crowd at the gas barrels, someone placed a pair of poles down for us, Matt taxied onto them and shut down the engine. Our agent, Len Morgan—also the local manager of the Hudson's Bay store—was there to meet us, together with all of the off-duty RCCS boys, a couple of the Mounties, and some of the other citizens.

The snow was still holding off but the overcast remained, keeping the temperature at a relatively warm and welcome -10°F. We were anxious to make use of the remaining hour of daylight so I started the servicing immediately. My first job, after draining the oil and installing the engine cover, was to have a word with one of our blow pots—the one that had been acting up that morning at Resolution. Serviceable blow pots were essential for winter operations, and morning was no time to be overhauling them. As I had spare jets with me, I made a quick change, then fired up the torch to ensure that its health was fully restored. Matt had volunteered to take care of the refuelling so that I could concentrate on our ski repairs. With the blow pot situation taken care of, I disconnected the ski harness—a cable and bungee assembly at the front to keep the ski level while in flight and a single check cable at the aft end to limit the rotation of the ski. I had jacked up the left side of the undercarriage in readiness for the ski removal when one of the Signals boys, J.B. Piercy—J.B. for short—volunteered to help me. This was most welcome as a ski/pedestal assembly weighed about 150 pounds. Removal and installation could be accomplished by one person using various blocks and levers, but it was far easier and faster with two.

With the aircraft jacked up and the ski harness disconnected, it required only a few minutes to remove the ski and meet our problem face to face. The cutting edge of the rock had been about three inches in width and this had inflicted a deep gouge in the brass runner, starting at about the centre

Damage to skis, such as occurred to CF-AAO at Fort Providence, was a routine part of winter operations. Here a repaired ski, once again involving CF-AAO, is being installed at the Snye at Fort McMurray by Casey van der Linden, Fred Little, Sammy Tomlinson and Lou Parmenter in January, 1934.

of the ski. It had cut through the brass, and a section about four inches wide by six inches in length had been folded back against the runner. Using a hammer and cold chisel I cut away the torn brass and then, using a flat file, smoothed the gouged area as much as possible. This was a laborious and slow process; anyone who has ever tried to file a flat surface with only a flat file for a tool will know what I mean.

By this time everyone else had returned to the settlement. "It's getting too dark to work, J.B.," I said. "Let's go up and have supper. Then I'll use your workshop to cut and drill the new piece of brass. If you can locate a gas lantern for me, I'll come down and finish the job after supper."

"I'll come and help you," he said. "I'm expecting a lot of mail from home, and if I open it now, I'll read it right away and there won't be any left for tomorrow. Besides, you'll need a hand to get the ski back on and hook up the harness again."

This latter point was most valid. Stretching the multiple strands of frozen bungee was a two-man job accomplished by placing a jack handle through the rubber bundle and then, with the handle extensions cradled in our arms, stretching the bungee far enough to make the connection. Making the actual connection was tricky. It required each of us to maintain the tension with one arm under the handle, then one man guiding the cable/shackle assembly into position with his free hand as the other man used his free hand to insert the shackle pin.

With a good meal behind us, the patch cut to size and drilled, and a Coleman gas lantern to guide us, we returned to the aircraft. We moved the ski into the tent and, in relative comfort and with the use of a hand drill, we fitted and secured the patch. The ski was re-installed, the harness re-connected, and by 9:00 in the evening we were back in the warmth and cheer of the signals station. It had not been such a bad day, really. It had been long—and cold at times—but quite bearable and much better than average. I could well remember others that had been worse. Our mechanical problems had been fairly routine and straightforward, the type that we anticipated and planned for. And the weather? Well, sometimes we were lucky. And at the end of the day we were standing on the same ground as some of the early aviation pioneers, we had faced and solved problems similar to theirs, and we realized that aviation hadn't changed very much at all in the previous 15 years.

8 Pilgrim's Progress

Readers with skiing experience or those with fond memories of toboggans and hillsides probably have a mental picture of our ski-equipped steeds gliding smoothly "o'er the snow" as though propelled by a Prancer instead of a Wasp. While true in most instances, sometimes our skis would become balky. The villain was overflow.

Overflows never followed any established pattern. Sometimes the cause would be a small stream that froze at its point of entry into the lake, allowing water to flow out under the snow layer and lie on top of the lake ice. Other times it was the result in a drop in water level that caused the ice to fracture and subside and water to flow into the depression. An average overflow might consist of six inches or more of slush, topped with a layer of snow. One of the frustrations of this condition was the almost total lack of any sign that it was lurking there, and from time to time we blundered right into one, resulting in some mighty oaths from the crew and the probable loss of all of our hopes of Heaven. Our encounters with overflow were not confined to milder temperatures. They could occur at very low temperatures, especially if there was a heavy blanket of snow to act as an insulator.

Matt Berry and I confirmed this in January 1936 when we were northbound in our faithful old Fairchild AAO after overnighting at Fort Resolution. As at most of our winter stopping places, at Resolution the company had arranged for an 8x12 wall tent to be erected close to where our aircraft would park for the night. The tent was equipped with a stove of sufficient size that our oil pails could be placed on its top. When the engineer made his appearance in the morning, he would light the fire in the tent stove, then carry on with the aircraft heating. The pilot would appear a bit later and take over the oil-heating duties. At posts where we seldom overnighted—Arctic Red River, Fort McPherson, Coppermine—our hosts, either the RCMP or the local HBC post manager—would heat the oil for us, carrying our pails into a warm area, sometimes even into their kitchens where our oil pails might be afforded a place of honour upon their kitchen stoves. The people at those northern posts helped us in every way they could, their kindness going a long way toward making our tasks more bearable. Their hospitality knew no bounds.

Such civilized arrangements were not available, however, when we had to spend a night in the bush (which might mean the Barrens if we were really down on our luck). Such occasions occurred when the weather got too tough, or we ran out of daylight, or the map disagreed with us. (We were never lost, of course. In cases of disagreement, we always blamed the map for our predicament.) For such contingencies I carried a pair of steel double-hooks of sufficient strength to hold the 50-pound oil pails. The hook on one end was large enough to fit over an exhaust or intake pipe so that in the morning I could heat the oil at the same time as I heated the engine. I never checked specifically with my colleagues, but I would imagine that they all carried similar devices.

The winter weather at Resolution was never great, and on that January 1936 morning it was far below average. As the -30°F temperature was accompanied by a strong wind, I placed two gasoline barrels against the upwind side of the engine cover to keep it in place, and then wrapped a small tarpaulin around the engine cover as an added windbreak. Even with these precautions it was over an hour before the frost line started to creep out along the propeller shaft—the one sure indication that the engine was internally warm. I refuelled the blow pots, then carried the two five-gallon pails of hot oil from the tent, adding this to the tank.

With our preparations completed, we were ready for departure. All we needed was some visibility, but the wind had kicked up a sizeable ground drift, and we had to kill the best part of an hour before we got underway. Our destination was Fort Rae, 160-odd miles to the north at the far end of the North Arm of Great Slave Lake. This old trading post had been built

The original Catholic church at Fort Rae. The short sections of log wall were a design feature necessitated by the stunted growth of the trees in the area.

on a peninsula jutting out into Marion Lake, which is just north of Slave Lake, and the location must have been selected with summer and mosquitoes in mind. It was treeless and windy with no shelter of any kind. When we arrived that day, the wind was blowing at about 20 mph and the temperature was -40°F. If wind chill charts had existed then, the reading would certainly have been off the scale. I put on the engine cover as soon as we stopped, but by the time I had finished refuelling, the engine was already stiffening up from the cold.

The temperature had also affected the hand-cranked inertia starter, and I just couldn't get it up to the proper speed. Matt had the engine primed in readiness, and he engaged the starter when I gave him the signal, but there was no response from the motor. It chugged over a couple of times and then died. Cranking one of those inertia starters, especially in winter, was one of the most physically demanding tasks that I know of. It required every ounce of energy that one possessed. Some of the big guys, the 180-pounders, could probably do three consecutive cranks without a rest break, but for us 140-pounders two was about the limit. With the -40°F temperature and that driving wind, our engine was fast losing its residual heat. I started cranking for the second time without much hope of success, but we were lucky this time. The engine fired up almost immediately, and we were soon on our way north again, heading for Cameron Bay.

Normally one can expect the air temperature to be some 20 or 30 degrees warmer than the ground temperature, but that day the air temperature was pinned at -40°F all the way. As we had a light load, I had access to the cabin heater outlet, but there was barely enough heat to warm my hands. Our agent at Rae (Bob Dodman, the Northern Traders post manager) had brought down some sandwiches, and we consumed these as we headed north into the failing light of the winter afternoon. The date was January 4 so our allotment of daylight was meagre, to say the least. With the single cockpit of the Fairchild there was little opportunity for conversation, but we both knew that all of our dim light would be consumed long before we reached Cameron Bay.

Matt had been hunched over, staring alternately through the left and right cockpit windows as he tried to identify landmarks in the dim light. Now he straightened up and half-turned his head. I knew the signal and moved closer. His first remark was a classic understatement. "That light's not very good," he said. "We'll try for Hottah Lake." The mining camp at the north end of Hottah Lake was the nearest outpost of civilization, but it was still 180 miles and two hours flying time from Rae. Matt continued, "If it gets much worse we'll have to spend the night in the bush, I guess." No reply was needed. We droned on. It is possible that there was a moon up there above the overcast because the light seemed to stabilize. It was bad but it didn't worsen.

To aid our nocturnal navigation, we were flying somewhat to the west of the normal track, following instead the distinct dividing line along the west side of the lake chain that extends from Rae to Bear Lake. To the east of this line there are lakes by the hundreds, leading off into the Barrens; to the west there are few lakes and the landscape is fairly well covered with timber. Fortunately, this division was plainly visible to us even in the poor light conditions. Though we could no longer see the thermometer out on the wing strut, we were too numb with cold to care. We just shivered and endured. Then at last the ten-mile-wide expanse of Hottah Lake came into view on our right, and we both brightened up. The lights of the mining camp were soon visible, but Matt hugged the western shoreline and then the northern shoreline, as the camp was at the north end of the lake. The lake surface to our right was a shadowless void, a winter version of the ever-dangerous glassy water condition of summer. Using the shoreline just off to the left for altitude reference and keeping the camp lights ahead, Matt eased back on the throttle for a slow descent. We were well past the camp when we felt the skis in the snow. As we slowed, Matt applied power to make the turn—and nothing happened. I had been looking through the side window and soon recognized our problem: we were stuck in deep overflow.

In the temperature range where overflow is normally encountered, a pilot can usually generate enough power to taxi through the stuff and perhaps make an escape to dryer terrain. But our temperature was an unbelievable -55°F, and because of the extreme cold our engine could not develop full power, and for the same reason the slush froze to the ski surfaces immediately. The only solution was to jack up the aircraft until the skis were clear of the slush and to block it up overnight until the slush froze. From previous experience with overflow, I knew I could work in the slush for a brief period without actually getting my feet wet, and I jumped out to survey the situation, then returned for the engine cover and the pails to drain the oil. But that night there was actually water at the ice surface, and it wasn't long before I could feel it seeping through my mukluks.

In the meantime Matt had climbed down from the cockpit and slowly moved around to the front where I was draining the oil. I realized then that he was doubled over, with both hands pressed against his abdomen. My first thought was appendicitis, and it was with considerable relief that I heard him say, "My hernia's giving me hell tonight." I was aware that he had this problem, but this was the first time I'd seen him in so much pain.

"Just take it easy, Matt. I'll run down to the camp and get someone with a sleigh!" I said.

"Let's wait a minute," he replied. "I've had these attacks before. They usually ease up after a bit."

I continued with my oil-draining operation, hung the pails on the hooks, and applied the engine cover. I got my kit bag and Matt's from the aircraft, and we walked back along our ski tracks, already well frozen. Matt was in bad shape, moving slowly and obviously in great pain, but eventually we reached camp, wondering at the same time why no one had shown any interest in our arrival. They had heard us land, of course, but strangely enough no one had come out to see why we had not taxied back. Normally if we were in trouble, the mining camp chaps would give us every possible help—but not that night. The helping hand did not function at such low temperatures. The cook, however, anticipating our arrival, had an abundance of hot food ready for us.

After supper I changed into dry footgear and returned to the aircraft with the small sleigh I had located, some blocks of squared wood and short logs. I strapped on my snowshoes and packed down the snow in the immediate area, then started the jacking operation. With each ski jacked as high as I could safely raise it, I used the jack handle and the shovel to clear off the worst of the ice that had frozen to the ski bottoms, then placed a couple of poles under each ski before lowering it again. (People familiar with hydraulic jacks will probably wonder what possible use a hydraulic jack handle could be as an ice scraper, but our jacks were Walker "Blue Boys," a mechanical type with a sharp-edged rectangular steel bar for a handle, which performed quite nicely as an ice scraper.)

With the aircraft in a more or less serviceable condition, my next thought concerned a runway for morning. I snowshoed two paths about a half mile in length, each path two snowshoes wide, and called it a night, remembering to take our two sleeping bags along in the sleigh. Matt's physical condition had been at the back of my mind all evening and I wondered, as I walked back, whether he would be able to continue tomorrow. It was about 10:00 p.m. by the time I reached camp for the welcome snack of a double serving of hot apple pie.

My last diary entry for the day reads:

> ***January 4, 1936:*** *Matt's hernia very painful tonight—could scarcely walk from the aircraft after we landed but feeling much better when I got back to camp about 10 tonight.*

In the morning our takeoff path was well frozen, but our windows were so frosted up that visibility was guesswork in the dim light. Matt kept the aircraft on my snowshoe path with great difficulty but we finally got airborne. Cameron Bay, our Bear Lake destination, was only about 55 miles distant but the light was poor, and we were constantly running into fog patches.

A view of Cameron Bay, looking west toward the main body of Great Bear Lake from the mining settlement.

After wandering around in this stuff for an hour, lost most of the time, Matt found our way back to Hottah Lake to spend our second night. This time, though, he landed in front of the camp and did two high-speed taxis to make a runway. We were now in good shape for morning, especially as there was no overflow in the camp area, but it was fortunate that we had left Resolution with full tanks and topped up at Rae, as there was no fuel at Hottah. My final diary entry for the day reads:

> *Found dry snow near camp so in good shape for tomorrow. Glad Matt feeling OK today/hernia not bothering him. Temp -60°F.*

January 6 proved to be a fairly routine day. The temperature remained at -60°F but, with the camp close at hand, it was a great improvement over the previous day. There were banks of fog and low stratus clouds, so it was close to noon before we got airborne. We went straight to Cameron Bay, where I jumped out into slightly warmer -50°F air and placed the poles in front of the skis. Matt taxied up onto them and shut down the engine. Our original plan had been to carry out a mail transfer here, then proceed to Camsell River to refuel. Normally we would have refuelled at Cameron Bay, but when Canadian Airways had absorbed Spence-McDonough Air

Transport, the company had inherited a sizeable gas cache at the AX Mining Syndicate camp near White Eagle Falls, so we would be making use of that gas on this occasion. However, as Matt opened the cockpit door, he made the welcome pronouncement, "Drain the oil. We've had enough for today." This gave us a full afternoon and evening of rest, warmth, and good food, a rare and infrequent happening.

Cameron Bay—deep, dark, and narrow—was always cold in winter and seemed to have an attraction for fog. The temperature on January 7 was normal for the season—about -60°F—but because of the reduced daylight and the fog that hung in layers in that gloomy canyon, the visibility was terrible. Our engine, unhappy with the low temperatures, refused to develop full power, backfiring repeatedly to show its displeasure.

Our first stop was the BEAR camp (Bear Exploration & Radium) to deliver a mailbag before we proceeded to Camsell River, 25-odd miles to the south, to refuel. The trip down was routine, except for the extreme cold and lack of cabin heat. We circled over the AX camp once to check for possible obstructions—water holes, snowbanks, ice chisels standing on end—and noticed the complete lack of ski tracks. Obviously we were the first aircraft to pay them a visit despite the company's edict that the AX fuel was to be used in order to conserve the Cameron Bay supply. Our landing was normal until we slowed down, and then we quickly stopped. For a moment thoughts of overflow crossed our minds, but what we had encountered was snow with the texture of coarse sand—and about as slippery. I got out and tried pushing the tail from side to side while Matt applied full throttle, a strategy that would usually get us started, but not that day. In any case, tail-pushing in the slipstream at -50°F temperatures was a rather desperate measure and one that could be endured for only brief periods. My face soon froze and my efforts gained us only a few feet of movement.

I then tried the next procedure in our bag of tricks. With the shovel I cleared a path down to the ice in front of each ski for a distance of 50 yards. Matt applied power, I rocked the wings to get him started, we moved ahead that 50 yards and became stuck again. This was repeated with no better success. On the third try we were lucky and reached the gas cache. The AX boys gave us a hand with the refuelling and urged us to stay. We were now westbound, however, with hopes of reaching Fort Norman that night, and though we gratefully accepted the sandwiches that their cook sent down, we cranked up AAO again and took another run at that frustrating snow. We went only a few yards before we were stuck again. Though the situation looked more and more as if an overnight stop was imminent, I shovelled a final path and this time we were successful. Matt kept up just enough power to keep the aircraft moving as I ran in from the right side and climbed onto the ski. He held the cockpit door open against the slipstream, I handed in the shovel and followed it myself, and we were airborne.

It was with profound relief that we headed west toward the Mackenzie. Our airborne weather was cold, but the bright sunshine created the illusion of warmth. Beneath us lay the rough and drifted surface of Great Bear Lake, 12,000 square miles of snow and ice. Even from our altitude the far northern horizon wasn't visible. Rarely travelled in summer, this inland sea was desolate and deserted in winter.

A half-hour of flying brought us to the north end of McVicar Arm, 15 miles wide and extending 60 miles to the southwest. From here we held to a south-southwest course, crossing into the south end of Bear Lake's Keith Arm, which was covered by hard-drifted snow, its texture plainly visible in the low light. It was obviously no place for a forced landing. With his characteristic caution Matt kept within gliding distance of the well-timbered south shore. If our luck ran out and our engine became weary, we would at least have shelter and firewood.

As we approached the western shore, we saw indications of the tiny Native community of Fort Franklin at the outlet of the Bear River. First, a few small columns of smoke and ice crystal fog rising vertically in the still air, then the small cabins of the Native settlement itself. Then far off to the west the Mackenzie Range came into view, always an interesting sight even on a January day. The sky in that area had a yellow-green cast to it—a sign of warmer weather, Matt claimed. But we had been on the move since well before daylight, and Fort Norman couldn't come too soon. Our AX sandwiches were but a memory and we were hungry as well as cold, the sun having disappeared behind the frost-haze to the southwest. Then at last Bear Rock came into sight, just downstream from Fort Norman.

Our summer landings were on the river in front of the post, but in winter this location was exposed to the constant sweep of the winds, leaving the ice drifted and rough. Fortunately, there was a small lake a mile or so to the north connected to the settlement by a bush trail, and it provided

Bear Rock, just downstream from Fort Norman, was one of the prominent landmarks bush flyers watched for.

us with a sheltered landing area, a bit smaller than we might have liked but adequate under most circumstances. Lacking radio communications, our agent there, George Douglas, would not have been aware of our approach, so Matt circled the village at low level to allow George to identify us, then we landed on the frozen lake. We were pleased to see the ski tracks of earlier visitors and to discover that we had left Bear Lake's granular snow behind us.

We turned and taxied back to the small tent where our oil was heated overnight. I hopped out and placed the short poles in front of the skis, and Matt taxied forward onto them and shut down the engine. By the time I had the oil drained and the engine cover in place, George had arrived, pulling a small sleigh on which to transfer our sleeping bags and overnight gear back to the village. We exchanged the usual round of New Year's greetings and health enquiries, then refuelled the aircraft and called it a day. George Douglas was one of those who had entered the north as an RCMP constable, taken his discharge at the end of his service period, but couldn't bear to leave the north. Although well past middle age, he still had a ruddy complexion, a twinkle in his eye and spring to his step, a northerner highly regarded by all who knew him.

As at Simpson and Aklavik, the RCCS staff at Norman would be our hosts.

We always looked forward to overnighting at these locations, to the comfortable beds, the fine food and the good company. During our brisk walk from the landing field, we discussed our plans for the following day, or I should say that Matt told us what he would like to accomplish. We had scheduled mail stops at Fort Good Hope, Arctic Red River and Fort McPherson, but with luck and an early start he figured that we might make all these stops and still enjoy the good food and good cheer of the RCCS station at Aklavik the next night. This would not be the easiest of tasks. Not that the distance of slightly over 400 miles or the six-plus hours of flying time presented any great problems, but daylight would be a factor. Norman is only slightly south of the Arctic Circle, the hours of daylight in January are limited, and the quality of light usually doubtful. Our necessary early start, therefore, must be preceded by an early bedtime curfew.

While this plan of action sounds elementary, there were problems associated with the early-to-bed part of it. For the people living at the small trading posts scattered throughout the north the isolation was felt most keenly during the long months of winter when the sun disappeared for weeks on end and outside activities were restricted to the barest of essentials. With little in the way of local news to share among themselves, they hungered for word of some fresh happening to break the monotony. Our infrequent visits were, therefore, special events. A pair of fresh faces (though not always well-shaven!) with a bit of news and gossip from up or down the river, from out on the Coast (as the Arctic was known), or from Outside. Two people who had read an Edmonton *Journal* that was less than six months old.

This was a need we thoroughly understood and we did our best to satisfy our hosts, but we had a major problem resulting from our daily activities. Our days were long, starting before daylight and finishing after dark, and cabin temperatures in January were only slightly above the freezing point. Working for long hours in this unremitting cold drained us of energy, and once we were settled for the evening, comfortable, well-fed, and warm, we had an overpowering desire for sleep. We tried our best to overcome this by sitting in hard chairs, by motion, by extending the conversations, but staying awake was a struggle. Our hosts understood this, particularly the two more senior members of the staff, "Snoot" Ross and Frankie Rapp, who had a few years of northern service behind them and knew of our struggle. Midway through the evening, aware of the odd head-nod, we could count on them to exclaim, "We've got to stop this and let you guys get some sleep."

We would protest, "No, no, we're okay," and move around a bit or go out to the kitchen to replenish our coffee, trying to convince them that we were the proverbial bright-eyed and bushy-tailed pair. This would be only a temporary measure, however, since we could not both be talking and the silent one would nod off in spite of his best efforts. Finally, regretfully, our evening would draw to a close. Minutes later we would be sound asleep. And minutes later, by our own estimates, we would be gently shaken awake again to face another day. An indescribable surge of pleasure and relief would fill us on the rare occasion when the message would be, "It's blowing a blizzard. You're here for the day." January 8 was not to be one of those occasions, however.

The temperature was a not unpleasant -53°F when I started along the bush trail to the lake, carrying my overnight packsack on my shoulders with my sleeping bag balanced on top of that. George, our most excellent agent, had preceded me, and the stove in the tent was doing its best to restore some viscosity to our two pails of SAE 50-grade oil. After a few brief words with George, I loaded my gear into the cabin, fired up the blow pots, and retired under the engine cover to endure the morning misery of heating the engine.

Matt arrived, and there was activity within the cabin as he loaded his gear and talked to George about mail or a possible fur shipment. It was after 9:00 when I extinguished the blow pots, refilled them and placed them beside the cabin door to cool. With the oil tanks filled, the pails cleaned and stowed along with the now well-cooled blow pots, our departure preparations were complete. Matt and George had defrosted the wings with a length of rope, sawing it back and forth and gradually sliding it toward the wing tip. There were only faint indications of daylight, but Matt said, "I think we've got enough visibility." With that I removed and stowed the engine cover, urged the Eclipse starter up to the desired pitch, and climbed aboard. It was barely 9:30 when we taxied down to the south end of the little lake, turned the aircraft, and waited for the blowing snow to subside. Finally, with the frost-covered trees at the far end of the lake just visible, Matt applied full power, and our day began.

The river—Mackenzie's route to the Arctic—faded into the dim light and mist off to the north. There was a horizon out there somewhere, but it was beyond our vision. The bulk of Bear Rock, just off to our right, was actually the southern extremity of the Norman Range, an unspectacular group of mountains paralleling the river for the next 100 miles or so, with an average elevation of 2,600 to 2,800 feet. Near at hand to the west lay the Carcajou Range of some 6,000 feet. Beyond lay the main range of the Mackenzie Mountains, where some mighty peaks reared up to the 8,000-foot level. Along the river itself there was little of interest until we reached Norman Wells, the site of the first oil discovery in the NWT. A small refinery occupied the site, operated during the summer months to provide fuel for the local riverboats and the Inuit schooners at Aklavik. A small supply of this fuel had also been purchased for use in our blow pots. It was our favourite blow pot fuel for, evil-smelling though it was, it would burn fiercely at the touch of a match, even at -60°F. The more highly refined product that was imported from Alberta would do the job but was not as volatile and harder to light.

As we passed over the refinery, the lone caretaker made a brief appearance. We had probably interrupted his breakfast, but our presence was not of sufficient interest to keep him out in the -60°F air for long, and he soon disappeared to return to whatever small activity he had devised to occupy his short days and long evenings.

After a further 60 miles the river makes a 90-degree bend to the north, but here a small mountain, a piece left over from some long ago geological construction job, had been deposited in the centre of the valley, and the river was forced to turn west to circumvent this obstacle before turning north again. Rock reefs were left in the riverbed, however, and this restriction, the Sans Sault Rapids, was a source of considerable annoyance to Captain Don Naylor of the HBC sternwheeler *Distributor*, especially during the low water of September, his last trip of the season. Two rivers flow in from the west at this point (although "flow" was merely a figure of speech on that January day). One is the Carcajou with its headwaters in the mountain range of the same name. The other and larger of the two streams is the Mountain, coming from far back in the Mackenzie Range.

We had been in motion for about an hour and a half when the Ramparts came in sight. These vertical rock cliffs constrict the river at this point from a width of two and a half miles to barely one-quarter mile. At the entrance to this narrow throat, the Ramparts Rapids lie across the river's full width;

The Ramparts Rapids

With its combination of rapids and fast water in summer and ice fog in winter, the Ramparts have always been a hazard to all forms of navigation. One of the early river travellers, Elihu Stewart, observed in 1906, "The steamer turned sharply to starboard and before us lay a narrow strip of shining water, appearing only a few hundred feet in width. Down this we glided at great speed between cliffs of limestone, on either side, of great height. These walls of perpendicular rock resemble huge fortifications, like another Gibraltar. For about 4 miles we hurried through this great gorge at almost railway speed."

here the river never completely freezes in winter, resulting in the generation of clouds of ice fog that shroud its surface. The river tumbles over the rapids and is funnelled at full speed into the narrowed passage between the cliffs, only gradually returning to normal over the next five miles of its course.

From the beginning of the Ramparts cliffs to the village of Good Hope is a distance of about eight miles. The settlement, a gathering point in those days for the Hare Indians who trapped to the north along the drainage of a river of the same name, is located on the top of a high, steep bank on the northeast side of the river. From the air the cluster of small buildings made their presence known to us by the vertical columns of ice-fog that rose from the chimneys. The buildings were typical of those small, northern posts: a Hudson's Bay store and warehouse, an RCMP station, a small group of Native log cabins, a church and the priest's dwelling. At larger settlements there would be two religious establishments, Anglican and Catholic, but at Good Hope there was just a Catholic church, one noted for its beautiful, hand-crafted interior decorations, the work of one of the earlier priests. The name of the village had, in fact, originated in the name he gave to his church.

We now searched for our landing strip, the tent and its associated group of gasoline barrels, finally locating them downstream from the post and out in the middle of the river. This was not an unusual state of affairs as our river landing sites were at the whim of the rivers during the freeze-up period. The ski tracks of previous landings were now faintly visible in the dim light, and we could see that the strip was a narrow slot through the surrounding rough ice with the tent barely visible at the south end.

We touched down, taxied to the end of the strip, and turned the aircraft to face north again, ready for takeoff. Because our stop would be brief, poles were not required under the skis, and as there was no wind I used only a small, lightweight engine cover. En route to the nose of the aircraft I noticed that the thermometer on the wing strut registered -63°F, a reading that might be experienced at any point in the north in early January, but without wind such a temperature was considered quite bearable. Matt had emerged from the cockpit, taking advantage of the brief stop to stretch his legs and restore his circulation. Engine cover in hand, I was up on the nose of the aircraft by this time, a vantage point that enabled me to check on the progress of our local citizens. Two of them were making fast time and were already halfway across the river. Another two were proceeding slowly and were some distance behind.

With the arrival of the first pair we learned that we were faced with an unexpected and unwelcome delay. We were to have a passenger on the trip to Aklavik in the form of Mrs. McGillicuddy, wife of the RCMP sergeant at the post. The two of them were making slow headway through the rough snow, and it was nearly half an hour before they arrived, breathless and apologetic. Because of the Spartan interior accommodation of our 71 and the less than adequate cabin heat output, I opened the snap-fasteners of my sleeping robe (this was the pre-zipper era) and spread the robe on the primitive rear seat—a section of canvas slung between two steel tubes. Then, with Mrs. Mac aboard and bundled up, we said farewell to Mac and the others, I uncovered and cranked the engine, and we were on our way again.

I chatted with Mrs. Mac for a few minutes, then crawled forward over the mail sacks to have a word with Matt. Our great plans of spending the night in the warmth and comfort of Aklavik now looked rather remote. "Guess we'll be spending the night at McPherson," was my cheerful opening statement. After a few minutes of silence Matt replied, "By the time we get away from Arctic Red, we'll just have time to make Aklavik if we bypass McPherson. We can deliver their mail when we make our southbound stop the day after tomorrow." (It was the custom to lay over one day at Aklavik to give the townspeople an opportunity to answer their mail.)

"Sounds like a great idea to me," I responded. "I was sure looking forward

A summer view of Fort McPherson with the Peel River disappearing north toward the Mackenzie delta. The winter landing place was a small lake off the photo to the right.

to that layover at Aklavik." We both lapsed into silence, watching the river surface and the frozen landscape that passed below us. It was nearly noon and the brightest part of the day, but the light was still poor and from then on would only get worse.

Matt had been wrestling with one of our few, poor-quality maps, and now he looked down through the front side windows, first to one side, then the other. Finally he pointed down and exclaimed, "There it is. D'you see it?" Not knowing what "it" was, I stared down at the frozen river surface, expecting a dog team or a cabin, but saw nothing. After a half-minute or so I had to admit defeat. "I can't see anything! What am I supposed to be looking for?"

Matt grinned. "The Arctic Circle! We just passed over it."

I pounded him on the shoulder as punishment for his trickery, then turned to smile back at Mrs. Mac. She was looking somewhat alarmed at what she perceived to be an outbreak of mutiny. She then beckoned me to come aft and opened a sizeable bag, from which she produced a half-dozen beautiful scones, still slightly warm. What a treat! With breakfast more than six hours behind us, they could not have been more welcome.

We passed over Little Chicago, the remains of a settlement established by a group of gold seekers who had hoped to reach the Klondike by descending the Mackenzie, crossing the mountains at La Pierre House, making their way down the Bell and the Porcupine, then up the Yukon to Dawson. Some of them had reached this point on the Mackenzie and spent the winter there before turning back. Some 40 miles farther on we passed the mouth of a river flowing in from the north, locally known as Thunder River, and looked down on an occupied dwelling, one of the few we'd seen along the river. What made it more unusual was the runway marked out with spruce trees on the smooth ice adjacent to the river mouth. "That's odd," commented Matt, "perhaps he is expecting an aircraft to land there." We droned on into the fading light of the afternoon, periodically beating our hands together and pounding on our bodies in an attempt to improve the circulation. I crawled back for a visit with Mrs. Mac, snugly wrapped in my sleeping robe and feeling quite comfortable—or so she claimed.

The river had now altered direction from southwest to northwest, and we watched for the tiny settlement of Arctic Red River, spotting it at last huddled on a barren point of land where the smaller river entered the Mackenzie from the southwest. Matt reduced altitude as we approached, and we checked over the landing area laid out on a smooth stretch of ice close to the settlement. We continued to the west, then turned in the direction of the settlement. The tiny group of residents was already down on the ice as we drew up and shut down the motor. The temperature was a bit warmer here, -55°F with no wind, so the engine cover was unnecessary. We soon learned that we were to have an additional passenger for Aklavik—another lady. Lady passengers were extremely rare, especially in winter, and to have two of them on a single flight was even rarer. Our new passenger was Mrs. Paris, wife of the Northern Traders post manager, neither of whom we had met before. With our exchange of mail sacks completed and our new passenger on board, we were soon on our way again.

Had we made a stop at McPherson as originally scheduled, we would have flown due west for 30 miles, but now, with Aklavik in our sights, we continued down the Mackenzie. McPherson is located on the Peel River, a fair-sized stream in its own right. Upon reaching the Mackenzie delta area with its myriad channels and islands, the Peel divides its output between two main channels before merging with the Mackenzie. The most direct of these is Peel Channel, and it is on the north side of this branch of the river that Aklavik is located. We continued down the main channel of the Mackenzie for about 30 miles before spotting the small Native village, just off to the west where the Peel Channel passes close to the Mackenzie. Normally we would have cut over and picked up the Peel route here, but the light was becoming dim so Matt stayed on the Mackenzie for a further 40 miles before he turned due west to Aklavik. As the Peel surface was exposed and usually rough, our winter landings were on one of its tributary channels, the Pokiak.

It was after three in the afternoon, and the lighted windows of Aklavik were just visible through the haze of frost crystals that hung over the area. As wind was not a factor, and there was neither reason nor necessity to make a circuit, Matt made a straight-in approach and landing. With power on again, we taxied across the Peel and pulled up beside the high bank upon which Aklavik was located. Our RCCS friends must have been checking their watches, knowing how long our expedition would take, and a couple of them were there to greet us, along with a few townspeople, HBC men and RCMP, all of them anxious to help. The poles for the skis were in place before I was even out of the cabin.

I drained the oil, which was promptly whisked away to be stored for the night in the warmth of the RCCS power house. I installed the engine cover, then turned to the final job of the day—refuelling. Here again, the Signals boys—and particularly "Red" Scarfe, whom I had known for some time—stayed to help. My helpers rolled a couple of the 45-gallon barrels over and manned the hand pump, while I climbed up onto the wing to carry out the refuelling. Finally, this quite average and uneventful day was coming to an end. I picked up my kit bag, Red carried my sleeping bag, and we toiled up the steep bank to the Signals station, our warm and comfortable quarters for the next couple of nights.

We had left McMurray on Thursday, January 2, and it had taken us seven days to reach Aklavik—not an unusual length of time for many of our winter expeditions. The Bear Lake diversion had been time-consuming, of course, but I now had a planned, non-flying day ahead of me. This included that greatest of luxuries—a morning sleep-in. As a further benefit, I could arise at any hour that I might choose and have a leisurely breakfast. All of these pleasant thoughts were occupying my mind as I washed up before dinner—also taking the time to eliminate a sizeable growth of whiskers from my face. Matt had been invited over to the HBC post manager's home for the evening, and to forestall the usual "head-nod problem" after a long day in the cold, he had decided to take a short nap. I promised to call him just before dinner.

After dinner there was enough activity to keep me well occupied for the early part of the evening, and the knowledge that I could sleep in the next morning made it easier for me to stay awake. Finally, with the most current gossip having been reviewed a couple of times, we had a round of coffee and I hit the sack. In spite of my intentions to sleep in, I asked Red to give me a call at 9:00 so I could carry out a bit of inspection and maintenance work on our companion, AAO.

With breakfast behind me and the first of the dim morning light creeping across the delta, my first job was to replenish our oil supply. At places like Aklavik and Norman we would bring our oil levels up to about 4.5 gallons in each pail; starting the day with a total of nine gallons on board would be sufficient to see us through the smaller, intermediate stations without having to add oil.

I then carried out a quick, external inspection of AAO. The left-hand shock strut was a bit low, and with the assistance of a small barrel, some wooden blocks, and my trusty Walker Blue-Boy jack, I raised the left side of the fuselage sufficiently to take the weight off the strut. I then fired up one of my blow pots and heated my shock strut pump by passing the barrel of it back and forth through the flames. With this encouragement the pump operated quite well, the air compression adding to the heat, and I was able to increase the air pressure in the strut. Not having a pressure gauge on the pump, this was strictly a guessing matter but one that was aided by the experience of similar activities in the past.

Our ski pedestals still had an accumulation of ice from the Hottah Lake overflow, but thankfully its removal was a job that could be accomplished without removing mittens. It was also one that would provide enough physical activity to keep me warm, but I deferred it until after lunch, as by that time Red had finished his shift at the station, and the two of us made short work of the cleanup, using a metal bar from the diesel shop and my jack handle. Daylight was fading by then, and the lights were coming on in the buildings that lined the riverbank. The RCCS diesel plant, which provided electrical power for the transmitters and receivers at the radio station, also provided electric lighting for their staff quarters, the only building in Aklavik to be so favoured. All of the other buildings used gasoline-burning Coleman lamps and lanterns. Farther down the scale were kerosene lamps and candles. Red took me for a quick inspection of the radio station. The high-powered, long-wave transmitters were massive things with bulky condensers and resistors; even the glass tubes where the necessary RF frequency was generated were huge.

As darkness fell, we returned to staff quarters for a quick coffee before the dinner hour. We met briefly with Matt, who was most apologetic for having accepted an invitation to dinner with Superintendent Curley of the RCMP and his wife. RCCS quarters were quiet that evening, but I had the opportunity for a long talk with the station OC, Frank Riddell. Although he hailed from eastern Canada, he was one of those with a natural aptitude for life in the north—a fact that he had proven during his several years of residence at Aklavik. Small, wiry, and tough, he was the owner/driver of an excellent dog team, and he had developed a reputation as one of the most experienced and accomplished travellers in the whole of the delta area and on the adjoining Arctic Coast. Because of my own experience raising and driving dogs, trapping, and bush travel farther south in the Athabasca area, Frank and I had much in common, and I was particularly interested in his stories of travel along the Coast and his descriptions of the experiences of various adventurers in that area, both Inuit and white. Finally, with the thought of an early rising in just a few short hours and of another long, cold day, we said our goodnights and I turned in.

I was already enjoying my breakfast the next morning when Matt joined me. "It's 52 below again this morning and it must be a bit overcast," I told him. "I went out for a quick weather check and I couldn't see the stars."

"We're going to have a bit of extra work this morning," was Matt's reply. "We have to do a test flight."

I stared at him in disbelief. "You must have been into the oh-be-joyful over at the Curleys last night!"

Matt laughed, then grew serious. "I'm afraid I've gotten us into a jam. During the course of the evening, Mrs. Curley remarked that she'd never been up in an aircraft and she was just dying to have her first ride. Without thinking for a moment that she would ever take me up on the offer, I said, 'Why don't you get up early in the morning, and I'll take you for a short ride before we head south?' Well, she jumped at the idea. She said, 'I don't mind the cold and I've got a good warm parka. Tell me what time you want to leave and I'll be there.' There was no way I could back down then," said Matt apologetically. "I'll take her up for a short flip just as soon as there's enough light. Right after breakfast I'll go over and let Mrs. Mac know that she'll need to be down on the ice as soon as she hears the aircraft taxiing back. It should only take a moment to get her on board, and hopefully we'll get away without too much time lost."

"Should work out okay," I replied.

"There's one other thing," said Matt. "Remember that landing strip we saw at Thunder River? Well, the Northern Traders have an outpost there—Bill Clark is their man—and they want us to stop and pick up a bale of fur from him."

As I made my way to the aircraft and commenced the heating job, I did some mental calculations. With our slightly delayed departure from Aklavik and one extra stop to make, it looked like a late arrival at Good Hope. But there was another factor that would work against us: eastbound our usable daylight hours would be reduced.

All the morning activities went as planned, and our delighted passenger had her ride, though in the half-light of early morning it is doubtful that she saw much of interest. The mail was on hand and ready to be loaded before the aircraft returned, and Mrs. Mac appeared on the scene shortly afterwards. As there was no need for engine covers or poles, we quickly loaded the mail sacks and assisted Mrs. Mac into the comfort of my sleeping bag. Moments later we were southbound up the Peel Channel at 500 feet on our way to McPherson. There was no need to fly higher, and Matt had no desire to waste precious time by unnecessary climbing. Off to the west the Richardson Range rose to 5,000 feet or so; had it been just a little later in the day, the peaks would have been pink-tinted by the noon sun, soon to make its first appearance.

By means of a homemade, unofficial transmitter, the Signals boys made short-range broadcasts to the area, and both McPherson and Arctic Red River had been alerted to our approximate arrival times and asked to have the mail ready. A small crowd of McPherson people, having no wish to miss

the excitement of an aircraft arrival, were at the small lake that served as our winter landing place to watch the landing and takeoff. As we taxied out, a number of little boys delighted in throwing themselves into the slip-stream to be bowled over by the blast.

The Arctic Red River people were equally prepared and cooperative. The actual mail delivery/pickup could have been accomplished without shutting down the motor, but these small far-northern settlements were so isolated and visitors were so infrequent that we did stop for a brief chat. We also advised them of our planned stop at Thunder River, 75-odd miles upstream, and asked if there was any danger of overflow where the little river (the Travaillant on today's maps) flowed into the Mackenzie. Not that we really expected any up-to-date advice on this

Short days and failing daylight resulted in one of our common winter experiences–a night spent in the bush. This photo shows CF-AAO, with its engine cover still on, while we were reloading the aircraft the following morning.

subject, but it did provide them with an opportunity to discuss local affairs, and one never knew when a casual question might produce some valuable information.

It was noon by the time we were on our way to Thunder River. The sun was somewhere ahead, just peaking over the horizon—not visible itself but briefly adding colour to the cloud bank to the south. We flew southeast for the first 25 miles or so then turned northeast as the river bent in that direction. We could see cabins at the mouths of a couple of the small rivers flowing into the Mackenzie, a slightly encouraging sight in winter when the possibility of a forced landing was never too far from our thoughts. Another half-hour of flying brought us within sight of the landing strip, marked with its spruce trees. Matt circled the tiny cluster of buildings, one

An Arctic Salmon War

The tiny settlement of Arctic Red River is located at the mouth of the river of the same name, flowing in from the southwest. The area is home to the Loucheux Native bands, who are also related to the fine people who make their homes at Fort McPherson. From ancient times the river has supported a major salmon migration in the late summer, a fact well known to both the Inuit who long ago made their homes in the Kittigazuit area of the Arctic Coast and the Loucheux of Crow Flats. Possession of this valuable resource was always in dispute, and apparently "might makes right" generally decided who would have salmon on the table next winter. According to ancient tales passed down by village elders, one particular year a large Inuit band secured all of the fish. The following summer the Crow Flats Loucheux assembled all of their warriors and with revenge in their hearts made their way downstream to where a small band of Inuit, not realizing their imminent danger, were already camped at the river mouth. The Loucheux made their attack in the late evening and the unwary Inuits were slaughtered, the entire band wiped out. To destroy the evidence—or perhaps just to clean up their camp site—the Loucheux then threw all of the bodies into the small lake just behind the village.

larger one that was doubtless both the home and the business establishment of the trader, a couple of smaller cabins, both occupied judging from their chimney smoke, and a line of dog shelters. Usually a hole in a snowbank was all that most dogs received in the way of shelter, so the sight of these doghouses gave us a warm feeling toward this man we had never met. He obviously took good care of his four-footed servants.

The landing strip was smooth and quite close to the buildings with no visual indication of overflow. The trader made his appearance promptly, and as we turned upstream for our landing we could see him on his way down to the strip, pulling a hand sleigh that obviously carried the fur bale. We were carrying a parcel for him from the Northern Traders post manager at Aklavik, which no doubt contained mail, a rare treat for a river dweller who might not see a letter from freeze-up to breakup. Matt shut down the motor and we both deplaned to simplify the fur loading, but Matt also had a couple of verbal messages for him from friends at Aklavik. This landing, brief though it was, provided a welcome break for the dweller of this isolated place—a meeting with a couple of strangers and a bit of fresh conversation. Our time was precious, though—Good Hope was still an hour and a half away. We would reach there with the last of our daylight, and the narrow landing strip would be difficult to find in the fog and half-light. We shook hands, Matt climbed aboard, I applied the crank, and we were soon on our way. During the fur-loading process we'd had a brief chat with Mrs. Mac, who claimed that she was still warm and comfortable. She added a warning, however: "You fellows had better hurry. Mac's no cook so I'll have to make our supper after we get home."

The Thunder River landing had greatly improved my personal comfort within the aircraft because instead of a pile of cold, uncomfortable mail sacks under me, I now had a comfortable bale of fur that retained a goodly measure of residual warmth. As we droned on up the river and into the gathering gloom of late afternoon, I gave some thought to a potential problem. This was one that Matt and I had not discussed because of lack of opportunity, but one that I knew he would be well aware of. Though it was the universal custom in the north for every traveller, no matter the season or the method of travel, to carry his own sleeping bag, our lady passenger was not equipped with one. If we were now faced with a forced landing—always a possibility—sleeping accommodations would become a very real problem. One approach would be to provide Mrs. Mac with one robe and then for Matt and I to take turns with the other, sleeping in three- or four-hour shifts. Another approach would be to open out both robes, then the three of us wedge ourselves in with Mrs. Mac in the middle. Modesty would not be a real problem as we always slept fully clothed except for our outer parkas, which were made of denim and were little more than windbreakers. To let Matt know that I was still part of the crew, I moved closer and commented, "I hope you're not planning on an overnight along the river. If so, we'll have a few sleeping problems." He half-turned his head, grinned, and nodded. "I'll match you to see who gets the sleeping bag!" he said. There was another moment of silence, then he turned his head again. "When we planned our gas load, I wasn't thinking of our test flight this morning, and I didn't know about our Thunder River stop. We won't have too much gas left by the time we reach Good Hope."

With that he resumed his concentration on the route ahead while I returned my thoughts to the best procedures to follow if our luck ran out. Our 8x8-foot umbrella tent barely provided shelter for two; it would definitely be crowded with three people. Though the temperature would certainly be in the -50°F range, our only heat would be from our Coleman gasoline-burning stove, and this could only be used briefly because of the fumes. Of course, there was always the possibility of making a lean-to shelter, with a wood fire to provide some measure of warmth, but while on the upper rivers there were good stands of timber adjacent to the riverbanks, the timber of the lower Mackenzie was scattered and of poor quality. Besides, we didn't carry a saw, only an axe, making the task of producing a fire from green, frozen wood, a fire large enough to keep three people warm, not an encouraging prospect.

All of these conjectures were optimistic. They were situations that we could endure for a day or for a single overnight if weather forced us down. If one were pessimistically practical, however, there were other very real possibilities to consider. Our forced landing might result from the failure of an engine or a component—cylinder failures were not uncommon. Or we might damage the skis or undercarriage while landing on rough ice. In either case we might have to wait for days before our non-appearance was noticed and a search started. Immersed as I was in all of these less than cheerful, though very practical, thoughts, I had been paying only casual attention to the world around us. I recalled that we had passed Little Chicago some time earlier, and I judged that we were still a good half-hour away from Good Hope. The light was failing badly and Matt had reduced altitude somewhat, trying to establish some measure of contact with the river and sort the smooth ice from the rough. But it was hopeless.

Slowly the river, a shadowless expanse of white, unwound below us. We strained our eyes ahead, watching for that high bank on the left side crowned with a few faint lights. Each turn brought to view another dim and empty expanse of river. Then finally success. I believe that Matt had remembered that particular river bend and had been watching ahead in anticipation, and as we passed on the left side of a large island, he exclaimed, "There it is!" Knowing the approximate location of the landing strip in relation to the village lights, he reduced altitude as we approached, intent on a straight-ahead landing, but suddenly the far riverbank and the lights disappeared.

CF-AAO after it collided with the fog-shrouded gas barrels and warm-up tent at Fort Good Hope. This photo was taken a day later, January 11, 1936, after the left side had been jacked up.

"Fog!" Matt called out, and we climbed back into the clear again. A low bank of fog was hanging over the whole river surface, covering the area where the landing strip was located. I saw Matt shake his head, probably with a mixture of exasperation about the fog and concern about our less than ample fuel supply. We circled to the right over the top of Manitou Island and downstream again for another attempt.

This time Matt started from well back and lined up with the village lights again, holding just enough power to stay airborne. We were still lined up with the lights as we drew closer, Matt reduced power, and we dropped into the fog bank. There were long, long moments with no visibility, then the comforting rattle of the skis on the hard snow. I could feel the tail drop as our speed decreased. Then pandemonium! There was a crash, people yelled, the aircraft violently swapped ends. And then there was silence.

Dislodged from my perch on the fur bale I found myself on the floor at Mrs. Mac's feet. We realized what had happened, of course: we had run over the tent and had collided with the gas barrels. But hearing all the shouting, we were certain that we had either injured or killed someone who had been in the tent. Fortunately, the welcoming committee—Sergeant Mac, the constable and the two HBC people—had been outside of the tent watching for us. The aircraft had been almost upon them before they realized it, and they had jumped aside at the last moment. We were also fortunate that none of the barrels had elected to come in through the side of the cabin. As it was, the three of us inside were without a scratch, though Mrs. Mac was a bit dazed and bewildered, scarcely comprehending what had happened until we pried her out of the cabin. When peace and order were restored again, the Macs started on the rough path across the river, while the others stayed to offer what help they could.

Our fine old Fairchild AAO was a sorry sight. The fuselage was lying low in the snow, the left ski inverted with the nose of the ski located in the spot in the cabin formerly occupied by myself and the fur bale. Both blades of the propeller were bent but it was too dark to determine the total extent of the damage. From force of habit I drained the oil and installed the engine cover. Then suddenly realizing that we were shivering—a combination of cold and reaction—we collected our gear and started for the village. And so ended Friday, January 10, 1936.

We had a large and late dinner, Mrs. Mac producing some treasures that had escaped the Christmas feast and Mac coming up with a bottle of distilled heather. Matt joined him in a couple of rounds of good cheer. I hadn't yet learned to appreciate the products of the Highlands so I kept Mrs. Mac company with the tea pot. On our last visit to the outdoors that night the thermometer registered -63°F. We slept on the floor but we had the luxury of mattresses, and bed never felt better!

As we turned in, Matt remarked, "Well, I'm glad you didn't have to try out all of those overnight camping plans you were hatching on our way up the river!"

"Yeah, me too!" I replied and then I was asleep.

We were up before daylight the next morning—not difficult at Good Hope in early January. A check of the thermometer through a frost-encrusted window told us what to expect for the day; it was -65°F. After we'd been there a few days we learned that the temperature only ranged a mere six degrees: -65°F at night and -59°F during the day. As soon as breakfast was over, Matt and I, accompanied by Don, the constable, made our way down to the river to assess AAO's damages. Fog still cloaked the landing strip and the aircraft looked forlorn, lying there in the snow, battered, bent, and covered with frost. Both blades of the propeller were bent, though not severely, and I judged these to be repairable. The left ski was broken in two places, both in front and behind the pedestal, with the broken front end protruding through the side of the cabin. The main undercarriage was undamaged as the upper end of the ski pedestal had absorbed most of the damage and was twisted almost at right angles. The left main wing strut had been damaged by direct contact with a barrel. There was no way that we could effect any repairs to it and we judged it to be serviceable enough for the flight home, assuming we could repair the balance of the damage. Two of the stabilizer struts were also bent but not badly; these we could reinforce.

But there was more damage to come. When I jacked up the left side of the aircraft to remove the damaged ski, we discovered there was internal damage to the aft part of the fuselage. A 10-gallon keg of frozen oil had penetrated the fuselage belly just aft of the cabin door, ripping open the belly fabric, bending one horizontal cross tube between the two lower longerons and tearing another one out completely. This latter item would certainly need my closest attention as it was the tube that carried the control cable pulleys for the rudder and the elevators. Having concluded that our poor old bird was repairable, we returned to the village with our broken ski in tow.

Fortunately, the Catholic church had a sizeable workshop where the church brother carried out various repairs both to the church's equipment and to that belonging to others in the village. Mac had already been in touch with them and they made us welcome. We brought the ski inside to thaw out a bit while we enjoyed the excellent lunch that Mrs. Mac had prepared for us. "Maybe we can find some wooden sleigh runners around the village," Matt said, "and bolt them to the bottom of the ski."

"How about dog boards?" I suggested. "I can't imagine a Hudson's Bay store without a stock of dog boards."

"What's a dog board?" Matt asked.

"Dog sleighs—that is, carioles—are made of two oak boards, each about eight inches wide. They're manufactured in some factory in eastern Canada where the front ends are steam-bent to the proper curve, and they arrive here stacked together in pairs to conserve space. Three individual boards would cover the bottom of the ski and we could cut off the surplus bend."

Mac joined the conversation at this point. "You're in luck," he said. "I was down there the other day and saw at least two sets of dog boards on hand."

"Dog boards have made a lot of aviation history," I explained to Matt. "That's what those Imperial Oil fellows at Simpson used to make those two famous propellers for their Junkers back in 1921!"

"Well," he said, "if they were good enough for propeller construction, they should be good enough for our ski."

Lunch over, Matt departed for the HBC while I returned to AAO to consider repairs to her twisted ski pedestal. Fairchild ski pedestals were constructed of a complex of welded steel tubing. The shock-absorbing function was provided by a set of bronze bushings sliding vertically, guided by lengths of square steel tubing. This cage of tubing provided a sliding capacity of about eight inches, the impact being absorbed by numerous turns of rubber bungee cord. As the pedestal was tapered, the small upper end had suffered the worst of the damage; it was an unlikely candidate for field repairs. The lower part of the pedestal was largely undamaged, however, and I realized that if the bronze sliding members that carried the axle were relocated to their lowest position, they would again be enclosed by undamaged material. I then cut away the rubber bungee cord and with the aid of a sledge drove the bronze sections downwards. Once clear of the damaged upper section they moved easily and dropped to the bottom of the slot.

While I was finishing up this job, Matt returned to the workshop, well pleased with the success of his expedition. He brought with him three dog boards, and he and the good brother immediately started measuring and cutting these to the proper length to fit the ski. It seemed almost desecration to cut off the graceful, double-curved bow end of the boards. We did, in fact, briefly consider retaining the curved sections for a triumphant return to McMurray, but as these would present about four square feet of drag to the slipstream, we abandoned that idea. The actual amputation of the curved sections did cause some pain, however. After the cut-off line was established, the brother, his saw in hand, lovingly stroked the smooth oaken curves before he reluctantly bent to the task.

Mac arrived on the scene about this time to check on our progress and to advise that the dinner hour was nigh. We had been working in the shop by the light of a gas lantern provided by our good host and had been so engrossed in our activities that we hadn't realized the lateness of the day. But we took leave of our faithful helper to spend another warm and happy evening with our kindly hosts.

CF-AAO's repaired ski, showing the dog boards bolted to the bottom of the broken ski and the wooden blocking used to reposition the axle and reinforce the damaged tubing.

The next day being Sunday, January 12, we were surprised to find the good brother in the shop when we turned up there in the morning, but as we learned later from Mac, the priest had given the brother special dispensation to work for us on the Sabbath. He had been on the job from an early hour; the shop was warm, the light was aglow, the frost had departed from the tools and metal parts, and the dog boards were all ready to be attached to the ski. Matt had discovered a supply of carriage bolts at the HBC store, and the brother had a sturdy, old-fashioned hand drill and bits from his native Brittany. He insisted on drilling the holes for us.

I was free to return to my pedestal problem. Having relocated the bronze slides to the bottom of the slot, I had to devise a method of retaining them in that position. Firewood was plentiful so I cut lengths of wood to fit in the various triangular spaces between the tubes, trimmed these to length with the saw and to size and shape with an axe. With the aid of the brother's sturdy sledge I drove these wooden wedges into place to reinforce the damaged tubing and block the slides to the bottom of the slot. A few spikes were added for good measure to ensure that the blocks did not desert their posts during the trip home. Next the right-hand axle of the undercarriage on the undamaged side would also have to be repositioned to the bottom of the slot in order to level the aircraft laterally. This was a simple job, requiring only enough blocking to keep it in the bottom position, and I took the necessary measurements and prepared the blocks. By this time the brother had completed the drilling job, and he and Matt began installing and tightening the bolts. This was carried out in stages, the ski gradually returning to a more normal shape as the bolts were tightened.

On Monday morning in the usual -65°F weather we returned to the aircraft and installed our repaired left-hand ski. Because of the repositioned axle, it was necessary to shorten both the main ski harness (a cable and bungee assembly attaching the front of the ski to the fuselage) and the safety cable that served the same function at the back of the ski. These re-adjustments were carried out with the aid of a couple of cable clamps from my emergency kit. The right-hand ski was lowered to match the left one by cutting the bungee lashing, and the axle assumed its new location automatically. The wooden blocks that I had prepared were driven into place and secured, and our undercarriage was again serviceable.

I crawled under the aircraft and removed the four pulleys that guided the rudder and elevator cables in order to repair the broken tube upon which they had been mounted. Sliding out the cotter pins and the quarter-inch pivot bolts was just next door to a bare-handed operation. For the occasion I wore a pair of cotton gloves; though they didn't provide warmth, they did allow for the necessary finger agility and prevented the tools from freezing to my fingers. Matt and I decided to reinforce the bent stabilizer struts with a couple of clamps. We took measurements, collected my remaining supply of heavy-gauge brass sheeting (normally used for ski bottom repairs), and hurried back to the shop. Then, thoroughly chilled after the morning's work, we made double-quick time to Mrs. Mac's for a hot lunch.

That afternoon Matt worked on the clamp project while I did some head-scratching over the repair for the cross tube. As this carried our all-important control cables, it would have to be a fairly skookum piece of hardware. My first thought was to use a piece of two- or three-inch diameter wooden sapling, notching the ends to fit between the longerons. While this wooden member, with the addition of cable for the tension, would have taken care of the compression loads, there was still the problem of how to secure the pulleys. Just then fortune smiled upon me in the form of a piece of half-inch wrought-iron water pipe! This object was far from the haunts of "hot and cold running" as there was certainly no indoor plumbing in the village, and it was some time later that I realized the original purpose of this priceless piece of pipe. Most of the boats in the area were powered by small, water-cooled inboard engines and their water systems commonly used half-inch pipe. I drove my piece of pipe through the damaged cross-member, slotted both ends with a hacksaw, spread the slotted ends, and wrapped them around the longerons.

Tuesday was a day of good progress. We made an early start and were pleased to find that our replacement cross tube fitted nicely. Double strands of "Pro Pelle Cutem" (the HBC trademark) fox snare cable were wrapped between the longerons to take care of tension loads, the ends were secured, and a length of split firewood was inserted between the strands. One turn of this produced ample tension, the "twister" was secured, and the repair declared "airworthy." At this point we noticed a cracked longeron in the same area, so we returned to the village to have some lunch and prepare another piece of the water pipe as reinforcement.

Wednesday was another good day, though we suffered greatly from the cold as we were immobilized with these small jobs. I re-installed the control cables and pulleys and applied the reinforcement to the longeron while Matt applied the clamps to the bent tail plane struts. Our fuselage repairs complete, we faced a finger-numbing sewing exercise in two areas: the left ski had created a sizeable hole in the side of the fuselage and the oil barrel had done its best to demolish our belly fabric. Sewing thread would have been useless for such an operation as it would slit the brittle, frozen fabric as soon as tension was applied. But for such repairs I carried a roll of rib-stitching cord, a braided material about two diameters thicker than store string. To sew it, I used a massive baling needle designed for sewing up sacking. This cord would not cut the fabric, and the needle was thick enough to be used with gloved hands. We did have some relief from the weather by this time as Mac and Don had re-erected the tent and re-installed the small stove, which surprisingly was none the worse for its experience. As Matt was rather handy with a needle, we took turns at the job, warming our hands—and ourselves—between shifts.

Thursday we expected to clean up the last of the small repair jobs and sewing, including repairs to some tears on the under surface of the left wing that Don brought to our notice. Shortening and re-adjusting the right-hand ski cables was another of the small jobs that we had left to the last. As we now had a measure of warmth in the tent, Mrs. Mac had provided us with sandwiches for a noon snack together with a kettle and the ingredients for tea, and we were in the tent enjoying these when we heard the sound of an aircraft. During the days that we had been at Good Hope we had given little thought to being rescued. We were thoroughly engrossed in our repair jobs and fully expected to return home under our own power, without any outside help. Now there was a hasty exodus from the tent, everyone anxious to see who the visitors might be. As the aircraft approached and flew over just to the east of us, we could plainly see the blue and orange colour scheme of another of our Fairchild 71s, ATZ, usually flown that winter by Art Rankin. This was confirmed a few minutes later when the aircraft pulled up onto the poles that I had prepared for them. Art appeared from the pilot's door on the right side, while engineer Bill Jacquot emerged from the left-hand cabin door.

There were greetings and handshakes all around, and Art asked with a big grin, "What on earth are you fellows doing here—running a trapline?"

"We just couldn't tear ourselves away," Matt said. "The weather here is so warm and pleasant and the grub's so good... ."

"Oh, sure," responded Art, "a real summer resort! I can see why you'd be reluctant to leave!"

"Well," kidded Matt, "it's a good job that we weren't in any serious trouble and depending upon you guys to come looking for us! We've been here nearly a week now. Mac is going to start charging us board any day!"

Art grew serious. "When you guys hadn't shown up at Norman by Sunday night, Wop [W.R. "Wop" May, our district superintendent] decided someone should go looking. But we had a load on board for Goldfields and had to deliver it on the way. We ran into some weather and only got as far as Smith that day. Tuesday night we made it to Simpson and to Norman last night. We've been searching all along the river today, thinking that you might have had a motor failure."

The repaired tent on the river in front of Fort Good Hope. CF-AAO's approach was from the left (north) so it was the left-hand wing struts which collapsed the tent.

At that moment Bill, who had been eye-balling our aircraft, said, "Say, what's the matter with your prop? It looks a bit tired!" With that, the banter was put aside, and we explained what had happened and the status of our repairs. "Why don't you fellows finish up the work on the aircraft?" Bill said. "Art and I will take off the prop and see if we can find something solid enough to straighten the blades."

"There's plenty of solid log cabins in the village," I told them, "and those over-lapping logs at the corners should do the trick! You guys go ahead with that. I'll drain your oil and put the engine cover on."

They removed the prop from AAO and started the tedious jaunt across the semi-darkness of the river path, the walking conditions made more difficult by the weight of the propeller that was balanced between them. After servicing ATZ, I rejoined Matt to complete the last of our small repair jobs. It was well after dark by the time we finished, but except for our prop, we were finally ready for departure. Art and Bill turned up at the RCMP station at about the same time we returned and reported reasonable success with their mission. They had dislodged a few logs in a couple of buildings during the blade straightening process, but the prop now looked reasonably healthy.

We had a crowded household that night, but with two more visitors from the south with new tales to tell, it was one that was thoroughly enjoyed by all, particularly our RCMP hosts, who now had enough fresh stories and anecdotes to keep the village entertained for the balance of the winter. After dinner, Bill volunteered to help Mrs. Mac with the dishes while Matt and I made the short trip to the church residence to thank the father and brother for their valuable assistance.

As far as Bill Jacquot and I were concerned, Friday morning was the start of another routine day. We carried the prop down and installed it while Matt, Art, Mac and Don followed behind with all of the kit bags and sleeping bags. With the tent stove doing its best to heat the frozen oil, Bill and I fired up our blow pots and started the engine-warming operation. It was a trifle warmer at -53°F, and this probably reduced the warm-up period by 10 minutes or so, but it was 11:00 a.m. before we got underway. Fort Simpson was our planned overnighting spot, with an en route landing at Norman for fuel.

Because of the repaired state of AAO, it was decided that ATZ would fly behind to keep an eye on us. Fortunately, we had no problems with our aircraft, either during takeoff or landing at Fort Norman; nevertheless, as in Robbie Burns' immortal poem, our "best laid schemes" certainly did "gang aft a-gley" minutes after our landing. I had placed the light cover on AAO's engine and had the refuelling equipment ready when Art, after following in our ski tracks as he taxied up, decided to circle around and approach the fuel barrels from the opposite side. What he had not noticed was a half-buried clump of willows, and he taxied right over it. The willows poked their way through the belly fabric of ATZ, ripping it from end to end. Art, unaware of this disaster, could not understand why I placed the poles in front of his skis and motioned him to taxi onto them. I could see Bill kneeling behind Art and a discussion taking place, then two questioning faces appeared in the side window, one above the other. I repeated my signalling with emphasis, Art shook his head in doubt, then advanced the throttle and taxied up onto the poles.

He was most apologetic about this mishap, particularly as he knew that Bill and I would be spending the balance of the afternoon lying in the snow under the belly of the aircraft sewing up the long tears in the fabric. With the knowledge of what had to be done, we started up AAO again, taxied her onto the poles, then drained the oil from both engines. Matt and Art, having nothing further to do, took the sleeping bags and our overnight kits and departed for the signals station. The temperature was only -45°F—a 20-degree improvement over Good Hope—and Bill and I took turns at our repair task with periodic warm-ups in the stove-equipped tent. Thus we spent the balance of the afternoon of Friday, January 17, 1936. We spent the following night at Simpson and finally reached McMurray on January19 after 18 days away, all of us still serviceable though somewhat the worse for wear.

The difficulties that Matt Berry and I experienced at Cameron Bay with extremely low temperatures and frost were the subject of a discussion I had many years later with Gene Schweitzer of Pratt & Whitney, makers of our Wasp engines. Gene was field service manager for the Canadian division of that company for many years and remains one of Canada's foremost authorities on aviation engine technology. "There are a number of variable factors affecting engine operation," he told me, "especially at extreme, sub-zero temperatures. Taken singly they may create only minor difficulties but in combination with others the adverse effect may be sizeable." He named the following as possible factors: a lean mixture as the result of dense air; inadequate fuel vaporization because of low temperatures; deteriorating spark plug conditions; less than optimum ignition timing (either slightly advanced or slightly retarded); or propeller loading, which can affect the ability of the fuel/air mixture to ignite, especially at low temperatures.

The start of combustion is known as the kindling temperature. Achieving it and maintaining combustion requires a certain minimum spacing of the fuel/air molecules. Therefore, the fuel/air ratio becomes a critical factor. Experience has shown that for adequate combustion that ratio should be between .06 on the lean side and .12 on the rich side, with a ratio of about .08 producing the best power. The fuel must be in the form of vapour and uniformly mixed with the air. Cold air entering the cylinders through the carburetor will narrow the fuel/air ratio band that can support the kindling temperature of the charge. If the mixture is too lean—below .06—then the fuel/air molecules will be too far apart and unable to support combustion.

One of the first of our pilots to experience those typical cold weather problems was Punch Dickins, who made his first winter flights in the Mackenzie District in the late 1920s. He complained about frost and ice in the carburetor at temperatures below -30°F. Frost problems also occurred if we were a bit careless when bedding down our aircraft for the night. Frost on the bottom of our skis created a situation akin to taxiing on wheels with the brakes locked on. Frost on the wing and tail surfaces completely cancelled the lift needed to get the craft airborne, and frost on windshields—and it was always there on winter mornings—caused problems with visibility when it was most needed.

9 His engine's quit! He's down!

It was April 18, 1936, and the bright spring day had drawn to a close. Twilight was deepening, and long shadows were creeping out of the woods and across the still frozen surface of the river. On the western horizon the sky was still bright with the afterglow that accompanies the lengthening days in the northern latitudes, while off to the east the last light had faded in the upper reaches of the Clearwater and the cool darkness was creeping down into the valley of the Athabasca.

In McMurray, the little settlement on the level benchland at the junction of the rivers, the silence was broken from time to time by the night sounds of the frontier—the hoot of an owl up on the wooded hillside, the clamour of a team of huskies as their evening meal arrived, and the sound of an axe blade biting into a rough birch log. The roads and paths between the houses were unpaved and unlighted while the single main street contained the only concession to civilization—a sidewalk of rough planks. Woodsmoke drifted on the air as evening meals were prepared, and yellow lamplight spilled from the windows.

On the Snye, the backwater channel joining the two rivers at Fort McMurray, a lone aircraft sat, the last of the ski-shod winter fleet. Her companions had been removed to safer quarters on higher ground out of the reach of possible floods; in the morning, it would be her turn. She was a Fairchild 71, registration CF-AAO, the aircraft that had been the loyal companion to Matt Berry and me all winter. Damaged when we had run into some gas drums at Fort Good Hope, she had been repaired and gone back

Engineer Frank Kelly.

into service. Meanwhile, Matt and Con Farrell were now sharing the pilot's duties on CAL's brand new Fairchild 82, CF-AXE, on which I had drawn the engineer's seat. Rudy Huess had taken over as pilot of AAO with Bill Sunderland as engineer.

On this particular night some of those responsible for AAO's health and well-being were gathered in a small house at the town end of the Snye Road, the narrow passage through the surrounding timber that linked the settlement and the Snye. This being a Saturday night and the playoffs underway with Foster Hewitt announcing "Hockey Night in Canada!" Don

Anne Goodwin, the pretty and popular wife of Canadian Airways chief mechanic, seated on a sleigh at the CAL's McMurray headquarters.

(L-R) Bill Jacquot, Don Goodwin, Fred Lundy and Cecil Piette pose for their photo at the Snye in April 1936. Piette was assistant to Lundy, Canadian Airways agent at McMurray.

Goodwin, our chief mechanic, was huddled over the old Stewart-Warner battery-powered radio, alternately cheering for the Maple Leafs and cursing the static that threatened to drown out the program. On the floor lay air engineers Frank Kelly and myself, studying plans in a magazine for a boat we intended to build and drawing up a list of the materials we would need. In the adjoining kitchen Don's charming wife, Anne, was attending to the wants and needs of their twin sons, Don and Doug, with some faint hope of hearing the last of the hockey game. "Come on, you guys," she admonished them, "finish your snacks so I can wash your grubby faces and get you off to bed." Just then there was a heavy knock at the back door and Anne called, "Can you see who that is, Don? I'm busy with the boys."

"You'll have to go, Anne," replied Don. "The score's tied and it's the last period."

A few moments later Anne entered the room to say, "It's Lundy, Don. Something about a trip in the morning. You'll have to talk to him."

The visitor was our senior agent, Fred Lundy. But the Snye Road being a sea of spring mud, and a fair percentage of it now coating his boots, out of deference to Anne's kitchen floor he had refused to enter.

"Sorry to interrupt the game, Don, but we have to send AAO on a rush trip north in the morning to Fort Smith. Cec and I have just finished loading it." Cec was assistant agent Cecil Piette, later killed at Goldfields in an aircraft mishap.

"Jeez!" This was Don's favorite expression. "Who planned this? The river's going to break up in the next day or so, and we don't want the aircraft stuck down at Smith over breakup—or lose it entirely if he has a forced landing in between!" Then as an after-thought he grumbled, "I wish we had pulled it out today as we intended to."

"Well," replied Fred, "I had a message from Wop and he says it's a shipment for McKay Meikle, the government agent at Smith, and pretty important, I guess. Anyway, maybe we'll be lucky—it's freezing hard tonight and that should hold back the breakup for another day. I'll stop by Rudy's place on my way home and let him know." All messages in McMurray were verbal affairs in those days, delivered by foot and mouth, because telephones had yet to be introduced there.

"This is pretty risky business," said Don, "but maybe we can get away with it if we get him off by daylight. It's only about a five-hour round trip plus a half-hour for refuelling. Kelly, will you stop by on your way home and let Bill Sunderland know, and Rex, you can take care of the engine heating and the oil in the morning."

Fred departed, the Maple Leafs won their game, and the twins lost theirs—having used up the last of their excuses they were marched off to bed, protesting loudly. Anne served tea, and as the four of us gathered round the table, our main subject of conversation was the impending trip. Still concerned about the risks involved with this late flight, Don wondered aloud, "Where would he go if he had a forced landing? Rex, you've been up and down the river enough times, is there any place where he could safely land?"

"Not too many," I replied. "If he had an engine failure along the Slave or Athabasca rivers, there would be no way they could get the aircraft ashore. Even if they landed near a trapper's or woodcutter's cabin and were able to field enough manpower and dogs to move the aircraft, they couldn't get it up those steep banks. If he lost an engine along the Slave his best bet would be to try for a landing on one of the salt plains or hay meadows, though he might have to argue a bit with some of the local buffalo."

Don stirred his tea in silence, considering my less than encouraging remarks. "How would he make out once he got south of Lake Athabasca?"

"His chances would be slim," I said. "Landing on the river would be out of the question—we'd lose the aircraft for sure when the ice broke up. But there are two sizeable lakes northwest of McKay. [Fort McKay is about 35 miles north of McMurray.] Namur and Legend lakes, and there's a small Native settlement there. They could probably assemble enough people and dogs to get the aircraft to the shore but the banks, as I recall, are quite steep and heavily wooded."

"So what then?" said Don with a grin. "Wait for it to go through the ice?"

Chuckling at Don's humour, Frank Kelly said, "AO would survive. She was born under a lucky star. But they'd have an interesting problem on their hands." He looked questioningly at me. "Maybe there's a gravel bar or a shallow place they could move it to before the ice melted."

I shook my head. "But there's some good-sized timber around the lake, and maybe they could jack it up and build a raft under the skis. If they used plenty of logs, we could fly the floats in after breakup and salvage it."

Frank intervened at this point. "What about those two small lakes about fifteen or twenty miles north of here—have you been in to either of them?"

I nodded. "I was back there moose hunting a couple of years ago. They have flat shorelines and the surrounding timber is small. If he landed there with a dead engine but plenty of speed, he might drive the aircraft up into the trees without doing too much damage."

"There's lots of muskeg on both sides of the river," Frank pointed out. "That stuff doesn't look too bad. At least, it's flat."

"Yeah," I responded, "The muskeg would be his only hope, I guess, other than those two lakes. Muskeg timber is pretty small so he could get down without doing too much damage."

Don had been a member of the McAlpine party, marooned on the Arctic Coast during the 1929 freeze-up. By frugal use of their meagre rations and the assistance of a family of Inuit, they had survived until the ice had frozen and then made the hazardous and difficult crossing to the settlement of Cambridge Bay. Now, perhaps thinking of his desperate trek across the fragile and yielding ice of Dease Strait, he said, "They'd have a long hike back to the river, and they'd have to hole-up with some trapper or woodcutter until after breakup."

"Hell! That would mean we'd have to leave the aircraft there all summer," said Frank in protest to no one in particular. "Then we'd have to go in after freeze-up to repair any damage and to make a runway."

"And then wait another month for snow and cold weather before we could fly it out," said Don, "so let's hope it doesn't happen. I'll have a talk with Rudy in the morning anyway and pass along our comments and opinions, for whatever use they might be. If he keeps plenty of altitude, he might be able to glide into a good spot if his engine quits. Anyway, maybe we're worrying without cause. We've gone all winter without a 'mechanical' so why should it happen on the last day?"

Everyone was lost in thought for the next few minutes, then Frank Kelly exclaimed, "Say, we'll have some extra work to do in the morning."

"How's that, Frank?" asked Don.

"Remember when AAO came in today? We drained the oil but we didn't top up the pails or put the wing covers on. If we need to add oil, we'll have to open a 45-gallon barrel of cold oil, and for sure we'll have a lot of frost to clean off the wings. Rex, you and I had better get an early start in the morning." With that, Frank and I said our thanks and goodnights and left the house, he heading to his bachelor quarters, I to my boarding house.

During the 1930s, winter and summer, the surfaces of the lakes and rivers were the airports of the north. But northern aircraft and the ones who maintained them were keyed to the cycle of the seasons in the same manner as the migratory geese and swans, the hibernating creatures, large and small, and the whitefish starting their long upstream journey to their spawning grounds. For us the cycle meant that every year flying had to be suspended for roughly a month during spring breakup and another month at freeze-up.

During the spring break we removed the skis, installed the floats, and converted the aircraft and engine systems for summer use. Then for the next few months, paddles and float pumps would replace the blow pots and engine covers of winter. While we looked forward to summer, there were still situations that could get one into the glue, though these were generally less serious than winter's problems and the solutions easier. But early summer brought mud and mosquitoes. Then came the forest fire season, cloaking the

"At the height of summer, nights became little more than long evenings, and through endless weary days we seemed to fly forever, watching the sun roll along the northern horizon like a red-hot marble, then rise again. We watched and flew on into another day." The author's multi-time exposure of the midnight sun.

river valleys with dense, blue-grey clouds of smoke. With visibility marginal—and at times non-existent—we "steamboated" along the rivers below treetop level, hoping that other airborne mariners were keeping to their own side of the stream. And then there were those glassy-water landings in the thick smoke. Nights became little more than long evenings, and through endless, weary days we seemed to fly forever, watching the sun roll along the northern horizon like a red-hot marble, then rise again. We watched and flew on into another day.

But summer always ended too soon. In no time the last trips before freeze-up were upon us, and early snowstorms had us down to periscope level, trying to dodge the monstrous snags that projected from the Slave River. It was a time when frozen ropes could be pointed rather than thrown, when ice-covered floats were traps for the unwary, when removal of the overnight snow accumulation from the wings and tail surfaces again became a necessity. With broom in hand, we would sit on the leading edge of the wing and gingerly make our way toward the wing tip, sweeping the snow and keeping a wary eye on the icy water below. Then, if luck stayed with us, we would ferry the last of the Barren Land trappers to their winter quarters and have a final rendezvous with our prospecting parties.

Rudy Heuss, the pilot of CF-AAO on April 18, 1936. Rudy began his aviation career as an air engineer, then took pilot's training.

A few hours after leaving Don Goodwin's house on that April evening in 1936, I was on the move again, stumbling down the Snye Road in the utter blackness, tripping over frozen hummocks of mud and crunching through ice-covered puddles. When I reached the Snye and inspected the aircraft, I found that Frank's prophecy was right on target: AAO was covered with a thick coating of frost. But to my relief, there was sufficient oil for the flight to Smith and return. I lit a fire in the large, wood-burning heater, placed the pails on top of it, and returned to the aircraft. Removing the two blow pots and the fire extinguisher, I fired them up at a safe distance and retired under the engine cover. Soon I heard Frank and Bill arrive, and a moment later Frank's cheerful face appeared in the opening of the engine cover. "How're you doing in there, kid?" was his morning greeting. "I'll check the stove in the oil shed and Bill and I will start cleaning off the frost. As soon as the heating is finished, we'll start the refuelling. Hopefully, we can be all ready by the time Rudy shows up."

With the engine heated to my satisfaction, I extinguished the blow pots and set them aside to cool, then brought the two pails of hot oil to the aircraft. Adding the oil to the tank was quite often a one-man operation, but it was quicker and easier with two, and now, with the defrosting completed, Frank assisted me by handing up the 50-pound pails of oil. Bill commenced the refuelling, it being standard practice for the engineer who was assigned to a particular aircraft to do this job so he would know exactly how much fuel was loaded and could cheat a bit and add a few gallons over and above the specified amount.

I have already mentioned the need to roll the heavy, 45-gallon barrels of aviation fuel to the aircraft and to refuel by means of a hand operated "wobble pump," so named because of the fore-and-aft motion of the handle. However, McMurray being our main base, we had become somewhat refined: a sizeable fuel storage tank was located behind our buildings and about 25 feet higher in elevation than the surface of the Snye, providing a substantial gravity flow and allowing one man to do the refuelling.

With our required tasks finally completed we still lacked one principal element—Rudy—and he was nowhere in sight. Daylight had returned and the sky to the east was bright with the promise of another fine day. To us engineers, accustomed to a daily winter routine of engine heating in the darkness of early morning, of unremitting cold, of difficult and often bare-handed repair jobs, of working in the propeller slipstream at temperatures far below zero, the tasks of this particular morning were pure pleasure. We stood in silence for a few moments, enjoying the cool, crisp air, the frost-covered trees, and the colours that were now lighting up the eastern sky. The ice shimmered and crackled in the small, frozen pools that lined the shore. Above us, a flight of early mallards swept by on whistling wings, searching for open water, the drakes resplendent in their spring plumage. Finally, little Bill—far from the heaths and moors of his homeland—made a comment that expressed all our thoughts: "Wouldn't it be great if all of our mornings could be like this?"

Our quiet appreciation of the scene was interrupted by a call from the top of the bank. It was the missing Rudy. We looked up to see him engaged in earnest conversation with Don, obviously about the pros and cons of forced landings and the best course to follow if his luck ran out. As Rudy and Bill entered the aircraft, I climbed to the nose and lifted up the heavy winter engine cover, now ballasted by the oil and grease of a winter's use. Dropping it to Frank to pack and stow on board, I reached back, took the crank that Rudy passed to me, and leaned into the inertia starter. Getting the heavy flywheel of the inertia starter up to the required speed of about 15,000 rpms needed five or six turns of the crank and 30 seconds of intense effort. I withdrew the crank and returned it to Rudy. He engaged the starter control, spun the handle of the booster magneto, and the Wasp sprang to life. After a brief warm-up he taxied a short distance toward the east end of the Snye, then turned and took off toward the west. Moments later he had rounded the corner into the Athabasca channel and was lost to our sight—and soon also to hearing.

We had a short conference with Don, who announced the plans for the day. "You guys go up and have breakfast and take your time. The other fellows will be down soon and we'll crank up the old tractor and get the last couple of loads up by noon. Rudy should be back by 12:30 or 1:00. We'll change the machine to wheels and pull it up the hill. Then we'll call it a day."

The morning went according to Don's plans. By the time Frank Kelly and I returned from breakfast, most of the winter equipment was on its way to the safety of higher ground. With the aircraft wheels and the jacking equipment laid out on the ice in readiness, everyone relaxed to enjoy the warm spring sunshine. Don checked his watch. "It's 12:15. He should be here soon."

"I'll bet you a dime he isn't here until after one," challenged Casey Van der Linden, our welder/base engineer, who was stretched out on one of a pair of skis. The rest of our group—Art Rankin, Bill Jacquot and Dick Leigh—had made themselves comfortable upon whatever piece of dry real estate they could find. Don occupied the seat of the tractor, I sat on the engine hood, and Frank perched on a ski pedestal. All of these men were destined to spend a lifetime in aviation and to achieve recognition of their expertise. At that time Dick, the younger brother of the famous pilot Lewie Leigh, was following the same path I had trod a few years earlier, working without pay to gain experience, but he, Don and Frank were destined to join M/E (maintenance/engineering) departments of Trans Canada Airlines (TCA) shortly after that company was formed. Bill Jacquot would finish his career with the maintenance branch of the Department of Transport. Art Rankin, though an expert pilot, was working for CAL as a mechanic until a flying job appeared. He also joined TCA, became one of their senior pilots during the early days of the airline, and had risen to an executive position by the time he retired.

During a break in the conversation, Art called, "Frank, how about a song?"

"Sure," replied Frank, "but seeing as it's Sunday perhaps we should have a hymn." With that he removed his cap, holding it in front of him to simulate his ukelele, and began to strum and sing a slightly irreverent verse to the tune of "Shall We Gather at the River." It ended with the words "and there's no bloody copper on the river that flows to the Arctic Sea."

There was general applause as he rendered the final chorus. After the laughter had died away, Bill Jacquot called across to Don, "I've heard that song so many times but never did know the source of it. Do you know, Don?"

"I believe it originated with some of the NAME boys back in '27 or '28," said Don. "Apparently some of their directors had been reading Samuel Hearne's book, and they were so sure they'd find a solid vein of copper up around Coppermine that they had a couple of their aircraft with crews and prospectors spend breakup there."

"They find anything?"

Don shook his head. "They staked some property over on Bornite Lake, I've heard, and did quite a bit of work on it before they finally gave up. I guess the song was put together by some disappointed prospector after a hard season with little to show for it."

Art spoke up then. "How'd they get the floats in, I wonder? Must have been by boat. They couldn't have flown them in."

"Yeah, probably by boat," replied Frank. "How about it, Rex? Your dad works for Hudson's Bay Transport—you must have heard something about it?"

"I doubt if they sent them down by riverboat," I said, "Back in '28 all of the Hudson's Bay posts in the Western Arctic were supplied by their own boat, the *Bay Chimo*, operating from Vancouver. That was the only way that anyone could ship cargo in. They were lucky to get their floats in, though. Some years, when the ice was bad, the *Chimo* didn't get as far as Coppermine."

"What became of the *Chimo*?" queried Dick. "Seems to me I heard she's still afloat."

"She was lost in '31," I replied, "on her way south at the end of the season, caught in heavy ice and abandoned south of Point Barrow. She survived, though, and was seen at different times over the next few years."

Everyone was silent for the next few minutes, doubtless with mental pictures of the old Arctic supply boat—a ghost ship without a crew—drifting endlessly through the ice floes.

Suddenly the silence was broken by Don. "I hear an aircraft! Casey, you've lost your dime." We were all quiet, listening, then the sound of an aircraft could be plainly heard, flying low up the Athabasca. As everyone watched, AAO came into sight, flying at about 200 feet, then roaring across town in one triumphant swoop to signal the end of the winter flying season. Rudy banked to the left and disappeared beyond our sight down the Clearwater, and we waited for him to reappear at the west end of the Snye. The engine noise grew louder and then there was silence. Only the fading echoes remained. For a moment we thought—and hoped—that the island on the north side of the Snye had blocked the noise. Then Frank Kelly shouted, "His engine's quit! He's down on that rough ice out on the Athabasca!"

But seconds later we had a brief glimpse of AAO as she flashed past the west end of the Snye with only a few feet between her skis and the ice hummocks below. If her motor failure had only been postponed for a few more seconds, Rudy would have had enough altitude to make a left-hand turn into the Snye and to coast to a stop in front of us. But it was not to be. As he later said with a rueful shake of his head, "If only I hadn't made that last pass over town."

The aircraft disappeared from sight, hidden by a point of land that was perhaps a half-mile distant. We all started running in that direction but Don stopped us. "Wait! We'll need equipment. That rough ice will have knocked off the undercarriage and we'll have to jack it up and get the skis back under it. Dick and Rex, you go back and get the small sleigh and load some blocks and jacking equipment on it. And bring anything else that you think we might need. The rest of us will go ahead." Then, as a fortunate after-thought, "Better bring along a spare ski, too."

Dick and I, being the youngest members of the staff, were accustomed to being the "gofers," and as we hated to miss out on the excitement, our mission was accomplished with commendable haste. The wooden blocks and jacking equipment for changing AAO from skis to wheels were quickly loaded onto the homemade sleigh normally used by Fred and Cec to transfer cargo and mail sacks to and from the aircraft. I took the opportunity to grab up my camera, which was always near at hand, before Dick and I set off in pursuit of the advance party, now scattered as lack of conditioning took its toll. With the enthusiasm of youth, we soon overtook the rear guard of the party and came in sight of our unfortunate AAO.

Our first concern was for the crew, and we were relieved to spot two figures surveying the mishap—big Rudy and little Bill. This being Sunday, a number of the townspeople, strolling in the sunshine moments before, were now streaming across the ice to enjoy the free show we had organized. Our group was soon joined by more CAL people who had been enjoying the luxury of a Sunday morning off—Archie McMullen, Frank Hartley, and our agents, Fred and Cec—added manpower that would prove a blessing. Even if the undercarriage was repairable, without engine power the aircraft could not be taxied, and manpower would be our only hope of salvaging it. During the next few hours everyone worked with extreme urgency as we all knew this warm day could trigger breakup, and we were well over a quarter-mile from the Athabasca's shore. If the ice moved, it would be a desperate foot race to reach safety. Though the banks of the river were high and steep, we knew that if we were sufficiently fleet-footed to get that far we could scramble up them. However, for our crippled AAO, there was only one escape route: back into the mouth of the Snye over the path we had just travelled because our graded slipway at the foot of the Snye Road was the only place an aircraft could be pulled ashore.

The gofers—Dick Leigh and Rex Terpening.

At first glance the situation looked most discouraging. The lower left side of the fuselage lay on the ice on top of a confused welter of undercarriage components. The left wing tip, obviously damaged, was imbedded in the ice. The steel rivets securing the upper attachment fitting of the left shock strut had sheared off. They had failed under compression-loading upon initial impact. The next bounce had applied tension and pulled them apart. But in spite of this harsh treatment there was no actual damage to the undercarriage components or to the ski and pedestal. On the right side the undercarriage was still intact but the upper tubing of the Fairchild pedestal had failed; not surprisingly considering the magnitude of the impact. The sturdy Elliot Brothers ski was undamaged and lay some yards away with the remnants of the pedestal. The tail ski was another casualty, having come out second-best in its encounter with the ice. It appeared to be our most serious problem as the entire structure had been torn away from the fuselage.

As the result of Don's foresight, we had brought a jack and we also had the use of the jack carried on board the aircraft. However, we were short of wooden blocking because Dick and I had loaded only the blocks that were readily available, so Cec and one of the local volunteers had to be sent back to the base for additional blocking. Jacking up an aircraft under unfavourable conditions with inadequate equipment proved a slow job, and as is usually the case, the more we tried to hurry the less speed we made.

While we waited for more blocking to arrive, as a first step we disconnected the right ski harness and removed the broken portion of the pedestal in readiness for the spare ski we had brought. As we lacked enough blocking to raise the aircraft high enough to re-attach the shock strut to its upper fitting—which fortunately was still attached to the side of the fuselage—we removed the left ski from the axle to get enough height to re-connect the severed members. Two of our stalwarts aided in this operation by raising the wing tip to gain a few extra inches. Fortunately, Bill had a good assortment of bolts in his tool box and these replaced the sheared rivets. Further trouble now confronted us: the undercarriage was repaired but since we'd had to remove both skis in the process, the aircraft was now sitting level but both axles were resting on the ice.

As soon as the additional blocking arrived, we began raising the fuselage so that the skis could be re-installed. This proved to be a frustrating exercise. The jacking pads at the base of the axle struts were now down at ice level so we were unable to insert the jacks. We tried to raise the aircraft with a single jack under the fuselage centre but failed because the load was too great for the old Walker mechanical jack. We then jacked under the longerons, raising one side at a time, until the axle pads were high enough for a jack to be inserted. After what seemed like hours, with everyone casting anxious glances upstream for signs of breaking ice, AAO was again on her own feet.

We now turned our attention to the tail ski—or rather, the lack of it. The ski itself was undamaged, but the supporting structure was in tatters, with the lower longerons imbedded in the ice. Our first thought was to jury-rig the ski back to its original location. Then a better solution appeared. The base party had brought the spare blocking on a small toboggan with a box mounted upon it and we instantly recognized its possibilities. Taking the axe from the aircraft kit we cut down the ends of the box to provide

Trying to gain an extra inch of lift as CF-AAO is jacked up after damaging her undercarriage, Dick Leigh and Bill Sunderland push up on her left wing while Frank Kelly crawls out onto her right wing to force it down.

Don Goodwin unloads blocks of wood from the sleigh and Bill Jacquot works the jack handle while Casey van der Linden, pilot Rudy Heuss and Dick Leigh look on.

The men manning the jacks get advice from Archie McMullen and Frank Kelly on the left and from Casey van der Linden, Don Goodwin, Cecil Piette, and Rudy Heuss. In the background is the base of the tar sand ridge which lies immediately behind the village.

Heading home to the Snye with CF-AAO in tow. Halfway there they were met by a team from Ryan Brothers Transport which took over the job.

clearance for the fuselage, threw in some sacks of His Majesty's mail for packing, and placed this under the fuselage. This contraption was placed well forward of the original ski location to avoid interference with the bottom end of the stabilizer support struts. We then extended a rope from one of the main skis to the nose of this toboggan to keep it aimed in the right direction. In the meantime, others had been installing the main skis. We were finally ready for the trip home, and we started turning AAO to face the Snye. We were still unsure of the amount of manpower needed to move the aircraft, but Don placed four men at the aft fuselage to aid in the gradual turn, while the rest were divided into groups, pushing against the wing struts and pulling on the ski harnesses. To our collective delight, the aircraft moved quite easily and we were soon headed for the home stable.

We had advanced perhaps a quarter-mile toward the Snye when Don called a halt for a breather. Preoccupied as we all were, no one had noticed what lay ahead. Coming toward us from the mouth of the Snye was a pair of hayburners from Ryan Brothers Transport with that company's expert teamster, Sammy Delorme, at the controls. Don whipped his slaves into action again and we closed the gap between ourselves and our new motive power. Babe and Prince then took over the towing operation—though not without a considerable amount of wide-eyed snorting and unrestrained flatulence—and we were underway again. We said our thanks and farewells to our town friends and climbed on board for a free ride back to our base. Then the reaction set in. The exertions and the tensions of the last few hours took their toll. Everyone was suddenly aware of a great sense of relief and weariness.

Those of us standing on the skis beside Sammy learned the details of his self-imposed rescue mission. The moccasin telegraph had quickly spread the news of our predicament around town, and Sammy, realizing the necessity of getting the aircraft off the ice without delay, had quickly gone to the stables, harnessed the horses, and set off to meet us. He towed us to the foot of the hill leading up to the Snye Road, then unhitched and directed his steeds toward home, with Don calling after him, "Make sure they get a good feed of oats, Sammy! They saved our bacon!"

We removed the main skis from the aircraft, installed the wheels, and towed her up the hill, her winter's work behind her. Once again AAO had proved that she led a charmed life, with a most influential guardian angel hovering over her. This was a craft that had been abandoned in the Arctic after the McAlpine party had been lost and later rescued. Rudy and I had gone through the ice with her at the east end of the Snye in November 1935, while in the January just past, Matt Berry and I, caught in fog and with our supplies of fuel and daylight nearly exhausted, almost wrote her

The entire salvage crew—CAL employees and townspeople—pose for their photo.

off while landing in rough ice at Fort Good Hope. As we parked her at the edge of the village, some of these thoughts must have crossed Don's mind, including Frank Kelly's prophetic utterance of the previous evening. "Kelly," he suddenly said, "you're right. AAO is a real survivor."

As AAO's motor had quit at the crucial moment, we needed to know whether or not an engine change was required, and the following day we carried out some troubleshooting. We checked that there was fuel in the tanks and that the fluid in the carburetor was actually gasoline, but lack of fuel had not been the problem. Could the cam drive gear have failed? A turn of the prop with a couple of rocker box covers removed eliminated that possibility. The magnetos were next and here we met with some success. The left magneto was not turning and we realized then where the failure had occurred. There were two horizontal drive shafts in the rear accessory case of the engine, the right one driving both the oil pump and the right magneto, the left shaft driving the left magneto and the fuel pump. Obviously, this left drive shaft had failed. Pratt & Whitney's reliable Wasp would no doubt have been quite agreeable to continuing the operation with only one magneto—but not without a fuel pump. I believe this incident was responsible for the mandatory installation of auxiliary hand fuel pumps on all Fairchild 71s after that.

If anyone wonders just how narrow our safety margin was on that long-ago Sunday, April 19, 1936, the ice broke up on April 21 at 6:50 p.m., just 48 hours later. And if anyone has witnessed the colossal force of a river breakup and wondered about the possibility of being caught between those giant, tumbling blocks of ice, 48 hours is a narrow margin. Those of us who were out there on that Sunday afternoon seldom mentioned it in later years and certainly never laughed about it. When the subject did come up, it was always with the question, generally unspoken, that had the ice moved, how many—or how few of us—might have survived?

Had we now exceeded our excitement quota for the season? Apparently not. The 1936 breakup caused one of the greatest ice jams and highest floods on record. The fact that a number of us had been perilously close to being an integral part of the excitement also made it a memorable event. As well, that ice jam nearly prevented us from the emergency launching of our first float-equipped aircraft of the season—to save a human life!

We had brought our damaged AAO onto higher ground to join the rest of the fleet near the village, in some cases in people's backyards. As we knew from our investigation, an engine change would be required as well as structural repairs to the fuselage. However, none of this could be dealt with until after the departure of the ice because, knowing our crane and shop would become unusable if a flood occurred, our shop equipment had been moved to a safer location. Meanwhile, there was plenty of other work to keep us occupied. The two Junkers aircraft, AMZ and ARI, together with AAO's sister ship, Fairchild 71 ATZ, were all to be float-equipped and prepared for summer operations.

Conversion from winter to summer flying mode related mostly to engine functions. Insulation was removed from engine oil sumps, oil tanks and plumbing, together with baffles and shrouds that either protected engine components from cold air or provided extra hot air for the engine induction system or for the occupants of the cabin and cockpit. Thankfully, removal of this extra hardware in the spring was always simpler than the installation had been during the previous freeze-up period. As the systems installed during the autumn layover were critical to the successful cold weather performance of the aircraft and the power plant, no slightest detail could be overlooked or left to chance. Each different make and model of aircraft had its own specific requirements, learned through years of experience by the operators. The spring conversion consisted of returning these systems to what the aircraft manufacturer, lacking detailed knowledge of cold weather requirements, had originally provided.

Having carried out the essential conversion of the airframe and engine, greased the rocker arms/push rods and adjusted the clearances, riveted patches on a couple of cracks in the engine cowling, patched the odd hole in the fabric, and painted the cabin floorboards (always a nice touch), we would give some attention to the aircraft's floats. These would have been removed in early November to spend the winter beneath the snowdrifts. Don would have inspected them for damage and ordered any needed materials. Float repairs and the accompanying paint jobs were some of the more pleasant of the spring tasks—unless, of course, the float you were patching belonged to a Fairchild.

The two Junkers had later model Edo floats and AAO had a pair of earlier models, but ATZ was inflicted with a pair of Fairchild Model P-7s. Not

An Air Engineer's Checklist, Circa 1935

Besides seasonal conversion of the aircraft systems, the on-board equipment and the emergency ration kits required our attention. Winter equipment consisted generally of the following items:

- Winter engine cover
- One pair wing covers
- Two blow pots
- Two five-gallon oil pails
- One mechanical jack, with handle
- One snow shovel
- One broom
- One container of spare fuel for blow pots
- Two 5/8-inch wing tie-down ropes, each 40 feet long
- Two pair snowshoes with extra lamp wick for binding
- One shock strut pump

Although details might vary between operators, an average summer aircraft operating kit would consist of:

- One summer engine cover
- Two paddles
- One float pump
- Two 5/8-inch mooring ropes, each 40 feet long
- One 1/2-inch rope for a tail tie, 50 feet long
- One 5/16-inch rope, 100 feet long, with a "turk's head" woven into one end. (Ropes of this type could be coiled and thrown for considerable distances—thus the name "heaving lines." They were particularly useful if your pilot happened to be junior in experience and cut the throttle when the dock was still beyond leaping distance.)
- One five-gallon oil pail (though smaller if available)
- Two mosquito bars (mosquito netting to cover our sleeping bags)
- Fly spray gun and fly spray (Fly-Tox was the common name.)
- Hand fishing line and lures
- A small fish net
- A float repair kit

Besides these basics there were certain items carried both summer and winter: a battery-powered emergency radio transceiver; an engine tool kit consisting of special tools for that aircraft's particular engine (spark plug wrench, oil filter wrench, cylinder hold-down wrench, induction pipe packing gland wrench, etc.); an axe; a tent; a ration kit; an emergency stove, either a kerosene-burning Primus or gasoline-burning Coleman; and a rifle. (The Marbles Game-Getter was the standard rifle, though some crews carried their own personal firearms. The Game-Getter was an interesting firearm, consisting of a single-shot mechanism with two barrels, one of which would handle either a .410 shotgun cartridge or a .44 ball cartridge. The other barrel—the upper one, I believe—was for .22-calibre cartridges.)

Each engineer had his own kit of tools plus whatever items of special equipment he felt to be necessary, as decided by experience, personal preference, and the type of aircraft. For example, a winter kit might include a baling needle and a ball of rib-stitching cord for repair of torn engine covers (and for torn belly fabric after a pilot tried a shortcut over a clump of willows); a chunk of brass for ski runner repairs; a spare generator; jets and jet cleaner for the blow pots; cable, cable clamps and bungee cord for ski harness and other repairs; one tin of a potent liquid cement known as Ambroid; a chunk of aircraft fabric; a roll of pinked edge tape; a length of ignition wire in case the engineer fried a couple of the lower ignition leads with the blow pots; and a roll of 14- or 16-gauge steel wire (otherwise known as haywire). An experienced engineer on a Fokker Super (noted for their fragile undercarriages) would also probably carry an emergency repair kit consisting of a couple of lengths of angle iron together with suitable clamps for reinforcing failed struts. Many a careful engineer would also carry in summer a section of lightweight canvas to stretch across the floats, below the engine, to prevent his servicing tools from joining the jackfish.

However, the most important item on board was the emergency ration kit, usually considered the joint responsibility of pilot and engineer. Check and then double-check was the rule that all crews followed where the ration kit was concerned. Each company had its own standards, but the ration kit of any prudent operator would certainly contain the following items, in varying quantities: dried vegetables, dried fruit, rolled oats, tinned ham or other meats, tinned butter, flour, sugar, tea, coffee, pilot bread (hardtack), pancake mix, syrup, peanut butter, jam, milk powder, baking powder, baker's chocolate, and matches (in sealed containers). Along with these food items there would be knives, forks, cooking utensils, candles for tent lighting, and a pot for making tea and coffee.

The need for careful handling and packing of ration kits was emphasized by the experience of Con Farrell and Frank Hartley during the summer of 1935. Misled by the early maps, they were totally dependent upon their ration kit for 10 days. Unfortunately, the Fly-Tox spray gun had been carelessly stored with the more perishable (and important) of the rations, and this contamination added greatly to the unpleasantness of their enforced stay. After that, the standard rule for all operators became "Never store the Fly-Tox with the rations!" In our day these ration kits were usually packed into one of those old, heavy-duty prospector's packsacks. This was a practical selection. If a crew had to walk out from a downed aircraft, the ration kit could be backpacked. In later years the ration kits were probably less used, and they were standardized and packed in sturdy containers.

that the model made any real difference—the hydrodynamics were poor on both the P-6s and the P-7s, while the internal construction was identical, as bad on one model as the other. Instead of using aluminum alloy for keels, formers and bulkheads, Fairchilds had elected to use one-inch-square oak for the internal members, and the aluminum alloy skin was attached to these wooden members with machine screws made of soft aluminum. As a crowning touch, the manufacturers had clipped off the projecting ends of the screws with cutting pliers, making them most difficult to remove when carrying out a repair and certainly guaranteeing that the threads would be stripped when removing the nut from the screw. But that was not all. As part of their misbegotten design, Fairchilds had coated the interior members with a sticky, tar-like substance. As it turned out, that spring ATZ's floats were in good condition so we were spared the misery of stripped screws and tarry hands.

One of the usual float overhaul routines on all types of floats was the replacement of water rudder pull-up cables and steering cables, a precaution taken at the beginning of each season to lessen the possibility of failed cables during some critical manoeuvre at a far-off northern lake or river. (I know of a couple of cases—perhaps not officially recorded—where aircraft and their occupants were nearly swept over Virginia Falls on the

Canadian Airways hangar jammed with ice blocks after the spring breakup of April 1936.

The breakup and ice jam of April 1936, looking along the Snye towards the Clearwater River. The ice had jammed downstream, causing this rise in the water/ice level and crushing the cabins closest to the shore.

Nahanni River when cables failed.) Pull-up cables were made of either $\frac{1}{8}$-inch or $\frac{5}{32}$-inch cable, and those for steering of $\frac{3}{32}$-inch cable. Renewal called for a considerable amount of cable-splicing talent—a craft in which Don particularly excelled, and it became a great opportunity to practise, particularly if one were a bit rusty. (How many readers recall the five-tuck splice—one under two to the left, one under three to the right, etc.?)

All of this aircraft activity was getting underway when the ice finally started to move on the evening of April 21, 1936. However, it must have been partially jammed at some point downstream because the water level continued to rise, and massive slabs of ice overran the shorelines, destroying everything before them. Although finally the ice movement ceased, the water level continued to rise for the next few days. These were the highest flood water levels that had ever been seen, even by the old-timers. When the water started to fill the ditches along Franklin Avenue, McMurray's main street, there was serious talk of a general exodus to the hillside behind the town. However, the ice jam broke before that eventuality, and the water receded rapidly, leaving the Snye Road a sea of slippery mud, and our hangar and the hoist area in a similar condition. Fortunately, no heavy ice had been left on the road itself as we had nothing with which to move it except our limited manpower.

With our seasonal conversions practically completed except for the actual installation and rigging of the floats, we left the aircraft at the townsite and started on the muddy job of cleaning up the hangar. And this was the situation on May 6, when we learned through the local grapevine that a pregnant resident, Florence Poitras, was seriously ill. Though there was a doctor at McMurray at that time, there was no hospital. By noon we learned that the woman's condition had grown worse. An emergency flight to Edmonton appeared to be her only hope—and we did not yet have an aircraft on floats. This was a serious matter—a life was at stake. We suspended all other activity and concentrated on preparing ATZ for immediate use.

We removed the last of the ice from under the crane and brought ATZ down the hill. Attaching the hoist, we lifted her high enough to remove the main undercarriage. The extended summer rudder and auxiliary bottom-mounted fin were installed at the same time. Then we lifted the fuselage a little more to get her to float-installation height, and by late evening the floats and water rudder cables were installed and rigged. Our standard

CF-ATZ prepares for takeoff on May 7, 1936, after her rush float installation and launching. The doctor and patient are aboard, and Dick Leigh and Don Goodwin stand on the float, waiting for pilot Archie McMullen to hand the crank out to them.

refuelling system was out of service because of the flood, so we brought down a wobble pump, a funnel, and a couple of barrels of aviation gasoline on a stoneboat pulled by the tractor, and the aircraft was refuelled as she sat under the crane. When we learned that the patient was still holding her own, we decided to knock off for the night—it was now dark—and launch ATZ the next day.

Bright and early the next morning we cranked up our venerable tractor and made the trip to the Snye with two men walking beside each float to keep them aimed in the right direction. Archie McMullen was the pilot, and it is my recollection that he wisely mounted to the cockpit before we left the hangar to avoid filling it with slippery mud. By the time we had ATZ back in the water, our patient had arrived, carried down from the town on a stretcher. There were no ambulances. Floundering in the sticky, slippery mud and perspiring under the hot spring sunshine, we loaded and tied down the stretcher. For anyone who has ever tried to shoehorn a stretcher into the side door of a Fairchild 71 on floats, it is an operation not soon forgotten. Our patient was only semi-conscious, which was as well—otherwise she would have been scared witless.

Standing on the float, Don gave our popular medico, Doc McCallum, a hand to board, took a final check of the cabin interior, closed the door and hopped ashore. Dick Leigh, in readiness to crank the engine starter, waited for Archie to pass the crank out to him. All conversation had ceased. Everyone waited in anticipation of the climax of our efforts—our own people and the townsfolk who had assisted with the stretcher carrying. The only one missing from the crowd was Florence's husband, Aime, a baker by trade. The higher wages of the mining camps had lured him to Yellowknife, and he was unaware of the family emergency. Only the rumble and crash of the ice as it broke loose from the piled masses and tumbled into the muddy water below broke the silence. The pause grew longer and the tension mounted.

Finally the heavy crank appeared through the side window, followed by Archie's face, wearing a sheepish grin. "I couldn't find the crank," he said, explaining the delay. His remark broke the tension and a chuckle rippled through the crowd. Relief from the worries of the past 36 hours showed on all faces. There was renewed hope that our efforts would not be in vain. Dick applied his considerable weight and muscle to the crank. The reduction gears of the starter commenced their dry, metallic whine, increasing in pitch with each turn of the crank. There is no sound quite like one of those old Eclipse inertia starters when the small, heavy flywheel reached its maximum speed. It's a sound like no other and it remains engraved in the memory of all aviation people of that era.

When the starter sound reached the proper pitch, Dick withdrew the crank, returned it to Archie, and stepped ashore. Archie pulled the starter knob, the prop turned, and the Wasp coughed to life, emitting clouds of blue smoke from the oil that had accumulated in the lower cylinders during the layover. Archie taxied rapidly downstream, dodging drifting ice masses, then completed a couple of wide circles at higher rpm in order to bring the oil temperature up to the minimum for takeoff. Finally ATZ turned to face the ice-studded takeoff route toward the Athabasca.

There was a pause and we had a mental picture of him saying a comforting word to Florence and asking Doc if he was okay. Then we heard the full-throated roar of the Wasp at wide open throttle, and a cloud of spray erupted from behind the aircraft. Rapidly picking up speed, ATZ was on the step by the time she passed us. A couple of minor power reductions were needed to effect course changes. Finally we heard the sound of maximum rpms as she became airborne and disappeared from our sight. Again all were silent as we listened to the fading sound of the motor as the aircraft turned, climbing southbound up the valley of the Athabasca, following the summer route to Edmonton.

It was a muddy and weary crew who plodded back up the Snye Road, returning to our hangar and the scene of our recent frantic efforts. There was little conversation, everyone mentally reviewing the events of the past several hours. Our tool boxes were open, our tools lying where we had dropped them. Normally an inventory would have taken place, with each tool carefully examined, cleaned and stored, but not today. Our tool boxes were placed inside the shop, the loose tools, slippery with mud and oil, piled on the workbench. Cleaning and sorting could wait. Bill Jacquot, searching for a spanner that he had dropped, was the last man to finish.

"Did you find everything, Bill?" Don queried. "If so, let's head for home, get rid of some of this mud, and take a couple of days off. We did a good stroke of business getting ATZ back on floats and away on this trip. Doc says an operation is the only thing that can save Florence now."

With that, we trooped up the muddy road and scattered to our respective dwellings and boarding houses. Among the townspeople we met along the way there was concern on every face. There were no strangers in our little village. Everyone knew Florence, her sister Mary and her widowed mother, Mrs. Bird. And so it was that later in the day a small crowd gathered in the vicinity of the government telegraph office on Franklin Avenue, anxiously awaiting some word from Edmonton. Charlie Summers, our lone operator, performed two very important functions in the village: he was our only link with the outside world, and he was the umpire for our softball games. A fine fellow, liked and respected by all. There was a notice board on the front of the building where messages of general interest were displayed, but on that day it was empty. As the crowd increased in size, there was an unspoken question on the face of each newcomer. The reply was a silent headshake on all sides. Time passed and the tension mounted. The afternoon sun had slanted down to the west when finally the telegraph office door opened. Charlie stepped out, a green telegram form in his hand. From force of habit, he turned toward the notice board for just a moment, then turned back to face the expectant crowd.

"I've just had a message from Doc McCallum," he said with a wide smile on his face. "Florence and the baby are both fine! Will someone run over and tell Mrs. Bird and Mary the good news?"

10 There but for fortune go you or I

In most of the winter experiences I have described there was always a sense of foreboding, a threat of disaster lurking around the next point of land—a desperate whiteout situation or an over-water expedition on skis where a motor failure would put an end to our worries. In contrast many of the summer calamities happened under the most innocent of circumstances. Sunny days, ideal conditions, nothing on the horizon that would cause anyone, even the most timid of souls, the slightest cause for worry. If threat existed, it was so remote that even the faint of heart would have forged ahead. Such was the case in May 1936.

Back in January, Matt Berry and I had partially demolished our faithful old AAO during an argument with the gasoline drums at Fort Good Hope, and our wounded steed had taken up residence in the company shop where Casey, our welder, and I worked on her between stints of servicing other aircraft. But with AAO out of service, Matt was missing the three-cents-per-mile bonus that pilots earned in addition to their monthly salary, and he was agitating to get his hands on another aircraft. We were still without wings on February 20 when the company's new Fairchild 82, CF-AXE, arrived in Fort McMurray. As this 82 was the first such model that any of us had seen, it was decided that the initial flights would be made with our chief pilot, Con Farrell, at the controls, and our chief mechanic, Don Goodwin, as engineer. Not that the 82 was any technological marvel, but she was a vast improvement over her first cousin, the Fairchild 71. To the delight of all of us engineers, she had a two-place

cockpit, and to the delight of our frugal and cost-conscious agent, Fred Lundy, she had a cabin of substantial size. And to add to her popularity, she was the first brand new, fresh-out-of-the-wrapping-paper aircraft that any of us had ever seen.

In due time, Con and Don, our test team, having decided that this new aircraft was a well-behaved creature, agreed that the rest of us common mortals could operate her with safety. Matt was, of course, the logical choice for her pilot, and as I had been flying with him all winter—that is, until the Good Hope incident—I drew the engineer's seat. We then operated AXE throughout the spring season with the flying duties divided between Con and Matt.

The performance of this aircraft was excellent, our only concern being the solid, non-shock-absorbing ski pedestals with which she came

Canadian Airways brand new Fairchild 82, CF-AXE, on the Snye at McMurray in March 1936.

equipped. Apparently, she had been ferried on wheels from the Fairchild factory to Winnipeg, the location of CAL's overhaul shops, and the skis had been installed there before the ferry flight was continued to McMurray. The only spare set of skis available at Winnipeg had solid pedestals, and those are what we received. Many of our landing places were anything but smooth, and after a few weeks of bone-jarring landings, we swapped the installed skis for a pair that were equipped with the excellent Fairchild shock-absorbing pedestals.

Prospecting activity was brisk that spring, and Matt and I made numerous trips into the Beaverlodge area, northeast of Goldfields. Other trips took us into the Yellowknife area, where considerable exploration was taking place. And there were routine mail and express trips to the river posts as well. Then in mid-March Matt took a few days off and was relieved by Art

Pilot Matt Berry (centre) standing in front of Fairchild CF-AXE with two prospectors he has just put down in the back country. Their supplies for the coming season are piled to the right of the aircraft.

Rankin, and it was with Art that I did the last trip to Aklavik before breakup. The weather was clear and mild—we had sunshine most of the way—and it was the most enjoyable Aklavik trip that either of us had experienced. This fine weather continued through to the end of the ski season after which, according to company surmise and gossip, Con would again become the pilot-in-command. Well, breakup arrived and the fleet became water-borne once more, but Con was elsewhere, and Matt and I were therefore delighted to carry on with AXE. Breakup, however, had not yet arrived at Yellowknife or down the Mackenzie, while Goldfields on Lake Athabasca was still ice-bound though unsafe for skis. The only posts to boast of open water were Fort Chipewyan, Fort Fitzgerald and Fort Smith. The first opportunity, therefore, for Matt and me to try out our new bird on floats came with a trip down the Athabasca River to Fort Smith.

We made our departure on May 28, 1936. In summer, flying the Athabasca was always interesting because of the variety of river traffic to be seen, and because both the river valley and the river itself presented such an attractive scene. This was especially so in mid- and late summer when the foliage was changing colour, water levels had receded, and the clear, brown waters were framed by the golden sand of the river bars. The river, however, was no thing of beauty in late May. The water was high and muddy, and driftwood lined the shores along with patches of stranded ice. Leaving this unattractive real estate behind us, we passed on down the Slave River to Fort Smith, where the local residents were delighted to receive their first mail of the summer season. Then hearing that Smith had received mail, the people in Resolution began clamouring for equal treatment and sent word that there was open water in the bay there. So this became our next mission. The Smith postmaster brought down the Resolution mail that had accumulated, adding it to the bags that we had brought.

At Resolution, Bob Porritt, our company agent, was on the dock to greet us, along with many of the residents. The spring breakup there, as in all those northern settlements, was a period of inactivity. The ice was unsafe for lake travel, and the snow too soft for bush travel. The local boats were ready for launching, but they had to wait for open water. Suffering from the breakup doldrums, Bob was anxious for company, and he tried hard to persuade us to remain at least for a few hours, but we had to decline. A couple of passengers were waiting in Smith for the trip to McMurray and we also had to make a local trip in the Smith area.

The Smith trip was to pick up a couple of trappers somewhere to the east. As we were unsure of the location of their trapline and had no accurate maps, we sought out one of their friends to obtain directions. Though familiar with the trapping area, he had only experienced it from ground level, but he sketched in the water courses on our maps and off we went. It took some little time to track down our prospective passengers, but once they were located, the rest of our operation was routine, except for a slight change in our expected passenger list. We returned to Smith late in the day with nine souls on board—six of them being dogs. Trips such as this one were often both frustrating and expensive for our company. The trappers would make prior arrangements to be picked up at some specific date at the end of the winter trapping season, but payment for the trip would be dependent upon the success of their winter fur catch. If that was less

Lives Lost in the Slave River Rapids

The name Fort Fitzgerald is a sure indication that this settlement was of Hudson's Bay Company origin as all of their early trading posts carried this "fort" designation, even though the later ones were far removed from the era of protective stockades. The name Fitzgerald commemorates a tragedy that is very much a part of northern history—The Lost Patrol. Inspector Fitzgerald of the RCMP was the leader of that unfortunate group who lost their bearings—and their lives—while on a winter patrol from Fort McPherson to Dawson City. Much has been written about that tragic expedition and many photos taken of their graves and the memorial at McPherson.

The 16-mile series of cataracts between Fort Fitzgerald and Fort Smith were sufficiently violent to earn the respect of the voyageurs, so those expert canoe-men would carry their trade-goods if they were northbound, or their fur bales if they were southbound, over the "carry" or portage rather than attempt the passage. A few unfortunates missed this opportunity, however. In one of the earliest recorded misfortunes on that stretch of river, the travellers had pulled ashore well upstream and out of sight of the rapids, and one man was detailed to walk along the shore and around the forward point of land to assess the risk. Their plan was simple enough: the scout would fire one round from his muzzle-loader if the rapids were considered passable. The canoe would then proceed, picking up the scout on the way. The scout completed his survey—a negative one, no doubt—and was on his way back to rejoin his comrades when, in a river backwater, he spotted a flock of ducks. With only his next meal in mind, he forgot the plan and fired. History has not recorded what effect this had on the ducks, but it was fatal for his comrades. Manning their canoe, they

than expected, payment to CAL would be partial or many times not at all. In this particular case, it was left for our local agent to resolve.

After our return to Smith there was still ample time to make the return trip to McMurray, but Mr. and Mrs. Farrow, our passengers, had disappeared. They had accepted a dinner invitation from friends and were nowhere to be found. Matt and I, therefore, spent the night—not unhappily—at Smith, swept forward around the point and into the cataract.

Another group of early victims—and I believe these were Catholic church people—were passengers on a raft of logs being floated down to the site of the present-day Fitzgerald. There they would be taken ashore, loaded onto ox-powered Red River carts, and hauled across the portage to present-day Smith. Unfamiliar with river travel, they had failed to correctly gauge the river current or the time and distance required for their journey. Ordinarily, log booms were manoeuvred close to the west bank of the river long before they reached Fitzgerald, where a line would be passed ashore and the landing made. Instead, the voyageurs found themselves still in midstream when they came in sight of their destination. Their situation was hopeless, and they were swept to their deaths.

Fort Fitzgerald is named for Inspector F.J. Fitzgerald of the RCMP, the leader of a four-man patrol who died when they lost their bearings on the trip from Fort McPherson to Dawson City in February 1911.

where we were entertained by the RCCS boys, all of whom were our friends and kept close track of our comings and goings. They were quick to sound the alarm if any of us were seriously overdue, especially when we were flying between any of the trading posts where the RCCS radio stations were located. As there was seldom an opportunity to make personal contact with them, this was a welcome layover on both sides.

The next morning we were up in good time, and with the Farrows on board, we were soon on our way south to McMurray. At the last minute, however, we were advised that a landing was required at Fort Fitzgerald, 16 miles to the south, but our time there was to be brief, just a matter of picking up a couple of bales of fur. The stretch of the Slave River between Smith and Fitzgerald is a series of cataracts that had claimed many lives, but those early-day misfortunes were far from our minds as we flew over the village of Fitzgerald. It was a fine Sunday morning, with billowing white clouds rolling across a sky of royal blue, pursued by a strong north wind, so Matt continued to the south, then turned and landed facing downstream into the wind.

In deference to the rapids, takeoffs at Fitzgerald were always upstream, to the south. Being cautious by nature, Matt had no wish to deviate from this standard, safe pattern, but our valiant 82, being somewhat headstrong, had other ideas. This model of aircraft had a long fuselage that was considerably affected by a crosswind, and she was reluctant to turn her nose to the south, even after a firm application of power. Adding to our difficulties was the fact that we were lightly loaded. With the floats riding high in the water, a turn against the wind was even more difficult.

After two unsuccessful attempts, Matt pulled the power and we drifted. "Well, I guess I could force her to come around, but I'd use most of the river to do it. We'll take off to the north. We've got no load and with that wind she'll jump into the air."

With that, he applied full power again, and in moments we were airborne. This was the first time that I had ever seen these mighty rapids at such close range, and it was probably a first for Matt as well. We stared down at the cataract below us—a mass of rocks and boiling water, river-wide and 16 miles in length. Matt turned from the side window and made one of his typically cautious understatements, "That would be a poor place for a forced landing." We climbed then, made our turn to the left over the portage, and were soon on our way south.

As we had a planned landing at Chipewyan and had a good tailwind, we stayed at a fairly low altitude to enjoy the river scenery, muddy though it was at this time of year. We had flown for about 15 minutes and had passed the government hay camp situated on the west bank of the Slave when the motor quit. No backfiring, no rough-running, no indication of trouble—just silence. I remember glancing quickly at the instrument panel and noting that we still had oil and fuel pressure and then at the ignition switches in case some ghostly hand had turned them off. The motor windmilled in the slipstream, producing absolutely no power. Matt dove for the river, at the same time heading for the west bank. He set the aircraft down beautifully. I made a hasty exit down to the float, grabbed a paddle and urged us in the direction of shore. With Matt steering with both the air rudder and the water rudders, we made our landfall at the hay camp. I could see that the left float would touch first so I scampered across the spreader bar and leapt ashore—into a foot or so of sticky mud. Normally, the river current would have swung the aircraft around to face the south, but the wind was strong enough to offset this, and I was able to hold the float by the front bollard while Matt grabbed a rope from the cabin and came forward to help me.

We had a moment—our first—to contemplate what had just happened. With the thought of the rapids still fresh in our minds, we exchanged a long look. "Boy! Were we lucky!" said Matt, shaking his head in disbelief. "I'd hate to think about where we'd be right now if that motor had quit when we were over the rapids!"

"Yeah! That was close!" I replied. "If we had gone down in the rapids, no one would have known about it. The aircraft would have been hammered to bits, and they'd probably spend days searching along the rivers for us!"

And as we contemplated our surroundings, we realized we were lucky in more ways than one: we could not have found a better place for an engine failure on the whole length of the river. This hay camp, some 30 miles above Fitzgerald, was maintained by the federal government as part of their Wood Buffalo Preserve operation. The helpful supervisor of the camp was Charlie Cooper, and his wife (whose first name I forget) was a good cook and a gracious hostess. There was assistance available, a workshop of sorts, material with which to make a work platform, good poles for a tripod for our engine change—and as a final, added benefit there was a telephone connection to Smith. Nothing was comparable along the whole length of the river.

As the buildings were all set well back from the river on the far side of the clearing, our hosts were not immediately aware of our presence. It being Sunday, they had been enjoying their day of rest. They had heard the aircraft going by, of course, but when they no longer heard the engine, they just assumed we had passed beyond their hearing range. But eventually someone happened to glance toward the river, realized there were visitors and hurried over to help us. At first we had difficulty convincing them that our engine had failed, that we had then landed safely, and paddled the aircraft to shore. After that, every resource they had was placed at our disposal. They couldn't do enough to help us.

Relocating the aircraft to a more permanent mooring was the first necessity, and here again we fared well. There was a tiny inlet just downstream, and we drifted the aircraft down to this location, nosed it in, and secured it. My next concern was to locate the source of our problem. As a result, I never did see our passengers again. Matt had helped them to disembark and they had been immediately made welcome by their friends, the Coopers. It was not until later, while we were having our first coffee break, that I realized they were no longer with us. There was a connecting road to Fitzgerald, and I was told that they had been driven back by car with, of course, quite an astonishing tale to tell their friends. Meanwhile, Matt had been busy on the telephone talking to the Signals boys at Smith, and they sent a message to McMurray to advise of our location and situation.

In the meantime I had obtained some planks from our helpful hosts and prepared to confront our reluctant Wasp. It was a matter of pride with us bush engineers that we should make every effort to repair damage and/or malfunctions in the field and return home under our own power. However, in this case, while there was little hope that the ailment was fixable, it did provide a splendid opportunity to examine the interior of the Wasp. The normal limit of our engine repair activities was a cylinder change or the replacement of the odd starter or carburetor. Anything inside the crankcase or nose section was out of bounds, except for shop specialists licensed for engine overhaul.

The fact that the oil and fuel pressures had been normal was a positive indication that the left and right drive trains were intact. (These were the two accessory drive trains in the rear section of the engine, the left one operating the left magneto and the fuel pump, the right one performing a similar service for the right magneto and the oil pumps.) Turning the propeller by hand disclosed nothing. I then removed a rocker box cover and watched the rocker arm as I moved the prop. There was no movement. Our trouble was therefore with the cam gear in the nose section of

CF-AXE at the federal government's hay camp on the Slave River south of Fort Fitzgerald after an engine failure. The nose cowlings and propeller are lying on the ground to the left, and the nose section and one cylinder have been removed.

The failed engine of CF-AXE. The push rods and their housings have been removed to allow the nose section to be taken off. Though normally the cam drive gear is hidden behind the cam ring, the ring has been removed to expose its missing section.

Tripod in place, engineer Casey van der Linden attaches the chain hoist to the offending engine of CF-AXE in order to install the replacement he has brought from Fort McMurray. Matt Berry stands by to help.

the engine, so I removed the propeller and then the nose section, using a hammer and punch to loosen the thrust-bearing nut. This gave me access to the mysterious world of cam shafts (or cam rings as they are known on the radial engines), cam followers, and the drive trains that connected them to the crank shaft. Exposing the disc-shaped cam ring with its numerous lobes, I discovered that there was no movement when I turned the prop; it was obviously disconnected from the power source. I then removed the cam ring—and this disclosed the source of our failure. A large section was missing from one of the cam drive gears. Wondering about the possibility of a field change for this drive gear in a case of some future emergency, I removed a couple of cylinders, providing access to the special nut that secured the cam gear supporting shaft. "Yes," I told myself, "it can be changed in the field without any tools more specialized than those in my tool box."

While all this was going on, we had been treated to a couple of meals and numerous cups of coffee by our hosts, the Coopers, and received word that a replacement engine was on its way. Our next requirement, therefore, was a tripod, but this was a simple matter as our hosts had a good selection of poles, ropes and chains, as well as a substantial chain hoist. We selected three sturdy poles, set up the tripod above the motor, and attached the chain hoist. With that accomplished, we knocked off for dinner. Meantime, the wind had died, and by the time Archie McMullen and Casey Van der Linden arrived, the spring mosquitoes were out in full force. Fortunately, there was some extra and well-muscled manpower available at the camp, which made the engine unloading operation much easier. Archie then departed, and we quit for the night.

Removing the failed engine was our first task the next day, May 31, and it was skidded out of the way with considerable help from the hay camp staff. We positioned the new motor under the tripod and hoisted it into position. It was well into the evening before we had the last of the motor mount bolts secured and locked. In discussion afterwards, Casey and I were unable to decide just which engine changes were the worst—summer with mud and mosquitoes or winter with temperatures of -50°.

The following day a stiff breeze kept the mosquitoes at bay as we fitted cowlings and baffles, installed the exhaust collector ring, and hooked up the exhaust stacks. We then ground-tested the engine, Matt came aboard and carried out a test flight, and we were almost ready for departure. Again assisted by some of the hay camp crew, we loaded the failed engine and tied it down, said our sincere thanks to our kind and helpful hosts, and were once more homeward bound.

Even though the hazards of summer flying were not as obvious as those of winter, they were still present, and in spite of all of the elementary precautions that might be taken, be it winter or summer, luck and the law of averages always played a hand. Matt was one of the most experienced, skilful and cautious of pilots. He always weighed the risk factors and his decisions were governed by caution, but this was the first time in all his years of flying that he had experienced a complete engine failure—one with absolutely no power. With such a sterling record behind him and a nearly new engine in AXE, he had decided that this was a no-risk situation—and yet moments later the engine had failed.

My dictionary says that the word "luck" means "that which happens by chance," a definition that can without any doubt be applied to our experience. In addition, of course, there are the adjectives "good" and "bad" with which to qualify this word. In our case, fortune had smiled upon us and we drew the good luck card.

11 Lost on the Barren Lands

Prior to the 1930s the only parts of the Northwest Territories that were mapped with reasonable accuracy were the main water courses, including the larger lakes. The vast lake-studded wilderness that lay between was little known, and to map it by ground survey methods would have been a daunting task. It was only when aircraft appeared on the scene that such mapping became a possibility. The RCAF made a start in 1926, using Vickers Vikings and later Vickers Vedette flying boats to survey the country to the north and east of Lake Athabasca. They did it with oblique photography—a series of photos taken at a fixed angle of view and altitude—a vast improvement over land-based observations but still not completely satisfying the precise needs of the map-makers.

The Vedettes were followed in the early 1930s by the Fairchild range of aircraft, first the smaller Wright J-5-powered FC-2s and later by the greatly improved Wasp-powered 71s, which could operate at 12–15,000 feet altitude. The RCAF equipped them with vertical cameras, which provided an overlapping sequence of photos, thus at last supplying the necessary accuracy for map-making. The air force also obtained a small number of Bellanca Pacemakers powered by the 300 hp Wright J-6 engine. Because of their smaller size, they came to be used almost entirely for photo work, while the Fairchilds, with their larger cargo capacity, could be used for transport work (setting up and relocating camps, ferrying gasoline supplies, etc.) as well as for photo work.

The very first mapping project of the area to the north of Great Slave Lake was carried out in the summer of 1931, using one Fairchild 71 and one Vickers Vedette. The detachment was under the command of Flt. Lt. Ralph McBurney, later to reach a well-earned air vice-marshal status, and now retired after a long and distinguished air force career. The other pilot on this ground-breaking mission was F/O Harry Winny, who later had a successful career in commercial aviation. By a coincidence that will be only fully appreciated later in this tale, two other members of this party were Eric Fry of the Dominion Government Survey & Mapping Division, and Joe Fortey, camera operator/aircraft mechanic. Eric, a key member of all those early photo/survey flights, used his sextant to provide the exact control points essential for accurate map production.

It is to the considerable credit of those who took part that their photo survey was carried out so efficiently with the marginal equipment then available. They flew over completely isolated and uninhabited country at a time when very few aircraft operated in the NWT, and virtually no aircraft had previously flown their routes. If they had become lost or experienced any of the mechanical problems that commonly plagued the aircraft of that day, their chances of rescue would have been rather remote.

Their photos provided basic strip maps of three important flight routes. The first of these was from the north end of Yellowknife Bay to Hunter Bay up in the northeast corner of Great Bear Lake. (This was before any mineral discoveries had been made in the Yellowknife area, and also before the LaBine strike at Eldorado had shifted the Bear Lake activity from Hunter Bay to Cameron Bay.) The second map was from Fort Rae northward to Bear Lake, and the third between Bathurst Inlet and Fort Reliance.

By the mid-1930s the RCAF were well organized with their aerial survey program. From their main base at Lac du Bonnet, Manitoba, the photo fleet would proceed westwards to McMurray, then north to their summer base on the Slave River, south of Fort Fitzgerald, becoming operational from there as soon as the ice departed from the lakes and rivers. By this time surveys had been completed of the area adjacent to Yellowknife to provide maps of reasonable accuracy for local prospectors. And by the summer of 1936 a survey of the area to the north and east of Great Slave Lake was underway, and the RCAF established a summer operating base at the site of old Fort Reliance with seven aircraft—two Fairchild 71s and five Bellanca Pacemakers.

Reliance had been occupied as a fur trading post by the HBC at various times from 1855 onwards, but by 1936 the only permanent residents were

Fort Reliance

Fort Reliance, now a national historic site, is a rather lonely piece of real estate, but because of its location on the threshold of the Barrens, it has been intimately connected with some of the earliest recorded history of the north. It sits on a sandy point that extends into Great Slave Lake's McLeod Bay, some eight miles from the mouth of the turbulent Lockhart River. The bay was named for John McLeod, who established the original Hudson's Bay Company fort there after he had been assigned the job of assisting George Back in his Arctic Lands Expedition of 1833. Back's name is, of course, well known to any student of early exploration in northern Canada. He was a member of Franklin's ill-starred 1819–1822 Barren Lands Expedition and was responsible for the ultimate rescue of Franklin and the other survivors. He returned with Franklin in 1825 to explore the Mackenzie, came back in 1833 to search for the members of the long-absent Ross Expedition, then stayed to explore the Great Fish River from its origin in Muskox Lake to its outlet on the Arctic Coast. (The Fish River later became the Back River.)

George Back also bestowed names on the major lakes drained by the Lockhart, the names having arisen from the public subscription list that financed the search for Ross. He wrote, "A large body of water to the north I named Aylmer Lake in honour of Lord Aylmer, Governor-in-Chief of British North America." Clinton-Colden Lake was named "as a mark of respect to the memory of those distinguished individuals," though he doesn't provide any further identification. Sussex Lake was named for "H.R. Highness, the Vice-Patron of the Expedition." Artillery Lake reflects the contributions—not monetary but physical—of his crew. "We soon got to the southern extremity of a lake," wrote Back, "which is about 40 miles long and 12 broad at the widest spot, and out of respect for the distinguished corps to which some of my crew belonged and from a grateful remembrance of the deep interest manifested by its officers for the success of the expedition and of their friendly courtesies to myself, I called it Artillery Lake."

In 1855 John McLeod's original Fort Reliance was rebuilt on a smaller scale by HBC chief trader James Lockhart to support the James Anderson

Expedition, which was organized to search for traces of the final Franklin Expedition. Lockhart's contribution was then commemorated in the name of the cataract-studded river that empties into McLeod Bay and in Lockhart Lake, some 130 miles to the northwest of Reliance.

Pike's Portage, which circumvents the cascades of the Lockhart, is a few miles east of that river's mouth, its name commemorating the travels of Warburton Pike. In earlier times the start of this portage was marked by a lobstick with the names of Pike and his guide, James Mackinlay, cut into it. (A lobstick—originally "lopped stick"—was a spruce or pine tree with all of the branches trimmed from its trunk except a few near the top.) Pike, whose name is also preserved in Warburton Bay at the west end of McKay Lake, used Reliance as a base while he collected information for his now long-out-of-print classic, *Through the Sub-Arctic Forest*. Pike was followed in 1907 by writer/naturalist Ernest Thompson Seton who continued as far as Aylmer Lake to research caribou and musk-ox for his book, *The Arctic Prairies*. In more recent times, John Hornby and his two young companions, Edgar Christian and Harold Adlard, struggled over Pike's Portage on their last fateful journey. Although by the time Pike, Seton and Hornby passed this way, the buildings of the second Fort Reliance had fallen into decay, the stone chimneys and fireplaces constructed by John McLeod's workers were still standing, and they were again put to use with new log buildings erected around them at the turn of the century.

John Stark, a more recent northern wanderer, fought his way up the cascades of the Lockhart, unaware of the existence of the portage route. (His name will be recognized by those who have read R.M. Patterson's tale of the Nahanni, *Dangerous River*.) In his later years Stark and his trapline partner, Gus de Steffaney, established a permanent camp on the headwaters of the Coppermine near a lake now known as DeSteffaney Lake. From here they ran their winter traplines out into the Barrens. Each spring an aircraft would fly one of them out with their winter's fur catch while the other remained in camp to care for the dogs and lay in a winter's supply of caribou meat. Stark, in particular, enjoyed these lonely summers in camp, but one autumn when de Steffaney returned, Stark was absent, leaving no clue to the trail he had taken. The north that had claimed his soul had now claimed his body.

Jack Stark and his trapline partner established a permanent camp at the headwaters of the Coppermine River. Here Stark (on the right) clutches a bottle of rum just brought for him by pilot Bill Spence (on the left). September 1932.

Bellancas made up the bulk of the RCAF's photographic survey fleet in the 1930s. This photo was taken at Lindsley Bay, Great Bear Lake, in the summer of 1932.

one RCMP constable and one Native special constable. Fortunately, a number of new buildings had been erected in support of this detachment, and these now provided accommodation for the RCAF's No. 8 GP Photo Squadron. That summer their photographic flights were normally carried out by two aircraft flying parallel courses that slightly overlapped one another, the map-makers having specified that the lateral overlap between flight strips should be 40 percent and the photos in each strip should overlap by 60 percent. Since their aircraft were not equipped with two-way radio communication systems, the use of two in tandem also provided a safeguard; if a mechanical problem was experienced on one aircraft, assistance was near at hand.

By early August 1936 No. 8 GP Photo Squadron's summer mapping project was approaching a successful conclusion. All that remained was a small block off to the north-northeast, and because of the distance from Reliance to the area to be mapped—nearly 300 miles—it was decided to set up a temporary camp at nearby Hunger Lake. Much time and fuel could be saved, and since near-cloudless conditions are necessary for mapping photography, it would also allow them to make better use of the mornings before the normal daily cloud buildup. Two photo aircraft and crews were assigned to this mission, Bellancas 604 and 610, which left Reliance on August 7 to establish the base camp. Completion of the job was expected to require only a few days.

Outbound from Reliance to Hunger Lake they would have followed Artillery and Clinton-Colden lakes and then carried on a further 25-odd miles to Healey Lake. If the weather was good, there would have been little need for them to refer to McBurney's strip map until they left Healey Lake. Steering a course about 70 degrees true for a further 80 miles would bring them to Hunger Lake which lies at about 104 degrees 15 minutes longitude and 64 degrees 45 minutes latitude. But the country between Healey and Hunger Lakes is a rather featureless area of the Barrens with no outstanding landmarks. I would guess that very close attention had to be paid to both direction and elapsed time in this last hour of the flight, especially under conditions of questionable visibility. The same degree of caution would be required when southbound again until Healey Lake was reached. Then south of Healey there are large and prominent lakes, distinctive landmarks in clear weather though much less so under low cloud cover. Fortunately, their strip map would have provided additional guidance. If the weather was down, however, and visibility was restricted by cloud and rain squalls, this southbound route had the potential for trouble, especially if one held a bit to the north of the normal course. The strip map corridor was narrow, and if it was overflown, the aircraft would soon be in the area of large lakes sprawling in all directions. In clear weather, flying at altitude, these could be easily identified. In poor weather at low altitude, map-reading would be required—and there were no maps!

About this time, the Reliance group was advised that one of their Fairchilds was needed in Manitoba and should be released as soon as possible. As the Reliance program was well ahead of schedule, it was decided that Fairchild 644 and its crew of Flt. Lt. Sheldon W. Coleman and crewman Joe Fortey could be released. Delighted with this turn of events, the men said farewell to their companions of the summer and left Reliance on August 12, pleased that their summer's work was now behind them and looking forward to reunions with families and friends.

On this same date Bellanca 605 departed for Hunger Lake to deliver food supplies and replacement film to the photo unit, though it was just possible that the Hunger Lake crew had already completed their mission and that the 605 crew might be able to assist them in breaking camp. All

three aircraft could then return to Reliance in a triumphant echelon to "shoot up" the base in celebration of the completion of their summer assignment. As the supply aircraft approached Hunger Lake they saw, as expected, two tents erected on adjoining patches of level ground, but to their surprise there was only a single aircraft nearby—and mapping was *always* done with two aircraft in tandem. As they circled to land, there

On August 12, 1936, RCAF pilot Flt.Lt. Sheldon W. Coleman and crewman Joe Fortey left Fort Reliance to return to Winnipeg in RCAF Fairchild 71 #644. When they overnighted at McMurray, they received a message to return to Reliance to aid in the search for missing Bellanca.

were no signs of life ashore. With growing concern they taxied in, hastily moored their aircraft, and proceeded to the silent and obviously deserted tents. The flaps of both were tied, their friends' last acts before departure. But departure for where? A quick check disclosed that all four men's sleeping bags and personal kit bags were missing, but there was no note of explanation. It was apparent that the four had left Hunger Lake in Bellanca

610, but why did they leave 604 behind? A check of 604's tanks showed plenty of fuel, and everything else appeared to be in order. Then a thought occurred: perhaps 604 had experienced an engine failure. Starting her engine, they were provided with a partial answer to the puzzle. The engine immediately began to backfire violently, emitting clouds of blue smoke from the exhaust, and they shut it down. Expressions of concern now gave way to ones of alarm. Their comrades had all boarded Bellanca 610—no doubt with the intent of returning to Reliance—but had never arrived. Their concerns would have multiplied had they noticed that the two aircraft emergency ration kits were still on board aircraft 604, which meant that the four men had only half rations for one week.

As the crew of Bellanca 605 refuelled their aircraft in preparation for the return flight, they encouraged themselves with the thought that 604's engine failure might have occurred on that same day, and their comrades might already be in Reliance picking up another engine. They might even have passed en route without seeing one another. And even if 610 was down along the standard route between Hunger Lake and Reliance, they might not have spotted it on their outbound flight as aircraft moored to shorelines are not always easy to spot, even when being searched for. They could easily have overflown it.

They maintained a careful watch on the nearly three-hour flight back to Reliance but had no success, and their final faint hope was dashed as they made a quick count of the aircraft moored along the shore. As their return was about at the expected time, only a couple of members of the party were at the lakeshore to assist them with mooring the aircraft. The CO of the detachment, Flt. Lt. Larry Wray, was engaged in conversation with Eric Fry in the little building that served as his office and map-plotting room. On its walls were such maps as were available of the area overlaid with copies of the strip maps with the intervening spaces marked out by flight lines indicating areas already photographed. Their conversation was interrupted by hasty footsteps, a quick knock, and the door swinging abruptly open. The pilot of aircraft 605 stood in the doorway. Quickly he outlined the emergency, finishing with, "And there was nothing to indicate the date they left."

"Which route did you follow," queried Wray, "going in and on the return?"

"The standard route both ways," was the reply. "As we had no reason to be searching on the way in, we could have flown over without seeing them, so we followed the same route on the way back, searching all the way, but saw nothing."

"They could be down five days by now," observed Wray. "We'll have to get Coleman back immediately—I hope he only got as far as McMurray today. In the meantime, we'll have to refuel all of the aircraft for an early start in the morning. And Eric, I'll need your help mapping out a search plan and preparing extra copies so that each crew will have a plot to follow." Wray then turned to the station's little battery-powered transceiver, and after establishing contact with the RCCS station at Fort Rae, he sent a message to be delivered to Flt. Lt. Coleman at McMurray.

As it happened, Coleman and Fortey had overnighted at McMurray and were preparing for departure the following morning when the fateful message was delivered to them. With a potential homecoming so nearly in their grasp, it must have been with mixed feelings that they again turned north.

Early the next morning Bellancas 607 and 608 flew north, Bellanca 605 now being held in reserve because of its high engine hours. They followed the strip map as far as Healey Lake, and then, with the aircraft flying within sight of one another eight miles apart, they started their systematic search along the parallel lines that had been laid down by Eric Fry on the previous evening. These lines used the strip map as a base and initially extended as far as Hunger Lake. Fairchild 629 also flew two lines, but farther to the south, and carried a load of spare fuel in ten-gallon kegs. These they deposited at a previously designated location on the strip map where the Bellancas would return for refuelling. The Fairchild then returned to Reliance for another fuel load, following new routes both inbound and outbound in order to make full use of both time and fuel. It was a weary and discouraged group who returned to Reliance on the evening of August 13, but they were somewhat heartened by the arrival of Coleman and Fortey in Fairchild 644. They would have an additional search and supply aircraft for the following day and two pairs of fresh eyes.

From information that I have been able to piece together, I have learned the missing group was located sometime the following day, August 14, on "610 Lake." I do not have any details, nor did I ever learn the location of 610 Lake, but I do know that a message was sent to HQ that night stating briefly, 4 MEN OK THOUGH FOOD EXHAUSTED.

The Reliance group now had two engine changes ahead of them. Bush engine changes always present something of a challenge, though slightly less at places where bush actually exists. Hunger Lake, however, well out in the Barrens and beyond the treeline, did not qualify in this respect. Resourcefulness and ingenuity were, therefore, the crew's key requirements, supported by manual labour in abundance. Equipment-wise, the principal ingredient was for three sturdy poles to form a tripod over the engine and hold the chain block to be used to remove and install the engines. Being fully aware of the absence of tripod timber out on the Barrens, the air force chaps had wisely provided themselves with a couple of portable tripods made of steel pipe. The platform that would be needed across the nose of the floats to provide a workstand during the changes would also be used as a gangplank during the loading of the new engine into the transport aircraft at Reliance and the subsequent unloading and reloading operation at Hunger Lake. All of the timber required for these labour-intensive operations would have been cut and prepared at Reliance, with the shorter pieces carried in the cabin and the longer pieces lashed to the floats as deck load along with the tripod sections.

Aircraft 610 being nearest, they apparently concentrated on this job first. With that engine change completed, they had another serviceable aircraft on hand. Then on August 15, Coleman and Fortey departed for Hunger Lake in 644 with an engine, crew and the necessary equipment to carry out the 604 engine change and bring the aircraft back to base. By the morning of August 17 the old engine had been removed and loaded into 644 together with a full load of empty ten-gallon fuel kegs, and around noon of that day 644 and crew departed from Hunger Lake, leaving the other crew to finish the job on 604 and fly it out.

When on August 21 neither Fairchild 644 or the disabled Bellanca 604 had returned to Reliance, F/L Wray dispatched a flight to Hunger Lake to check on their progress. And that was when they learned that 644 had left five days earlier and that its crew had left their rifle and one of their two ration kits behind because the engine change crew were running short of supplies. HQ in Winnipeg and Ottawa were advised immediately that 644 was either down with mechanical problems or lost and that the base at Reliance was extremely short of fuel, due to the amount consumed in the search for aircraft 610.

Extra fuel was ordered for boat delivery from Fort Smith, and arrangements were made for immediate airlifting of more fuel from an RCAF cache at Camsell Portage on Lake Athabasca. Stan McMillan and Bob Hodgins of Mackenzie Air Service carried out this airlift with their Bellanca Aircruiser AWR, but to permit an immediate start on this latest search it was necessary to utilize the remaining RCAF Fairchild, 629, to ferry fuel from Yellowknife, a distance of about 200 miles. With all Bellancas now serviceable the search was carried on from daylight to dark. First they concentrated on the route between Hunger Lake and Reliance. Then they covered the area west of Artillery Lake as far as the Yellowknife basin. Other aircraft carried out a patrol, covering the boundary of the largest area that Coleman might have flown into, to the south, then to the west, and finally to the north again into the Yellowknife Basin. All this was based on an estimate of the amount of fuel that Coleman had on board at the time of departure from Hunger Lake. The problem was that no one knew exactly how much fuel Coleman might have had, though even with only full wing tanks he would have had a range of over 400 miles.

Within days it was apparent that the long hours were taking their toll on the members of the group. First there had been the two-day search for aircraft 610, followed by the urgent requirements of the two engine changes, then the new daylight-to-dark search. On top of this were the demands placed upon the crews after their return to base. "Further," Wray later wrote, "refuelling, servicing, base duties, cooking and messing were being carried out by the same personnel. Coupled with the anxiety and nervous strain, sufficient rest was not being obtained. Because of the constant and extreme stress under which all personnel were operating it has become necessary to ground some of the search personnel because of extreme fatigue."

Another problem was the lack of suitable clothing. All air force personnel were still dressed in summer-issue garments and suffered increasingly from cold and exposure as the first of the autumn storms swept down from the Barrens. It also became obvious that additional observers were needed to aid in the search. Ideally there should have been a minimum of two per aircraft to permit the pilot to concentrate on his map-reading and keep in touch with the other aircraft of their flight. The RCMP responded to this need by moving three constables from other posts in the area to Reliance, and this five-man force worked alongside RCAF personnel, aiding them in every way possible, including long hours spent as observers.

On August 25 RCAF Fairchild #629, taking off from Yellowknife with a full load of fuel for the aircraft searching for the lost Bellanca #610, struck a huge wave which bent the right float up at a steep angle.

Flt. Lt. Larry Wray, meanwhile, besides planning and directing the search activities, was also taking direct part in the daily searches. Then during the evenings, in conjunction with Eric Fry, he updated search records and made plans for the following day. In addition, he had to plan for a continued supply of fuel and tend to message-handling duties. This latter duty was particularly time-consuming. All messages to RCAF HQ in Winnipeg and/or Ottawa went out in CW (Morse code) from Reliance's small, battery-powered transceiver to the RCCS station at Rae and were relayed from there to Smith, to McMurray, to Edmonton, then transferred by telegraph to Winnipeg, and finally to AFHQ in Ottawa, each message being handled a half-dozen times. As the days passed and no good news arrived from Reliance, air force headquarters in both Winnipeg and Ottawa became increasingly concerned over the gravity of the situation, the logistical problems, and the lateness of the season, and plans were made to supply reinforcements. In the meantime another impending shortage of fuel required further air ferrying of fuel from Yellowknife, and Fairchild 629 was sent on this mission, reducing the size of the search fleet by one. It was a mishap on one of 629's ferry flights that brought Matt Berry and myself into the picture.

On the morning of August 25 when F/O Blanchard in 629 took off from Yellowknife Bay with a full load of fuel, he started his takeoff run toward the southwest in the direction of the open lake. Acceleration was slow because of the load, but the Fairchild was on the step and almost at flying speed when it struck one of the big, smooth waves that roll in from Great Slave Lake. The impact threw the aircraft into the air. Fortunately it remained airborne, but the wave had struck at a slight angle from the right side, with the result that the right-hand float had been bent upwards at a steep angle from a point just forward of the spreader bar. Blanchard must have had a difficult return flight with a full load of fuel on board and numerous square feet of float bottom exposed to the slipstream.

Three days later, on August 28, 1936, a lone aircraft—the Canadian Airways Junker W.34 registered as CF-ARI—droned its way south over the Athabasca. The river valley was bathed in the warm sunshine of late summer. The water was clear, though stained with brown residue from the discharge of countless tributaries, the small and placid streams that drain this muskeg-covered land. A few red and amber leaves from the balsam-poplar were already afloat, signalling the approach of autumn. The water level was dropping, and the exposed sand bars glowed gold in the mellow light. A chorus of strange and plaintive calls could be faintly heard—the migrating calls of the sandhill cranes, the first of the seasonal birds to make their way south, their ragged, high-flying formations barely visible against the hazy blue sky.

CF-ARI was carrying a load of mail in the striped canvas bags that were then favoured by the Postal Department, and these provided seats for four passengers. The crew of the aircraft were pilot Matt Berry and engineer Frank Kelly, two of the best in the business. Frank leaned across the cockpit to comment, "Seems odd the air force would need two floats, Matt."

"I wondered the same thing," Matt said. "The aircraft's waiting for them in Reliance, but the order came from air force headquarters to our Edmonton office. There was no explanation, but I'm guessing they're for one of the aircraft searching for Coleman and Fortey."

"There's clear water in all of those lakes and rivers in the Reliance area," Frank mused. "You can see the bottom through ten feet of water so I can't see how they could have run onto rocks. Of course, they might have been moored on a rocky shoreline and got caught in a blow. Do you intend going through to pick them up in Edmonton tonight?"

"I'm planning on it," came the reply. "The days are starting to shorten up a bit but I should still have time to make Cooking Lake before dark. If they can load the floats tonight, I can make an early start in the morning, and I should be in Reliance by tomorrow night."

A few moments later there was a tremendous clatter from the engine. "Shut her down, Matt," Frank shouted. "That sounds like a broken connecting rod!" Matt pointed the nose down and to the right where the Athabasca River waited for them.

Downstream from Point Brule, in an eddy below a river bend, the occupant of a Chipewyan skiff was engaged in a practice that has been followed by river-dwellers in these parts for countless generations, setting his net in preparation for the beginning of the whitefish spawning run, a food source for man and dog for centuries. This was old Pete Peterson, years and miles removed from his native Denmark, a land he would never see again. This was the life that he loved—trapping in winter, hunting muskrats in spring, cutting cordwood for the sternwheel steamers in summer, drying fish and hunting moose in autumn, picking berries in season. Pete, with his Native wife and his covey of youngsters, was a contented man. He lived off the land, helped his neighbours, extended hospitality to all travellers, and paid his debts. Humanity produces no better specimen than Pete. On this warm day of late summer, as he finished setting his nets, he looked up at the sound of a southbound aircraft, but as he watched, the sound suddenly died away, and the aircraft commenced a long glide toward his section of the river.

Meanwhile, the SS *Athabasca River*, one of the sternwheelers operated by the Transport Division of the Hudson's Bay Company, puffed her way placidly upstream, pushing a 200-ton barge with another 100-ton barge lashed to its left side. Because of the crooked channels and numerous sandbars along the river and the need for abrupt course changes, all barges were pushed rather than towed. And because of low water periods, especially in the fall, most cargo was carried on these shallow-draft barges rather than as deck load on the boat. The passenger deck, once thronged with travellers, was nearly empty. Most of the people who had once travelled on these boats for weeks—sometimes for months—to reach their destinations, now travelled by air. Staff rotations in the ranks of the HBC and the RCMP, the two most visible organizations in the north, were now accomplished in a matter of days, and the sternwheelers were increasingly relegated to

Canadian Airways Junkers CF-ARI secured astern of a barge pushed by the sternwheeler *Athabasca River* as it heads upstream to Fort McMurray. August 28, 1936. Matt Berry stands on the deck of the barge enjoying the view.

the transport of cargo. But already the end of this service was in sight; these fine old steamers, the last of their species to be used in the north, would soon be replaced by diesel tugs.

Down at deck level the chief engineer, John Sutherland, leaned on the lower half of the dutch door on the port side of the engine room. Coffee cup in hand, he was enjoying the warm morning sunshine. Apprenticed to the mechanical trades at Caithness in his native Scotland, John had joined the HBC in 1883 at the age of 21 and had spent a long lifetime in the service of the company. Up in the pilot house the captain, Harvey Alexander, lounged in his round-backed chair, swatting at an occasional horsefly and rifling the odd round of tobacco juice at the brass spittoon in the corner. At the wheel nearby stood another veteran in the company's service, pilot Alex Linklater. A son of the north and a riverman all his life, he had been known as Big Alex in his youth, but now with the slow advance of the years he had become Old Alex. Though a big man still, his back was rounded from the punishment of the track line and the portage in his youth when he had run the scows down through the miles of rapids above McMurray.

As the boat proceeded upstream to the steady urging of the big paddle wheel, the conversation in the pilot house was concerned only with subjects that were of importance to their small and peaceful world—whether the water level was lower than the previous year, the possibility of an early freeze-up, and when the whitefish run would start. Suddenly Alex pointed upriver and called, "Cap! Look! Airplane!" and they watched as ARI landed in the river close to Peterson's cabin.

Matt landed ARI without difficulty and turned toward shore with the last of his landing speed. Frank supplied the motive power for the last several yards with one of the canoe paddles that were stowed for emergency uses on each float. They were only a short distance below Pete's cabin, and within a few moments Pete pulled in beside them and shut off the motor of his skiff. While Frank was securing the aircraft, Matt opened the cabin door to reassure his rather startled passengers. "We've had an engine failure, gentlemen, so you may as well get out and stretch your legs. This was all well planned, though," he added with a grin. "We've arranged for the sternwheeler to pick us up—she'll be along in just a few minutes."

The steamer pulled in to shore just upstream from the aircraft. Assisted by Pete and his skiff and with considerable shouting and hand-waving, ARI was secured beside the bow of the boat immediately astern of the smaller barge. Then just before they departed, a white-clad figure emerged from the bow of the boat and ran to the front of the barge. It was the tall and affable Asian cook, Charlie, with a fresh-baked pie for Pete. Being a fish lover, Charlie was making an advance payment on the first netful of the season's whitefish.

It was noon by then and Matt, Frank and the rather delighted passengers were treated to the finest lunch that the HBC had to offer. The trip to McMurray was pleasant and uneventful and late in the evening they arrived at the Snye where the Junkers was cast adrift and paddled ashore. Some little time later, Matt and Frank sat in the living room of our slightly incredulous chief mechanic, Don Goodwin, recounting their adventures and making plans for an engine change on the following day.

First thing the next morning, August 29, ARI was pulled from the water and removal of the faulty engine was soon underway. Blessed by fine summer weather, unhampered by mud, rain or mosquitoes, and with a substantial crew of expert engineers on the job, the failed engine was quickly removed and lowered to the ground. At the same time two of the engineers had opened the box containing the spare engine, removed the bolts, and attached a sling in readiness for the installation. At that moment Don, who had just stepped over for a routine inspection of the new engine, called out, "We've got a problem. This engine isn't an SC-1. It's an old Model B Wasp."

There was a chorus of disbelieving comments—suitably embellished with profanity— but there was no doubt about it. The identification tag on the box stated that it was an SC-1, and there had been no reason before this to open the box to check the contents. But such a mistake was easily possible. Both these early Wasp engines were of the same 1,340-cubic-inch displacement, and all of them—the Bs, the Cs and the SC-1s—were nearly identical in appearance. The only outward clues were the cooling fins on the cylinder heads. On the older Model Bs these were horizontal. On the Model C and its derivative, the SC-1, the cooling fins were more numerous and vertical—that is, perpendicular to the cylinder head—and to differentiate between them, each of the induction pipes on the SC-1 was stamped with a small rectangle of yellow paint. What Don had spotted were the horizontal cooling fins of the Model B and the lack of yellow paint. The problem now was horsepower. The SC-1, the standard power plant for the Junkers, was rated at 450 hp, this being achieved by use of a 10-to-1 supercharger drive ratio. The horsepower of the B Wasp, because of its marginal cylinder head cooling and its 8-to-1 drive ratio, was only 420 hp.

A somewhat agitated discussion now took place among Casey, Dick, Bill and Frank. Various suggestions were made as to the best course of action, but after a few moments this clamour died away and everyone turned to Don who had not expressed an opinion. "Getting a replacement engine from Winnipeg might take a week or more, and that's if we made the right train connections. This old B Wasp will give us more than the Junkers had originally, so let's go ahead with it." There was no disagreement with this logic. Someone said, "You're right, Don," and with that the work proceeded at top speed.

While this was going on, out beyond the timber line on the edge of the Barren Lands, the first blizzard of winter had already dusted the hilltops with snow, and the smaller ponds were covered by a thin film of ice. Moored to the rocky shoreline of a small lake sat a yellow, float-equipped aircraft with RCAF markings. A small tent was pitched on the hillside beside it. Within it sat two men, Coleman and Fortey, clad in their lightweight summer uniforms. They had made a trip on their first day to the only timber in the area for firewood and poles for their tent. After their return, Fortey had realized that the bow struts—the eight-foot-long aluminum alloy tubes that were fastened between the float fitting and the wing root—could be removed from the aircraft and used for two of the tent poles, thus conserving their firewood supply. Now, after 12 days, their fuel supply was exhausted, little food remained, and they waited and hoped that rescuers would find them before winter closed the Barrens to float flying.

12 Search on the Barren Lands

That summer I was flying with Con Farrell in our Fairchild 82, CF-AXE, but at the time the events of the last chapter were unfolding, I had been just completing my annual vacation in the Edmonton area. When I checked at CAL's Edmonton district office in search of a flight back to McMurray, Wop May, our district superintendent, advised me of the status of the Coleman/Fortey search and the RCAF's float requirements, then told me to go out to Cooking Lake to load the floats onto Matt's Junkers and return north with it.

Cooking Lake, about 20 miles to the southeast, was—and perhaps still is—the seaplane base for aircraft operating in and out of Edmonton as it was the closest sizeable lake. It had been used by float-equipped and amphibious aircraft ever since Jack Caldwell and Pete Vachon had landed their Vickers Viking, G-CAEB, there in September 1926, and during the 1930s it was every bit as important as Edmonton's municipal airport. Aircraft would be ferried from the municipal airport on wheels, towed to the crane at the waterfront, and there changed to floats for summer operation, a procedure that was reversed in the fall.

I was on hand at Cooking Lake when the Junkers arrived the next morning. I didn't expect an engineer to be on board, knowing that we were slightly short-handed at the time, so I was agreeably surprised to see Dick Leigh open the cockpit hatch and step onto the stub-wing. He was still waiting to write his air engineer's exams, but Don had been able to arrange a few days' work for him. I could well remember how much I had appreciated the occasions when Don had been able to place me on the payroll. In such cases we were designated as crewmen rather than engineers, and the daily airworthiness signature in the log books would be applied by the pilot. I was happy to see Dick, but on this occasion our greetings were brief. Matt was already a day late, and as we both knew the urgency, we started immediately on the float-loading project.

During the bush flying activities of the '30s, and especially after mining exploration started, our aircraft were expected to carry anything that our customers proffered. If it was too large or too bulky to fit into the cabin, it was carried on the outside, tied to the undercarriage or the floats, under or on top of the fuselage or, in the case of our low-winged Junkers, under the wings. Securing and lashing down these external loads was one of the standard duties of the engineers.

Surveying the floats, Dick and I judged them to be only slightly larger and heavier than many of the canoes we had hauled. Their weight would not be a problem, we concluded, especially as there would not be a cabin load. Because of their regular shape and flat decks we decided that they could be most easily secured if carried in the inverted position. We arranged three planks (two-by-twelves, as I recall) across the top of the Junkers' Edo floats. The Fairchild floats were rather slippery rascals, as they were curved and tapered in every direction, so we placed them on top of the planks and secured them with large quantities of half-inch manila rope tightened with numerous "chokers." Just as we finished, we heard someone ask, "Aren't you guys finished yet? You've been at it for hours!" It was Matt, of course, with a wide grin on his craggy face. He had been up at the lodge for a snack and a visit with the Robertsons. Neville Robertson, who had been in the RAF in WWI, was the seaplane base manager, and his wife, who was generally known as Mrs. Robbie, presided over the kitchen and dining room with a stern eye and firm hand. Knowing of our problem loading the floats, she had sent Matt down with lunches for Dick and me in order to expedite our departure.

While Dick carried out the refuelling, I checked the engine oil quantity. Then I removed a cowling from each side for a quick check of the newly installed engine. This would normally have been carried out at McMurray after the test flight, but with time-saving in mind Matt and Don had agreed that the trip to Cooking Lake would serve as the test flight, though a rather

Dick Leigh and the author lash down two replacement floats for the RCAF's Fairchild #629, placing them in the inverted position on top of the Edo floats of Canadian Airways Junkers CF-ARI. Edmonton, August 1936.

long one. My inspection was a double-check on the safety locking of the engine controls and the security of the fuel and oil line connections. But everything was sound. The McMurray boys had done a good job.

With the refuelling complete, we climbed aboard, Dick in the cabin and I in the right-hand cockpit seat. As I had spent the better part of two years flying with Matt, we were happy to be together again, even for this short flight. Following a brief engine warm-up, Matt looked over, grinned, and said, "Well, here we go." He opened the throttle and we started down the lake, fully expecting to have a normal Junkers' response—up on the step and quickly airborne. But it didn't happen. We were doing nothing except stir up mud and weeds, burn up lots of fuel, and elevate the head temperatures of our poor engine. We were still ploughing water with no indication that we might get on the step, when I saw that the cylinder head temperature had passed the 500°F mark, and I tapped it to bring it to Matt's attention. He cut the throttle and we drifted awhile to let the motor cool off. Cooking Lake with its 2,500-foot altitude has always been known as a difficult takeoff spot, and our conditions—a warm and windless day in late August—were doing nothing to improve our chances, but we were still puzzled.

"I can't believe that she wouldn't come up on the step," Matt observed. "Of course, we're down a bit in horsepower and there's absolutely no wind, but we have no load to speak of. We'll give it another try and if we don't make it, we'll cool her down again and try in the other direction."

Our second attempt was no more successful than the first. Once again we had to heave-to until our Wasp had cooled her fevered brow. We were now beginning to suspect the truth of the matter—that the negative pressure on the inverted floats was the source of our trouble. We made one more takeoff attempt—admittedly a rather half-hearted one—this time toward the west and then called it a day.

After dinner, Dick and I returned to the dock and commenced re-positioning our troublesome floats. As our planks were already in place, it was merely a matter of turning and re-tying the floats, which became increasingly heavy as the evening wore on. Balanced on their keels they were now somewhat unstable laterally and none too secure in a longitudinal direction. If we'd had time, daylight, and better facilities, the application of wooden blocks, strategically placed, would have corrected all of those problems. Having none of these but having plenty of rope, we finally completed the job and returned to the lodge to Mrs. Robbie's welcome teapot and sandwiches.

Matt had already returned from his home in Edmonton when Dick and I finished breakfast at 8:00 and together we returned to the dock. We had been hoping for a slight drop in temperature and perhaps a capful of wind, but we were disappointed in both cases. We carried out a joint inspection of our evening's work and found that some of the lashings, applied by flashlight and by feel, didn't look that great in the light of day. As we had no desire to have either or both of our floats become airborne without benefit of our professional guidance, we spent a further half-hour correcting the problem. After the usual warm-up we were soon at full throttle down the lake, scattering the mudhens before us. As we held a southeast course to the far end of the lake, the aircraft had a different feel to it and this was encouraging. She would appear to rise in the water and seemed to be on the point of climbing onto the step, but finally high cylinder temperatures forced us to call a halt. Obviously, what we lacked was that extra 30 hp that an SC 1 would have given us, together with the slightly cooler cylinder heads on the C Wasps. There is no doubt that the inadequate cylinder head cooling and high piston temperatures were combining to rob the engine of power. Even the rated 420 hp just wasn't there. We made three more attempts, two to the west and one more to the east. By then outside air temperatures were climbing with still no hint of wind. There was, very obviously, not the slightest hope of a takeoff. We returned to the dock to wait until late afternoon, slightly cooler temperatures, and perhaps that elusive breeze.

It was time to give some thought to our fuel supply. Originally we had loaded enough fuel for McMurray plus a small reserve, perhaps a total of 80 or 90 gallons. Like most aircraft of that era, the Junkers aircraft were not provided with an accurate fuel gauge system, and we usually worked with a combination of estimated reserves plus a fairly accurate estimate of the fuel added. After our numerous full-throttle cruises down the lake, we were doubtful that we had enough fuel left to make McMurray, but as ARI had shown no eagerness to become airborne with her present load, we were certainly not about to add to it with more fuel. We kicked this around a bit, and Matt finally came to a decision. "She was so close to coming onto the step a couple of times that I'm sure we'll make it next time. It will be a bit cooler, and we've less fuel on board. If we can get her off, then we'll go into La Biche for fuel. [Lac la Biche, a small settlement at the east end of a large lake of the same name, is about 100 miles north of Edmonton.] There's always a breeze on that big lake and we'll have no trouble getting off there."

We retired to the lodge for a late lunch, after which Dick and I returned to the aircraft and tightened up some of the float lashings. In search of anything that might give us an advantage, we checked all of the compartments of ARI's Edo floats, even though we knew these were in excellent condition and virtually leak-proof. We did have the satisfaction of removing perhaps three gallons of water, an amount that we would have scorned under normal circumstances but we were thinking about the 30 pounds that it represented. By late afternoon the sky had become overcast and slightly cooler, with a hint of rain clouds to the northeast. Everything looked promising as we cranked up the engine again and cast off from the dock. After the usual warm-up Matt grinned. "We'll make her this time," he said and with that he applied full power.

In spite of our optimism and the hint of breeze, we only dragged along in much the same manner as before while the head temperatures steadily advanced. Then finally the aircraft climbed onto the step. Our speed began to increase, though ever so slowly, as we rapidly consumed the available lake surface. By this time the head temperature was approaching the pin at 600°F. The end of the lake, complete with the old railroad station, was fast approaching when at last ARI commenced a slow and reluctant climb, and we skimmed over the trees at the lake end with only yards to spare. Across country we went, over the farm yards, scattering livestock and farmer's poultry, and creating general havoc. We were still at full throttle with the head temperature gauge now solidly against the pin at the 600°F mark. I couldn't believe that the Wasp would continue to operate under such conditions and expected her to shed a cylinder head momentarily or burn a piston through. But gradually we picked up a bit of altitude and levelled out at perhaps 200 feet. Matt reduced power slightly—very slightly, as our airspeed was only about 75 mph. Fortunately, the terrain below us was flat with plenty of farmer's fields, and a forced landing was possible, although not necessarily right side up. From the time we began our takeoff until the head temperatures started to scale back must have been close to a half-hour, although one tends to lose track of time during situations like this. There had been no words spoken up to this point but at last Matt turned, and with a quick half-grin, exclaimed, "I wouldn't want to do that every day!"

There were no connecting doors between the cabin and the cockpit on any of our Junkers aircraft. Dick would have had only limited visibility through the cabin side windows and must have spent a fairly tense half-hour watching the terrain fly by at low level, wondering how long we might remain airborne. I do not recall Dick's comments when we discussed the takeoff later that evening, but I do remember thinking I was glad to be up front enjoying the luxury of a seat belt.

The weather was overcast though still quite flyable. Our short flight to La Biche was without incident. The town is located at the east end of the lake and was the centre in those days for a sizeable commercial fishing enterprise. For this reason it was provided with a substantial wooden dock where we could tie up. There were, however, no dockside fuelling facilities as the town was not a frequent aviation port of call, it being right on the Northern Alberta Railway line leading to McMurray and also well provided with roads.

It was some time before we were able to contact the local fuel agent and replenish our tanks. It was still only early evening and the visibility was fair, but Matt said, "I think I've had enough flying for today. I'll get the fuel agent to give me a ride to the railroad station in his truck, and I'll send telegrams to McMurray and Edmonton to let them know that we're not down in the raspberries."

Our float customers, the RCAF, were also advised, probably from our Edmonton office. It was interesting to learn many years later that this information had somehow been mishandled by the rather laborious communications systems of the day. After passing through a number of offices in the chain of command, the message received at Air Force headquarters in Ottawa stated: CANADIAN AIRWAYS AIRCRAFT FLYING FLOATS FOR AIRCRAFT #629 FROM EDMONTON TO WATERWAYS FORCE LANDED 40 MILES SOUTH OF MCMURRAY STOP UNABLE COMPLETE TRIP UNTIL TUESDAY SEPTEMBER 1.

The next day the weather was fine with a light breeze from the west and a slightly rumpled lake surface, both factors in our favour. Our takeoff was a bit slow but there was no real difficulty, and after a slow climb, Matt turned to the right to follow the valley of the Athabasca River. As Matt completed his turn, he said, "The rudder control feels odd—sort of soft and mushy. Maybe it's turbulence from the floats." It was at this point that I remembered that when we were loading the floats I had tried to gauge the area of keel surface they represented and just what percentage of it was ahead of the centre of pressure. I now realized that this matter should have received much more of our attention. Unfortunately, we were so accustomed to carrying such a variety of external loads (though nothing this large) that caution and judgement were at a low ebb, especially when coupled with the urgency of the float delivery. But a suspicion began to form in my head that our aerodynamic situation was badly out of balance. During the spring conversion from skis to floats, most of the bush aircraft of that period were fitted with an extra fin on the underside of the fuselage. This was mated with a longer rudder, adding nearly 100 percent to the fin area and probably 25 percent to the rudder area. Both were needed to compensate for the considerable keel area of the floats. This keel area was well ahead of the wing centre of pressure, about which the aircraft would normally pivot during a turn. Junkers aircraft, with their short, stubby fuselages, were particularly in need of this extra keel area and control surface material. My mental arithmetic told me that the additional fin/rudder area added for summer operations amounted to about 35 percent, but we had just sacrificed this by adding an extra set of floats. The 65 percent we were left with was probably the amount of effective rudder control that we had left. We were still comfortably controllable with power on, but an engine failure could have changed our situation drastically.

"Matt, do you think we should relocate those floats once we get to McMurray?"

He stared at me for a moment or two in silence, then returned his gaze to the winding valley of the Athabasca. He was obviously contemplating the pros and cons of the situation before replying. "No, I think we'll carry on. The weather is good, the temperature is cool, and there is no turbulence. McMurray's elevation is only about 1,200 feet above sea level, so our takeoff performance will be better. Also, I'll need to make only one 90-degree turn to get into the Snye and one more after takeoff. We'll have to land at Fort Smith for fuel, but we'll land and take off to the north so there won't be any turns needed. From there to Reliance it's almost a straight line." There was another pause before he added, "They need these floats at Reliance so they can get another aircraft serviceable."

I never had an opportunity to again discuss this matter with Matt, but I'm sure that in time we both realized that it wasn't much more than engine power that had kept our faithful steed aimed in the right direction. If the engine had failed, there was a strong possibility that ARI would have swapped ends, thus terminating her airborne condition. To quote from an ancient expression, "Where ignorance is bliss... ."

As we approached McMurray, Matt kept well to the west side of the river. He then made a very gradual right-hand turn toward the Snye and a normal—though slightly down-wind—landing. At this point I deplaned as I was scheduled to rejoin Con Farrell on our Fairchild 82, AXE, but I gave Dick a hand with the refuelling. While this was underway, I checked that our float lashings were still snug and needed no further attention. With Matt again in the cockpit, Dick applied his considerable muscle to the hand crank. The whine of the inertia starter increased in pitch, and the Wasp coughed into life. Dick climbed into the cockpit as we pushed the aircraft clear of the dock.

Conditions on the Snye were somewhat less than ideal. There was some

Matt Berry talks to Casey van der Linden atop Junkers CF-ARI after finally arriving at McMurray with the Fairchild floats, this time lashed aboard right-side-up.

shallow water with a rocky bottom at its west end, which was normally not a problem because the aircraft would be on the step by that time. Today it was a source of concern for our under-powered Junkers with its bulky load. There were a couple of favourable factors, however: the temperature was down and there was a light west wind. Matt taxied eastward and around the bend into the Clearwater, then turned and applied full power. ARI was moving briskly when she came into sight again. Shortly after passing the floating docks where we stood, she was on the step and gaining speed. They were airborne just before reaching the Athabasca, and we watched them climbing slowly, outlined against the valley hills far to the west. Finally, a gradual turn to the right and they were gone from our sight.

While Matt, Dick and I had been striving to deliver the Fairchild floats to the RCAF at Reliance, the freighting of fuel from Camsell Portage had continued as search planes again combed the areas to the west and south of Hunger Lake, then into the Aylmer and Walmsley lakes area and west of Artillery Lake. One flight covered the water route west of Aylmer Lake to 40 miles west of McKay Lake and then south to Slave Lake. However,

Ferrying Floats with a Fairchild 82

A few years later Al Brown and Page McFee, flying a late model Fairchild 82 for Mackenzie Air Service, were called upon to ferry a pair of floats from McMurray to Yellowknife. Their 82 was powered with a 550 hp H Wasp and equipped with a constant-speed propeller. With such a modern and high-powered piece of equipment and no load except one pair of floats (and these only slightly larger than the Fairchild floats that we carried on that August day in 1936) Al and Page did not anticipate a problem. Using the same line of thought that we had first attempted at Cooking Lake, they laid planks across the 82 floats and secured their load in the inverted position. To their utter amazement the 82 refused to become airborne. They made two attempts without success, then returned to the dock, gave the floats a quarter turn, so that they were lying on their sides, and re-tied them. They were then able to take off, but with no great margin of performance. By comparison, our Junkers, with 130 less horsepower and a fixed pitch prop, had struggled into the air from Cooking Lake at an altitude 1,200 feet higher than McMurray. Those old Junkers W-34s were truly amazing aircraft!

as all flights were hampered and delayed by rain squalls and low visibility, it was difficult to be certain that all areas had been thoroughly covered.

Meanwhile, the RCCS had suggested that they could transfer their one-operative radio station from the small mining community of Outpost Island, some 30 miles north of Resolution, to Reliance for the duration of the search. This would provide the Reliance squadron with a professional operator, together with more powerful and reliable equipment. The suggestion was immediately accepted. About the same time Canadian Airways was able to divert one aircraft to the search, this being Fairchild CF-ATZ flown by Rudy Heuss with Dick Leigh as crewman, and since Rudy was unfamiliar with search routine he was assigned the task of transferring the radio equipment and the RCCS operator. In his report to HQ, Wray would later state, "Up to this time the detachment commanders had been handling all traffic in schedules with the RCCS station at Ft. Rae. The volume of traffic was becoming so heavy that several hours were spent each night in clearing this

Stan McMillan in the cockpit of Mackenzie Air Service's Bellanca Aircruiser CF-AWR.

Mackenzie Air Service's Bellanca Aircruiser CF-AWR.

Point Lake Noted For "Boisterous Weather"

Samuel Hearne, returning from his epic journey to the mouth of the Coppermine 165 years earlier, made some pointed observations on the subject of the weather he experienced at this same time of year and at nearly the same place Coleman and Fortey awaited rescue. "On the 3rd of September [1771]," he wrote, "we were at a small river belonging to Point Lake but the weather at this time proved so boisterous, and there was so much rain, snow and frost alternately, that we were obliged to wait several days before we could cross in our canoes."

and great difficulty was being experienced in obtaining reliable inter-communication. Consequently the addition of the RCCS operator with more reliable equipment relieved the communication problem and assisted tremendously in the administration of the operation."

Two other new developments also raised the searchers' spirits. A chartered boat-load of fuel arrived from Resolution, and pilot Stan McMillan appeared in Mackenzie Air Service's Bellanca Aircruiser with another load of fuel from Camsell Portage. Together they established an adequate supply of gasoline for the first time in the search. But Stan also brought another welcome addition to the camp—D.B. McNeal, a cook who had been hired at Goldfields. With these reinforcements on hand the RCAF was able to set up a temporary base and tent camp at Steele Lake on the upper section of the Thelon, and aircraft were then able to search the Thelon/Hanbury River courses. They also covered the area north to the Back River and east as far as Dubawnt Lake, though their searches were constantly hampered by low ceilings and heavy rain and frequent periods of below-freezing temperatures at night. They also made an attempt to reach the Lac de Gras area but all aircraft were forced back by rain, low clouds and gale-force winds. By this time the fuel supply was again becoming critical, and Stan McMillan took advantage of a cancelled flying day to begin ferrying more fuel from Smith in his Aircruiser, while RCAF crews prepared Fairchild 629 for its float change.

By September 2 Coleman and Fortey had been lost on the Barrens for 17 days. The same weather that had made the search difficult that week—and at times impossible—had also taken its toll of the lost pair. Because of

Crewman Joe Fortey of Fairchild #644 with the stove he constructed from an empty gasoline keg.

their meagre clothing and the frequent rains they were confined to their tent for much of the time, but the time had not been wasted. The resourceful Fortey had realized that one of the small gasoline kegs from their load might be converted into a stove. Using a hammer and chisel he had cut an opening in its front and devised a set of hinges to reattach the cut-out piece as a door. Then removing a metal panel from the interior of the aircraft, he converted it into a chimney to project through the side of the tent. Now for the first time since they landed they were able to enjoy a measure of warmth within their tent and had a means of making tea and soup. Whenever there was a break in the rain storms, they made the two-mile trip to the small grove of trees that was their only source of wood.

On Thursday, September 3, Matt Berry arrived at Reliance in Junkers CF-ARI with the much-needed floats. These were unloaded immediately to allow him to proceed to Yellowknife that same evening to carry on with urgent charter work. With the weather still making it impossible to continue search activities, the Aircruiser made a return trip to Smith to take Wray to consult with Squadron Leader Stevenson, who had arrived to handle logistics from the Smith base. Another welcome addition to the search staff was W.H.B. Hoare, on loan from the National Museum's department of biology. Hoare, who had carried out the original survey of the Thelon Musk Ox Preserve in 1927 and spent many years in the Arctic and on the Barrens, had been employed that summer on game research work in the Thelon area. About the same time another Canadian Airways flight arrived from McMurray, bringing a couple of reinforcements for the search party and a Canadian Army medical officer, Major Hunter. His secondment had been requested by Wray because of his concerns for the health of the searchers as well as the knowledge that, should Coleman and Fortey be found, they would probably be suffering from freezing as well as starvation.

It was now becoming a very real possibility that the search might continue over the freeze-up period, and messages were exchanged between Grandy at Winnipeg, Slemon at Ottawa and Wray at Reliance over the logistics of continuing the search. Wray persuaded them that Reliance would be the best freeze-up base because the sheltered bay there normally froze early, but they would continue the search with float aircraft on the larger waterways even after the smaller lakes froze. On September 8 a stores officer departed from Winnipeg by train with skis and full winter equipment for all aircraft; this would be delivered to Reliance on the last boat before freeze-up. Meanwhile, Fairchild 629 with its new floats was returned to the search fleet, and a barge deposited another 4,000 gallons of gasoline at Reliance, replenishing the dwindling fuel supply. Now all they needed was improved weather conditions.

Unfortunately, at this point Mackenzie Air Service recalled the Aircruiser to Edmonton for an engine change, and Fairchild 629 had to be diverted to ferrying fuel to forward areas, thus once more reducing the size of the search fleet. By now they were encountering heavy snowstorms, and there was a general drop in the temperature—a reminder that winter gales were imminent. The searchers who had started out with such confidence in mid-August were becoming more and more depressed. All of the country to the north and east of Reliance, roughly 24,000 square miles, had been combed, and the search was now moving into the western block, but they all knew that time was running out because Coleman and Fortey had left with only enough food for one week.

Toward the end of the first week of September there was some slight improvement in the weather, permitting a number of the aircraft to penetrate into the Lac de Gras area. Until this time the searchers had been unaware of the presence of Jack Stark and Gus de Steffaney in this area, but one of the flights happened upon them travelling on the Barrens some distance east of their cabin. When questioned, the trappers told of seeing an aircraft of the same type and colour as the missing Fairchild on August 17. They were of the opinion that this aircraft had landed and then taken off again, flying north. Their observation later proved to be correct.

Finally there was a ray of hope. All flights resumed the search in the Lac de Gras area but were unable to penetrate farther north because of the return of poor weather, and the restricted visibility resulted in numerous forced landings to await improvement. They made a further attempt the following day under difficult conditions, but the weather went from difficult to impossible by the time they reached Aylmer Lake, so all aircraft returned to base. At this time CAL's ATZ, which had been ferrying fuel to Aylmer Lake, had to be withdrawn for an engine change, following which it would remain at Smith over freeze-up. However, the RCAF was promised

A 1935 Barren Lands Search

Pilot Con Farrell and crewman Frank Hartley in CF-AMZ had become lost and out of gas while returning to Fort Rae from the Barren Lands in the summer of 1935. Here AMZ is moored beside a lake while Con sits on the shore.

Of considerable interest to the crews scouring the north for Fairchild 644 was a search that had taken place the previous year. During the summer of 1935 Con Farrell, one of Canadian Airways most experienced pilots, had become lost with engineer Frank Hartley in this same general area. He had been returning to Rae after taking a party of trappers to their winter grounds in the Barren Lands. To make this 1935 incident even more interesting to the 1936 searchers was the fact that Special Constable Adolph Fabian, now a member of the Reliance RCMP detachment, which was working with the RCAF, had been acting as spotter for Matt Berry and Frank Kelly when they found Con and Frank. In another coincidence, in the later stages of the 1936 search both Matt Berry and Frank Hartley would also become involved, though Hartley was one of the searchers this time.

In 1935 after Con failed to return, there had been no great concern expressed at CAL and no immediate search was organized because he carried one of the company's radio transceivers, and he had quickly made contact with our radio operator at Rae, a very resourceful individual by the name of Hank Roth. During these brief radio contacts, Hank learned that Con had lost his bearings and was out of fuel, but Con also advised him what he thought was his location. Matt, who was servicing geological parties from Rae at the time, then searched the area Con suggested, but he had no success. Now, Con was not the most patient of individuals, and after a week of this he had some pointed remarks to make to Hank concerning the abilities of the searchers. His words were both loud and profane, which was unfortunate as he later had to eat them.

Canadian Airways radio operator Hank Roth in front of the company's radio station at Cameron Bay on Great Bear Lake. Roth was responsible for pinpointing CF-AMZ's location.

Hank then decided to apply a little modern technology. He constructed a direction-finding loop antenna and attached this to his receiver. During Con's next radio contact he had a local volunteer gradually rotate this home-made DF loop while he monitored the radio receiver until he determined the direction of the strongest signal. Taking a compass reading on the heading, he applied this to the map and was able to give Matt a direct line to follow. Matt flew this heading on his next outing and had no difficulty in locating Con's Junkers on Sussex Lake, just north of Aylmer Lake. But Matt and his engineer, Frank Kelly, had not forgotten Con's disparaging remarks about their search efforts, and instead of letting the two downed fliers know they had seen them, they flew on until out of view, then sneaked back at low altitude to surprise them. Con Farrell and Frank Hartley had been missing for 10 days at this point, and it was mainly due to Hank Roth's efforts that they were found without a full-scale search.

a replacement aircraft by the following day, this being AAO with Matt Berry as pilot and Frank Hartley as crew.

It was not until Thursday, September 10, nearing the end of the fourth week of the search, that Bellanca 607 with pilot Rutledge and crewman Walker, searching north of Lac de Gras, spotted some small gasoline barrels and stopped to investigate. There they found a note from the lost men, written on the day they had disappeared. It advised that they had only enough fuel for another half-hour of flying, that they would proceed in a southerly direction for 30 minutes and then land. With renewed hope the searchers concentrated on the area between Lac de Gras and Great Slave Lake. They were confident now that the search was ending and that their comrades would soon be rescued.

As Coleman's note indicated that they must be within a radius of perhaps 50 miles from the location of the gas drums, Wray decided to set up a tent camp at Aylmer Lake. Although it was now necessary to send Bellanca 605 south to McMurray for an engine change, the four remaining Bellancas moved to the tent camp to maintain the search until the last possible moment before freeze-up. Much of the area near at hand had been searched to the extent permitted by the weather, but a further and more intensive search was conducted of the area south of the newly named Drum Lake. Fuel was supplied to them by RCAF Fairchild 629 and one Mackenzie Air Service Fairchild, CF-AKN, flown by Marlowe Kennedy. While all search aircraft had been operating in pairs up to this point as security against possible further engine failures, when Matt Berry arrived in AAO with Frank Hartley, they were assigned to search the Snare River drainage area alone because of Matt's experience and knowledge of that country. That search proved fruitless.

Meanwhile, out on the Barrens as a means of passing the cold and often dreary days, Coleman and Fortey played checkers. They had marked out a "board" on a spare piece of canvas, and for checkers they had removed two types of nuts, one brass and one steel, from the unserviceable engine they had been freighting back to Reliance. The game took their minds off the bitter cold and their empty stomachs. They made wood-gathering trips whenever weather permitted, but these were becoming more and more difficult and energy-consuming because of the cold, the wind, and their increasing weakness. They had been able to augment their rations at first by picking berries but this resource was now coming to an end. Though they had fishing tackle as part of their equipment, in spite of numerous attempts they never got a single nibble. They saw both wolves and caribou, and either would have served as food but they had no rifle. That week, however, Fortey devised a snare and caught a ground squirrel. "We put that squirrel in the pot that Fortey here had set up," Coleman wrote. "We left the squirrel right there in the pot and boiled him and boiled him and stewed him some more to get the soup. Pretty weak at the end but not bad. And in the end we ate him. Then, on the day that our rations ran out, and we had eaten the last of our berries, we caught another squirrel. He was a nice, big fat one—the daddy of the family."

In the sometimes sketchy reports compiled later, there is no indication that any of the air force searchers had ever visited Stark and de Steffaney's cabin or even knew its whereabouts. The flyers' earlier contact with them had been made while the trappers were travelling on the Barrens, probably on a caribou hunt. Matt, however, was well acquainted with the location of their camp, having flown Gus to their winter quarters in early August, and on September17, a day that was cold, grey and overcast, he decided on a quick visit to the trappers' cabin. They repeated their story: they had seen a yellow Fairchild on August 17, and it had flown north and never returned.

Matt knew that there was no time to lose. He took off to the north, following the 15-mile length of Providence Lake until he reached the southeast end of Point Lake, which extends northwards for a further 15 miles before it turns west-northwest. From there to the northwest end of Point Lake where it drains into Redrock Lake, it is roughly 50 miles. A detailed search of its extremely rugged shoreline with its numerous bays, both large and small, would have taken hours of search time—more hours than Matt knew would be available to him before the weather broke, and he elected instead to fly along the centre-line of the lake, checking the shorelines on either side. Toward the northwest end of the lake there is a large island, about six miles by eight miles in area, and here Matt made a fortunate decision. He could have followed either the south or the north route around the island; fate made him select the north. Close to the main shore on this north side is another mountainous island and over the top of this, as they drew closer, Matt spotted the objects of so many weeks of anxious searching. A short distance back from the shoreline stood a white tent and moored in front of it was the missing Fairchild. Coleman and Fortey heard the aircraft at about this time and lit a small signal fire—one they had prepared weeks before with the fading hope that it might still be needed. So, at about 1:00 p.m. on a grey and overcast September 17, with ice covering the small ponds and the smell of winter in the air, the long search came to an end. Coleman and Fortey, weak from hunger but still in good condition, had finally been located.

Once their rescue was assured, the lost pair, unable to face the cold in their inadequate summer clothing, returned to their tent and their sleeping bags. As Frank hastily moored the aircraft, Matt went to the tent to shake hands with the occupants and greet them with, "What are you guys hiding out here for?" When asked later what their response had been, he said, "Lord! I don't remember! But they are real stout fellows, I can tell you, and showed little emotion at their rescue."

There can be little doubt that Coleman and Fortey had finally given up all hope of rescue. They knew they had but a few days remaining. Coleman said later, "That same day before Matt came along, we had shaved... ." Obviously they had sensed that the last portage was in sight. With regard to their flight on the day they were lost, Coleman said that they had been "flying high—never less than 2,500 feet—and when we looked for the chain of lakes that we were supposed to be following, we couldn't find them." He thought that they must have been flying through a storm when they crossed out of the strip map area. After they realized they had missed the identifying marks on the map, they had made an emergency landing. "We came down on what we later found to be Lac de Gras and left the gasoline drum there with the note saying that we were flying south. We couldn't see any trappers around there, though we later found that there were a couple [Gus De Steffaney and Jack Stark] just about 10 miles away and we flew right over them. We did fly south after we took off from there, too. We flew south for about twenty minutes then swung off to the north and northwest again in order to get into the timber. We wanted to get near timber so that we could get a fire going. We knew then that we were lost. We came down between an island and the mainland on what we later found was Point Lake. As soon as we landed, we tried

Matt Berry's CF-AAO moored beside RCAF Fairchild #644 by the shore of Point Lake on September 17, 1936. *Photo: Matt Berry*

(L-R) RCAF pilot Flt.Lt. Sheldon W. Coleman, crewman Joe Fortey, and Canadian Airways pilot Matt Berry who found them. *Photo: Matt Berry, courtesy Provincial Archives of Manitoba*

to find out our position by figuring back our compass routes, and we decided that we were about fifty miles south of our actual location."

After their near-starvation diet, food was uppermost in the minds of the two lost airmen, but Matt knew the dangers of allowing them to eat anything solid or substantial. Instead, he took powdered milk from his ration kit and added this to water heated on their improvised stove. Then he flew them to Reliance, pausing en route to signal his success to the RCAF search party camped at Aylmer Lake. The lost pair were then placed under the care of Major Hunter while Matt, after spending a joyous evening at Reliance, returned to Yellowknife. As a measure of the proximity to tragedy, the day following the rescue the Point Lake area was blanketed with snow and the temperature dropped far below the freezing point.

Both during and after the search there was much conjecture about compass deviations and proximity to the north magnetic pole. In discussing this later, Matt was of the opinion that their compass had been adversely affected by their cabin load—the failed motor and the gasoline drums. In addition, we who were very familiar with Fairchild aircraft had always found their compass readings unreliable because the compass was mounted adjacent to some of the heavy steel tubing that formed the centre section. Because of this, it became common practice for experienced Fairchild crews to include a hand compass in their equipment, permitting the crew at times of uncertainty to land and obtain an accurate reading.

The compass bearing from Hunger Lake to Healey Lake was west-southwest about 240 degrees true, and the distance was about 80 miles. From there a further 25 miles on the same heading would have brought them to the north end of Clinton-Colden and the unbroken water route to Reliance. It would seem likely that Healey Lake would have been the point ("the identifying marks on the strip map") at which they should have turned south toward Reliance. If they had been flying over cloud at the time of passing Healey Lake and if they had continued in a west-southwest direction, they should have passed over or within sight of Aylmer Lake, some 50 miles to the west. With a length of some 30 miles from north to south, Aylmer would have been hard to miss.

As they eventually landed at Drum Lake, which was slightly north and west of Lac de Gras, without ever seeing Aylmer Lake, it would seem that they had been well to the north of their intended track ("I guess we were flying through a storm"). A compass error of 30 degrees would not have been too noticeable, especially on the nervous compass card of a Fairchild 71. These were mounted behind the pilot's head and to one side, and had to be read through a mirror, thus requiring the numbers on the compass card to be reversed—an arrangement not conducive to accuracy. A 30-degree error would have taken them in a straight line from Hunger Lake to the Lac de Gras area. As in the case of many who have been lost, however, the compass is often disbelieved. As Matt remarked, "After their note was found, it was a matter of deciding which way was south to them."

Although the search was now ended, there was still unfinished business for Larry Wray and his crew: the recovery of Fairchild 644 from Point Lake and the salvage, if possible, of the tent camp on Aylmer Lake. In spite of the lateness of the season, they felt that Point Lake and the other large water bodies would remain open for another couple of weeks, and there would be a good chance of success. On September 18 Fairchild 629 and Bellanca 610 departed from Reliance with an extra crew for 644, plus spare fuel. After an hour's flying under low ceilings and intermittent rain and snow squalls, they hit a solid wall of weather—an intense blizzard. The aircraft had been flying in close proximity so as to maintain contact, and both now landed, mooring their aircraft against a lee shore.

The snow continued for about four hours, and they were considering a return to Reliance when suddenly it cleared. They pushed on over country white with the first heavy snow of the winter season, reaching Point Lake without further incident, but still there were problems. Although they knew the exact location of 644 from Matt's description, because of the heavy snow cover, they had great difficulty locating it. There was no doubt in their minds that the rescue had been accomplished on the last possible day.

By the time 644 was fuelled and serviced, the bow struts replaced and the tent dismantled and stowed, the weather was closing in again, and since it was already late in the afternoon, they decided to remain overnight. It was obviously better to stay where they were, together and securely moored, rather than chance an uncertain landing on some unknown lake. As there was little cabin space in 644 because it was carrying the failed engine from 604, the six men spent a cold and uncomfortable night in the other two aircraft, with no warm food, not even hot tea or coffee.

RCAF Fairchild #644 on Cooking Lake on September 24, 1936, after delivering Coleman and Fortey safely from Fort Reliance via Fort McMurray. Cpl. L.A. Parmenter stands on the float.

They awakened the following morning to another wintery scene but with some promise of a fair flying day—overcast but no additional snow overnight and a 500-foot ceiling together with the usual north wind. An hour's flying brought them to the south end of Providence Lake, then they turned east toward Lac de Gras. A strong northwest wind was now blowing, the ceiling had lowered, and the first snowflakes had appeared. By the time they reached Lac de Gras it was blowing a gale, the snow was falling with blizzard intensity, and the lake was a sea of wild water. The aircraft were forced down to an altitude of 50 feet or less, keeping contact with each other with the greatest of difficulty. A landing on stormy Lac de Gras was out of the question, but another 15 minutes brought them to calmer water, probably one of the smaller lakes between Lac de Gras and Mckay Lake, and all three aircraft were able to land. Two were still in contact with one another, but the third had disappeared from sight. Hours of taxiing were needed before these two managed to tie in to some boulders on the lee side of an island.

About seven that evening the snow abated somewhat, and with improved visibility they were able to locate a more sheltered mooring and secure the aircraft for the night. Unless a person has been engaged in similar activities under like circumstances, it is difficult to appreciate the hardships that these men would have undergone. There is no way that one can moor an aircraft on a shallow, rocky shoreline without getting very wet. And it was still blowing a gale during this time with temperatures near the freezing point. With no way to dry or warm themselves, they spent a long, cold night in the unheated aircraft with only their sleeping bags for covering.

The following morning they spotted the missing aircraft anchored to an offshore boulder on the opposite side of the lake. Rifle shots attracted the crew's attention and the three aircraft were soon reunited. However, much of their fuel supply had been used up during the flight and in the hours of taxiing, and now there was insufficient for all three aircraft to reach Reliance. They drained fuel from two of the aircraft, 10 gallons at a time, and transferred it into F/O Blanchard's Fairchild 629, then the six half-frozen souls climbed aboard and completed the last lap of their journey to Reliance.

Then on that same day they flew two loads of fuel back to the two abandoned aircraft, and the flights then continued to Aylmer Lake. They found that the tents had been completely destroyed by the violence of the blizzard, but they dug the equipment out of the snow, loaded it into the aircraft, and flew back to Reliance to complete a summer that will remain forever in the minds of all those who had any part in the operation. The following day the RCAF closed up their operation at Reliance for the season, returning their equipment to the main base above Fitzgerald. During this process Bellanca 605 experienced an engine failure while taking off from Smith. This is the same aircraft in which, barely a week earlier, a newly overhauled engine had been installed at McMurray. I would guess that after such a dismal season the RCAF carried out a full investigation into the quality and performance of their engine overhaul contractors.

While all this was happening, Coleman and Fortey had remained at Reliance, recuperating and regaining their strength. Then they were flown south, overnighting at McMurray on the way, and on September 24, in the same aircraft in which they had been lost—now flown by F/O Blanchard—they landed on the calm waters of Cooking Lake and taxied up to the dock. Following the final engine change on 605, all the aircraft were ferried back to the main RCAF base at Lac du Bonnett via McMurray, Churchill Lake and Cormorant Lake. The total flying hours expended in the search by both service and civil aircraft amounted to 802 hours; the area searched was calculated at 93,100 square miles.

The Search Team

The names of those involved in specific incidents in this account were not always available to me. I have, therefore, refrained from using names except where there was no doubt as to identity. Fortunately, F/L Wray did include in his final report a list of the names of both service and civilian parties who took active part or provided support to the search activities. These are included below.

Bellanca 604	Pilot Sgt. W.F. Tourgis	Crewman Cpl. E.H. Macauley
Bellanca 605	Pilot F/Lt. L.E. Wray	Crewman LAC R. Inglis
Bellanca 607	Pilot F/O H.C. Rutledge	Crewman Cpl. E.F. Walker
Bellanca 608	Pilot Sgt. J.W. McNee	Crewman Cpl. K.S. Regan
Bellanca 610	Pilot W/O/2 A.S. Horner	Crewman Cpl. W.F. Johnson
Fairchild 629	Pilot F/O S.S. Blanchard	Crewman Cpl. L.A. Parmenter
Fairchild 644	Pilot F/Lt. S.W. Coleman	Crewman Cpl. J.A. Fortey
Fairchild 644	Pilot F/Sgt. G.E. Cherrington	F/Sgt. A. Holdsworth
MAS Bellanca AWR	Pilot S.R. McMillan	Crewman R. Hodgins
MAS Fairchild AKN	Pilot M. Kennedy	Crewman J. Austin
CAL Fairchild ATZ	Pilot R. Heuss	Crewman R. Leigh
CAL Fairchild AAO	Pilot A.M. Berry	Crewman F.L. Hartley

Other personnel engaged in search activities were:

Major Hunter	Royal Canadian Army Medical Corps
Eric Fry	Topographical Surveys
W.H.B. Hoare	Department of Biology, National Museums
D.B. McNeal	Cook, Goldfields, Sask.

Courtesy of Dr. William Beahen, RCMP historian, the following are the names of the RCMP personnel who aided in the search.

Cst. W.J.G. Stewart	Cst. R.W. Thompson	Cst. D.A. MacDonald
Cpl. J. Robinson Spl.	Cst. A. Fabian	

For the exemplary service provided by these members of the force, all of them received Commissioner's Commendations "for outstanding performance during Search Operations for DND personnel lost in the Great Slave Lake area of the NWT."

13 Orphans of the snows

It was a typical autumn morning on the Snye at McMurray—clear and cold with remnants of the overnight frost still present, the small pools at the water's edge covered with a layer of ice. The trees were bare. The last of the fall foliage, once resplendent in hues of yellow and red, was now drifting with the current. Overhead, two long strands of Canada geese, the last of the fall migration, added their melancholy comments as they made their way south.

The date was September 29, 1936. Con Farrell and I had just returned the previous evening in Fairchild 82 CF-AXE from Nonacho Lake, south-east of Great Slave Lake, where we had taken supplies to a geological survey party and had been weather-bound by wind and snow for an additional two days. AXE was now tied to CAL's floating dock. Next to it was Fairchild 71 CF-ATZ, which pilot Rudy Heuss, with engineer Dick Leigh, had flown during the search for the lost RCAF fliers, Coleman and Fortey, located only 12 days earlier. On this particular morning I had made an early start as I wanted to track down a small but annoying engine oil leak. With the side cowlings removed and flashlight in hand, I was concentrating upon this problem when I heard Rudy's friendly voice. "Rexie, what are you looking for in there?"

There were handshakes and some friendly banter, and then he remarked, "I guess they've had a tough time with ice down on the Arctic Coast this year."

"Yeah, sure have," I responded. "Some of the posts are going to be really short on supplies." While the HBC post managers tried to keep a year's goods in reserve, it was inevitable that they would run out of some of the essentials before the next shipments arrived, but that year freeze-up had come so early that many of their supplies had been stranded on the riverboats and hadn't even got as far as Aklavik.

"There's talk of one of our machines spending freeze-up at Rae," Rudy said, "so we can make an early start on moving some of that freight."

With this bit of news I realized that there was, perhaps, a message behind the casual comments of my friend. Only too aware of being the most junior of our staff of engineers and Rudy being the most junior of our pilots, I abandoned my oil-leak search. "Rudy, I have a suspicion that you know more about this freeze-up project than you're letting on. If it's going to happen, it won't be hard to guess who the lucky individuals are going to be!"

"I was just trying to break the news to you gently," he said, chuckling. "Yes, you and I are the fortunate pair who will spend an interesting freeze-up at Fort Smith. Apparently this was decided a few days ago. We're to take ATZ, and Don is already checking and servicing the winter equipment for it."

"Well, at least we'll have a bit of preparation time," I said, "but I want a word with him because there's a particular pair of blow pots that I want, and there's a few extras we'll need."

Fast forward to October 20 and a vast change in the weather. Rudy and I in ATZ, loaded down with skis and winter gear, were fighting our way through thick weather. We'd been into snow ever since leaving McMurray, and now just north of Chipewyan we were "steamboating" along the Slave River. This is a rather tense experience, especially under heavy snow conditions, but we pressed on, giving up precious altitude as the visibility decreased, always hoping that we were through the worst of it. Experience in this sort of flying is valuable but can lead to serious consequences. Experience tells you that you've had it this tough before, so you press on, but the limits are hard to define. If you pass the limit—and there are no signposts for guidance!—you can find you've left it too late for corrective action.

To make matters worse for Rudy and me, forward visibility in a Fairchild 71 was almost non-existent, especially at low altitudes, and this section of the Slave River had a particular danger, one that every pilot was well aware of: snags. Riverbank failures had deposited the remnants of large trees in the water, and these would drift with the current until one end became imbedded in the river bottom, leaving the remainder projecting as

Plying Northern Rivers and Arctic Waters

After establishing trading posts along the Arctic Coast early in the century, the Hudson's Bay Company had been forced to set up a transportation system to provision them, and their posts along the rivers, as no commercial shipping company existed in the north at that time. Thus, from the end of steel at Waterways, three miles east of McMurray, to Aklavik, near the mouth of the Mackenzie River, the commerce of the north moved on the decks and in the cabins of the tugs, barges, and sternwheel steamers of the company's fleet. From Aklavik initially, and later from Tuktoyaktuk, supplies were transferred onto small coastal schooners for delivery to Herschel Island in the west and all the posts that lay to the east—Baillie Island, Read Island, Coppermine, and Gjoa Haven. But besides supplying their own posts, they also made this service available to the RCMP and other branches of the federal government, to the Anglican and Catholic churches, and even to their competitors, the so-called free-traders. It was a service provided, of course, without any hint of government subsidy. The only ship not flying HBC colours in northern waters belonged to the Catholic Church. Having a need for more than the annual trip of the HBC supply boat, the church had decided to provide its own service and arranged to have a 55-foot schooner built. This craft, christened *Our Lady of Lourdes*, became one of the most successful boats in the Western Arctic.

much as 10 or 20 feet above the water's surface. A collision with one of these monsters was dangerous for a boat but fatal for an aircraft. On this occasion when we lost touch with the shoreline momentarily, due to a slight bend in the river, one of these mighty snags flew by just below our wing level. Rudy's hand had been on the throttle for some time in preparation for a fast landing, and I certainly thought the moment had arrived. Moments later the snow suddenly eased off, and we were able to scramble back to a more comfortable altitude. I had been kneeling on the floor just behind Rudy's seat, staring forward, our heads at about the same level. Now he turned his head for a moment and we exchanged glances. "J—-s, that was close! If we'd hit that snag they'd never have found us!"

The Hudson's Bay compound at Fort Smith with the HBC store on the right and the Mackenzie Hotel on the left. The only hotel in the North, the Mackenzie's existence was due to the vagaries of the sternwheelers' schedules.

Thankfully, the rest of our brief flight to Smith was routine, and in another half-hour I was securing the tie-down ropes for the night while Rudy removed our overnight packs from the aircraft. Normally we walked the quarter-mile from the waterfront to the HBC's Mackenzie Hotel. Today, however, with the freighting season at an end, one of Ryan Brothers' trucks appeared, its driver having come to enquire whether his truck would be needed the next day to haul the aircraft to the landing field. That point settled, we were soon at the hotel, guests of manager Paul Kaiser and chef Joe Lanouette. Over coffee Rudy and I discussed our close call in the snowstorm. "That's the sort of thing I hate about these last flights before freeze-up," he said. "So much of the time you're bucking dirty weather and you don't always get away with it. We were just lucky!"

The Mackenzie Hotel, owned and operated by the Hudson's Bay Company, was the only such establishment in the north, its existence entirely due to the vagaries of their marine schedules. The 16-mile unnavigable stretch of rapids between Smith and Fitzgerald meant that northbound cargo and passengers were delivered to Fitzgerald by the sternwheeler *Northland Echo*. Passengers continuing beyond there, however, were at the mercies of the northern fleet's schedule, particularly that of the company's other sternwheeler, the *Distributor*. If she was delayed in her long

Changing CF-ATZ from floats to wheels at Fort Smith, October 21, 1936. Pilot Rudy Heuss and crew Rex Terpening.

trip to Aklavik and return, the passengers were obliged to wait—and thus the need for the Mackenzie Hotel. There were few winter hotel guests but the Hudson's Bay people found it more practical to keep the hotel open year-round in order to retain their staff. This was a move that we airline people strongly endorsed.

At Smith, Rudy and I took a day off, the first either of us had taken since the start of the busy fall season. The next day, with ATZ on wheels, wings folded, and tail secured to the deck of a Ryan Brothers' truck, we made our way to the landing field. This was a series of meadows adjacent to the village and of adequate size for our activities. My first job there was to insulate the oil tanks and lines, then add baffles and other hardware to the engine to improve the hot air supply to the carburetor. Rudy's comfort was not overlooked, either, as I closed off the many small gaps and openings adjacent to the cockpit. As we had a substantial snowfall while I was doing all of this, it was then time to install the skis. Rudy and I did a careful check on our emergency equipment—tent, stove, ration kit and the numerous small items that experience had taught us were necessary or at least desirable. Finally, we did an engine run-up, I changed the oil from SAE-120 summer grade to SAE-100 for winter, and we were ready for action.

All these activities were of great interest to the residents of Fort Smith, mostly because there was little else for them to do at this time of year. During the navigation season Fort Smith, being the northern terminus of the portage past the rapids, was a busy place. All cargo for northern trading posts, both along the rivers and on the Arctic Coast, passed through it during those brief summer months. However, most "summer help" departed on the last southbound boat before freeze-up, with the remainder going out on the last southbound planes. The winter residents consisted of a handful of non-Natives—HBC people, RCMP and RCCS—a few trappers, both white and Native, and the considerable number of bodies that were required for the operation of the sizeable Catholic mission and hospital. Naturally, in this closed community Rudy and I injected a welcome element of change to the normal freeze-up routine, and we were under constant observation.

Our preparations were completed by November 6, and we carried out a short test flight followed by a trip to Resolution and return to bring back some of the boat crews stranded there by the early freeze-up. That flight was typical of our early winter trips—overcast, low clouds, snow showers—and such thin ice on the smaller lakes and rivers that an emergency landing would have been extremely hazardous. Our next mission was also to Resolution, this time to pick up trading goods destined for the HBC post at Coppermine. Loading problems there caused some delay as the post manager had made a list of priority items for the first load, and it took some little time to fit them all into our limited space.

Then we were airborne—though only for a brief time. Great Slave Lake was still wide open, of course, and our normal crossings were made about 30 miles east of Resolution, from the south shore to the Gros Cap on the north shore, a distance of about 50 miles. On this occasion it was a potentially dangerous operation because the lake was still unfrozen and we were on skis. With sufficient altitude this would have been no great worry, but snow and poor visibility kept us down close to the water. We started the crossing in light snow with a bare 200 feet of altitude and soon were well on our way. If the snow held off and our motor kept operating, we'd make it, but when we were almost halfway across and feeling optimistic, the snowfall increased. Reluctantly, Rudy reduced altitude but the heavy snow continued. I had been perched on the load just behind him, and now he turned his head and shouted, "I'm going to turn back while I still have

The first flight after freeze-up over Great Slave Lake. While all the surrounding land and small lakes are solidly frozen, there is still open water on the big lake. November 1936.

enough altitude to make a turn." With that we began retracing our route—another 20 minutes above those heaving, grey waves, which we tried to ignore by staring ahead. The low willow flats of the delta shoreline finally appeared through the gloom, and minutes later we had snow beneath our skis again. A double sigh of relief filled the cockpit. Another 30 miles and we were back at Resolution where we were heartily welcomed by our agent, Bobby Porritt, always happy to have an evening of different faces and new stories.

To Bob's considerable pleasure, for the next two days we had a blizzard—wind, snow and near-zero visibility. This brought us to Wednesday, November 11, Remembrance Day when, the weather finally showing some improvement, we were able to get on our way again by mid-morning. This time we reached Gros Cap safely, and another 45 minutes' flying time brought us to Yellowknife Bay and the only habitation in the area. A small company, Burwash Mines, was sinking a shaft there, and the dozen men in the little camp were delighted to have some mail—delayed at Smith since freeze-up—and a bit of news from the outside. I'd expected we would push on to Fort Rae, another 120-odd miles farther up the North Arm, but the warmth and good food of the mining camp appealed to Rudy, and he decided we should overnight there.

As it turned out, the following day was another rest day. The cook, who was first up, was pleased to deliver the news: "There's a blizzard blowing, fellows. You're here for the day." By the following morning the weather had moderated, and we were able to make an early start, refuelled at Rae, and with the last bit of low quality light touched down at Cameron Bay, about midway up the east coast of Great Bear Lake. The small lodging place there was operated by a man-and-wife team whose names I do not recall. The wife was an unseen body—always in the kitchen. The husband served the meals but had little to say. An odd pair!

It had been our plan to make the 160-mile flight to Coppermine the following day and be back in Cameron Bay for the night, but in the morning after heating the engine, I discovered a small oil leak, and tracing it slowed our departure. Our route from Cameron Bay to Coppermine took us north for about 30 miles to Hunter Bay, once the supply centre for a possible mine site at Dismal Lakes, another 60 miles farther north. From Hunter Bay we flew northeast for about 50 miles to the Big Bend of the Coppermine River, crossing the Arctic Circle in the process. Here the rugged hills and timbered valleys of the Cameron Bay area slowly give way to low hills and scattered timber, and we soon left the last of the trees behind as we entered typical Barren Land country—flat, featureless, and devoid of landmarks. Navigation here in summer was often difficult, in winter often dangerous. But November 11 was a clear day, and we were able to make a direct flight from the point of the Big Bend to the settlement of Coppermine, a distance of about 80 miles. (On days when we had to follow the river, it was more than 100.)

It was early afternoon when we reached Coppermine, but by this time there was not enough light to make the return trip safely, and we prepared to overnight there. This small settlement, named Fort Hearne by the HBC, lies on the Arctic Coast a mile or so west of the Coppermine River. The few white residents—two HBC employees, two RCMP members, and one representative of the Anglican Church—were all there to welcome us, eager for mail, for the sight of new faces, and news of any sort from the other posts we had passed through. The HBC people immediately set to work unloading their supplies from the aircraft while I started the oil-draining operation. This was always a special experience in Coppermine because I was immediately surrounded by 15 or 20 Inuit of all ages, anxious to be of

RCMP Constable "Frenchie" Chartrand beside his dog team at Coppermine, November 1936. Chartrand died of heart attack while serving aboard the RCMP patrol vessel *St. Roch* a few years later.

assistance. In order not to lose any of the oil, it was necessary to hold the pail close to the drain valve, and as soon as they understood this, a couple of them relieved me of the pail, my only task then being to operate the drain valve. When the pails were full, there was something of a competition to see who would carry them to the RCMP station. Next my crew of Native helpers rolled two barrels of fuel to the aircraft, and there was another competition, this time to decide who would operate the wobble pump. For them and all of the Native villagers, completion of the refuelling process was an important moment. There was always a gallon or more of gas remaining in the hose and pump, and since it was a scarce commodity and every family owned one or more gasoline-fuelled cigarette lighters, not a teaspoon of this would be lost or wasted. Every lighter in the village was refilled that afternoon together with an assortment of small containers that had been hoarded for this special occasion. It was not that the villagers were nicotine addicts; the lighters were used as the primary ignition sources for the wicks in their seal-oil lamps and, for those families fortunate enough to own one, to light their primus stoves.

Our hosts at Coppermine were RCMP constables "Frenchie" Chartrand and Derek Parkes. Both had served in the Arctic for some years, having been previously posted to Herschel Island and Aklavik. Because of his outgoing nature and constant good humour, Frenchie was well known along the Arctic Coast. Unfortunately, he was destined never to leave it. Several years after this visit he died of a heart attack while on the RCMP patrol boat, *St. Roch*. He rests on a high ridge overlooking Paisley Bay, where the cairn erected by his crew members reads: "Cst. Chartrand, RCMP—Reg.#10155. 8 Oct 1904–13 Feb 1942." Frenchie would have wished for no better or more fitting resting place than this.

That evening I renewed my acquaintance with Tommy Tingmeak (Goose), an Inuit who worked for the RCMP as a special constable, interpreter, dog driver, igloo-builder and general handyman. Born at Port Hope, Alaska, in 1902, he spoke English fairly well, so communicating was not a problem for him. In fact, when Tommy had been living in the Bathurst/Burnside River area just a few years earlier, it was he who had made the all-night trip to Burnside to alert the search parties that the McAlpine party had reached Cambridge Bay. Tommy's wife, Molly, whose dimensions were about five feet in both directions, was also part of the organization.

Special constable, interpreter, dog driver and igloo builder Tommy Tingmeak (Goose). Coppermine, November 1936.

An Inuit family in front of their igloo.

Besides caring for their three boys, Roy, Wallace and Jack, she made mukluks and caribou-skin clothing for the RCMP constables. The family lived in a small, government-provided house and thus were the leaders of the local Native social circle.

During our visit Tommy enquired if I had a snow knife with which to cut snow blocks for a shelter, and he showed concern when I said I didn't, a snow knife being essential equipment for anyone living on the Arctic Coast. Then he told me that he had a spare that only needed a new handle, and it would be mine once he had repaired it. Thinking of all my future trips to the Arctic and possible emergencies where I would need a snow knife, I accepted his generous offer.

The next morning a weather report received by the Department of Marine station at Coppermine from the RCCS station at Cameron Bay advised that the weather there was down. (The marine navigation season along the Arctic Coast was brief—perhaps three months at the most—and we often wondered what the operator did for the remaining nine months of the year. I had no chance to ask as we never did see the gentleman who operated the Coppermine station, as it stood at the extreme west end of the settlement.) Taking advantage of another enforced free day, I toured the settlement, camera in hand, with Tommy as my guide, and we were invited into some of the Inuit dwellings for tea. This early winter period was the most uncomfortable time of the year for the Inuit. Lacking the hard-packed snow needed for igloo-building, they were forced to live in tents of canvas or caribou skins, sheltering these structures from the wind with the few snow blocks available.

Finally on Tuesday, November 16, the weather at both Coppermine and Cameron Bay was clear, and we made an early departure—though an early start from the Arctic Coast in November was not before 10:00 a.m. Aboard were four passengers: the HBC district manager for the Western Arctic, R.H.G. Bonnycastle, generally known as "Bonny," and three members of the crew of the HBC coastal supply ship *Fort James*. Normally the *James* would have returned to its home base at Tuktoyaktuk, but early freeze-up had caught her at Bernard Harbour, west of Coppermine. The skipper, a Captain Summers, and two seamen had elected to remain with the ship for the winter, but the rest of the ship's crew had made their way back to Coppermine. Our load included the cook and one seaman and the engineer, Gurth Claydon.

An Icy End for the Fort James

The Hudson's Bay schooner *Fort James* in the foreground with the old northern supply ship *Bay Chimo* off shore. Coppermine, 1931. Both vessels were crushed by ice, the *Bay Chimo* in 1931, the *Fort James* in 1937.

In the early winter of 1937 the crew of the *Fort James* again had to be flown out of Coppermine, but the circumstances were different on that occasion. En route to Tuktoyaktuk, the *Fort James* was crushed in the ice in Dolphin and Union Strait. The crew were rescued by the RCMP patrol boat *St. Roch*, westbound from her winter quarters at Cambridge Bay and fortunately near at hand.

At Cameron Bay Rudy and our passengers had a brief meal break while I refuelled the aircraft, then we were airborne again, heading south to Fort Rae. Rudy had brought along a huge sandwich for me—roast caribou meat between thick slices of homemade bread! Delicious! As Rae lacked a commercial lodging place, we stayed at the house of the Northern Traders manager, Bob Dodman—all of us sleeping on the floor, of course.

Gurth Claydon, being an engineer, had an interest in all things mechanical and elected to help me prepare ATZ for takeoff the next morning. The extra manpower couldn't speed up the engine heating process, of course, blow pots having their own speed and BTU output, but a second pair of hands did make a difference when it came to adding the two pails of hot oil, refilling the blow pots and refuelling. Because of this we made an early start from Rae with hopes of reaching Smith that day. The weather was normal for that time of year—overcast with a low ceiling—as we proceeded down the east side of the North Arm, but a few minutes after passing Yellowknife Bay we saw the first snowflakes. By the time we reached the Gros Cap it was snowing steadily. I watched Rudy shifting back and forth in his seat, looking out first one side, then the other, a worried look on his face. He was obviously going through mental torture, trying to decide whether to attempt the crossing or turn back, but we still had some ceiling—perhaps 500 feet—so he forged ahead. Our passengers, who had been chatting among themselves over the roar of the engine, became suddenly very quiet and turned their worried faces to the windows. There was nothing but open water below, and the consequences of a forced landing on skis were obvious! We droned on through the gloom, but as the snow increased, we were forced down closer and closer to that dark water. I checked my watch. We had been flying for almost 25 minutes so it was too late to turn back. We should soon be across, but then the snowfall became even heavier. Forward visibility was nearly zero. The only thing we could see was the black water just below the skis. We flew on like this for perhaps a desperate minute or so when Rudy suddenly called out, "We've made it!" and the willows of the delta flashed beneath our skis. Rudy closed the throttle, and moments later there was the comfortable sound of the skis bumping over the frozen hummocks.

Rudy and I had experienced hair-raising crossings before, but this was definitely the worst, so we were as silent as our somewhat shaken passengers as we climbed down from the cabin. As it was still snowing and the visibility remained poor, I installed the engine cover—we weren't going anywhere for awhile. I then took out one of our blow pots while Rudy dug into our emergency kit for tea, sugar and mugs. Placing a pot filled with snow on the rack that formed the top of the blow pot, I put the torch into action, and before long we were all drinking hot black tea. Up to this point there had been very little discussion regarding our recent experience, everyone alone with his thoughts. Then as Bonny refilled his tea cup, he leaned toward Rudy. "Tell me," he said, "Do you do this often?"

This bit of humour broke the tension and there was laughter all around. With a grin Rudy replied, "All the crossings are bad, but I have to admit this was the worst one I've experienced." Suddenly everyone was recounting his own reaction to the experience. More snow was melted, more tea drunk, and as we were rinsing out our cups with snow, Bonny quietly said, "Quoanna puk puk," the words for "thank you" in the Inuit tongue. "Puk puks" are the equivalent of "very"—the more "puk puks," the greater the appreciation.

Visibility had improved by this time, but our takeoff area didn't look too promising—soft snow with many hillocks of varying consistency—and Rudy announced, "I think I'd better make two trips." I told him I would wait for the second trip. "Gurth knows how to crank the starter so you can take him on the first trip. But just in case you don't get back for us tonight, we'd better keep the ration kit, the tent, our sleeping bags, and one blow pot here."

Gurth, the cook, and the other seaman climbed aboard, I cranked the starter, and the Wasp sprang to life. With power applied, I pushed the tail around so that the aircraft was lined up with our arrival tracks. Rudy applied full throttle, and ATZ was airborne in a cloud of snow. The aircraft climbed, turned, and came past us with a final waggle of the wings. Bonny and I had much to discuss in the hour or two we waited there on the delta. With his HBC background, he knew a great many HBC people in the fur trade and in the transport division where my father was employed. Then Rudy was back, bumping toward us over the hillocks of snow. We loaded our gear, climbed aboard, and were soon in Resolution.

Although our primary mission that November was freighting supplies from Resolution to Coppermine, it is probable that we would have taken Bonny and the *Fort James* crew on to Fort Smith the following day, but warm weather had melted the snow on the meadows there, leaving no place for a ski-equipped aircraft to land. Our next trip would therefore be north again, and I took advantage of the two-day wait and the unseasonal but most pleasant weather to deal with various small problems on the aircraft and motor. Meantime, Bonny, familiar with the needs and shortages at the Coppermine store, had been supervising the selection of our next load and helping to load it aboard. The night before our departure Rudy received a wire advising us to prepare for a trip to the mission at Paulatuck on the Arctic Coast to pick up Bishop Fallaize and party who had been stranded there by the early freeze-up. The wire didn't specify when we were to do this, but we immediately gave our maps with their questionable accuracy some close attention. We could see that Paulatuck was about halfway between Coppermine and Aklavik—about 400 miles in either case. It would be a long trip to make both ways on one of winter's shortest days.

Even though we had a heavy overcast the next morning, I heated the motor in preparation for an early departure, but the overcast dissolved into heavy snow. Had our route been along the rivers we would not normally have been delayed by such conditions, but our recent open-water experience was still fresh in our minds, and we had no wish to cast off in the direction of the Gros Cap without good visibility and a ceiling. However, toward noon the snow stopped and, though it was still overcast, there was a good ceiling so that this time our "ocean voyage" was a relaxed affair.

Because of our late start we overnighted at Rae, but uncertain weather delayed us again in the morning, resulting in yet another late start. The flight to Cameron Bay from Rae took about two and a half hours, but as the route was well marked with numerous well-defined lakes of various sizes, even in overcast weather it presented few navigational problems. Next morning the overflow at Cameron Bay was so bad we could barely taxi through it, and once out of it, we had to jack up the aircraft to clean some of the ice from the ski bottoms. I say "some" because much of it was beyond the reach of my ice scraper. We then unloaded half of our cargo and made two trips out onto solid ice. It was about 1:30 by this time—late for a Coppermine departure—but we felt we could just make it. Navigation is always a problem on the Arctic Coast and the treeless Barrens; with good light one can just distinguish the landmarks—the hill formations and river valleys—but in poor light they simply disappear. And so it was on that day.

In the dim light we felt our way with difficulty to the Big Bend of the Coppermine, welcoming the sight of the well-defined rocky hills in the broken country lying to the north of it. Here we turned north but were soon faced with a solid fog bank. "We can't make it!" called Rudy. "We'll have to turn back." And he swung away from the fog bank, flew south for a few minutes to get clear of it, then turned southwest toward Hunter Bay. But the fog had closed in behind us so we had to turn south to follow the river. This proved to be difficult—the rounded hills along the river were almost invisible in the failing light. Fortunately, there were still patches of open water wherever rapids occurred and we could use these for landmarks. They were all we had. Obviously, we would have to find a place to land, but landing on the boulder-strewn tundra—even if we could find a flat place—would almost certainly demolish our undercarriage or worse. Our only hope was to find a lake, and our maps were of no help, even if we could have read them in the dim light within the cabin. The minutes passed and the tension mounted. The terrain below us flattened out and there were fewer patches of open water—and thus fewer landmarks—as we continued upstream. Then suddenly Rudy called, "There's a flat place just back from the river! Looks like a small lake!" Sure enough, at the head of a small draw was a flat area, its boundaries outlined with underbrush. Using what was probably the last of our limited daylight, Rudy dropped the nose, made a half-turn and we landed, hoping that the surface was as smooth as it appeared.—and fortunately it was!

Because of the absence of timber this far north, on our trips to the Arctic Coast we carried some small poles with us, and before Rudy shut down the engine, I put the poles under the skis to prevent them from freezing down. While I drained the oil and carried out the rest of my routine duties, Rudy set up our tent. This had a square base that was pegged to the ground, and the structure was supported by a single adjustable pole in the centre. It was not as roomy and comfortable as a wall tent but was compact and easy to erect and didn't rely on local timber for a pole. With our emergency kit and sleeping bags inside, and a single candle for illumination, our little camp was cheerful and cozy. Our cooking device was a gasoline-powered stove, which did an excellent job, though it had the same drawback that the blow pots had: it emitted enough fumes to make the air almost unbreathable. During the actual cooking we would partially open the tent flap for ventilation—then close it to retain a measure of warmth after the stove was turned off. Our meal consisted of canned meat, sliced and fried, and this was followed by cheese, hardtack, jam and plenty of tea. As we settled for the night, Rudy said, "You know, we were damned lucky to find this lake. If it had turned out to be tundra, we'd have ripped the bottoms off our skis or worse and been stranded here—maybe for weeks." He was right, of course. Winter flying hadn't yet started in the south; there would have been no one to search for us!

The weather was relatively warm—around zero—and the night started out pleasantly enough, but around midnight we were awakened by a violent flapping as our tent threatened to become airborne. There was nothing available in the way of anchors, so we removed some of our HBC cargo and packed this around the tent in lieu of tie-down stakes. Thus stabilized, we survived the night. By morning the wind had died but it was overcast or foggy—we

Pilot Rudy Heuss and engineer Rex Terpening use shovels to cut snow blocks to shield their tent from the wind. An unnamed lake east of Great Bear Lake, November 1936.

couldn't tell which—and definitely not flying weather. Donning our snowshoes, we followed a draw down toward the river and found a patch of scrub timber, most of it dead and dry. As we had a small collapsible wood stove in our emergency equipment, we returned to camp for the axe and cut a supply of wood. We also used our shovel to cut some snow blocks—rather anemic-looking ones—to add to our tent shelter and put out more of our HBC "anchors." As we had plenty of rope, we also extended guy ropes to the wing struts.

The next morning it was still overcast and the light was poor, so we enjoyed a leisurely breakfast before checking our tent moorings. I took some photos of our campsite. A survey of our landing field showed us a rocky hill just beyond where we had landed. "If I'd made a circuit the other night," Rudy said, "we'd have run right into that hill! I never even saw it in the dim light!" When the ceiling suddenly began to lift in early afternoon, we scrambled to break camp and were on our way again. The remainder of our trip to Coppermine was uneventful though very interesting as we seldom had an opportunity to fly over this off-course part of the country.

At Coppermine I made a quick call on Tommy and Molly Goose to deliver the fabric I had purchased for Molly—duffle cloth, denim and some bright calico—and she was delighted! Then Tommy, with a grin on his round face, said, "I have something for you." He produced the snow knife he had promised me, but now it was complete with a carved bone handle, and I was more than pleased to receive it. Knowing of my interest in photography, Tommy then showed me some of his photos. He had learned the craft of film developing and photo printing somewhere during his travels and had many interesting pictures, some of which he presented to me. Finally I said my farewells and returned to the police station to show off my new snow knife.

The Goose family didn't fare well in the years that followed. The next summer their eldest son, Roy, went swimming in front of the village where river water created a current along the shoreline. By Coppermine's standards it was warm there and some of the local boys—hardy types!—used it as a "swimming hole." Unfortunately, Roy got in over his depth and disappeared. Constable "Red" Abrams (who had replaced Frenchie that spring) heard the cries of the other boys, stripped and plunged in, diving repeatedly but to no avail. The Goose family then moved to Holman and there experienced further problems. To quote from Sergeant F.S. Farrar's *Arctic Assignment* describing the voyage of the RCMP patrol boat *St. Roch*, "At ten-thirty that night we had tied up at Holman. On our arrival at the island landing we were greeted by a small group of anxious Eskimos, a priest, and a Hudson's Bay official. A little Native boy, Jackie Goose, had been shot through the face by accident while playing with his brother. The injured boy was out of danger but needed treatment. We promised to take him to Aklavik." I never learned the outcome of this misadventure.

In later years the family moved to the Aklavik area and there Molly contracted tuberculosis. After lengthy hospital treatment at Edmonton she was pronounced cured, and the night before she was to return to the north there was a *Hello, The North!* program broadcast from the hospital. Molly was one of the featured speakers, and she told her friends that she was now well and would be returning home. But Molly died of a heart attack the following morning. And Tommy? He lived out his life in the Inuvik area as a father figure and senior citizen. Years later I made contact with a grandson, Louis Goose, who told me that Tommy had died July 8, 1964. Should I have the opportunity to visit Inuvik, I will surely stand beside Grave 47, Plot 12, to let my old friend know that he is still remembered.

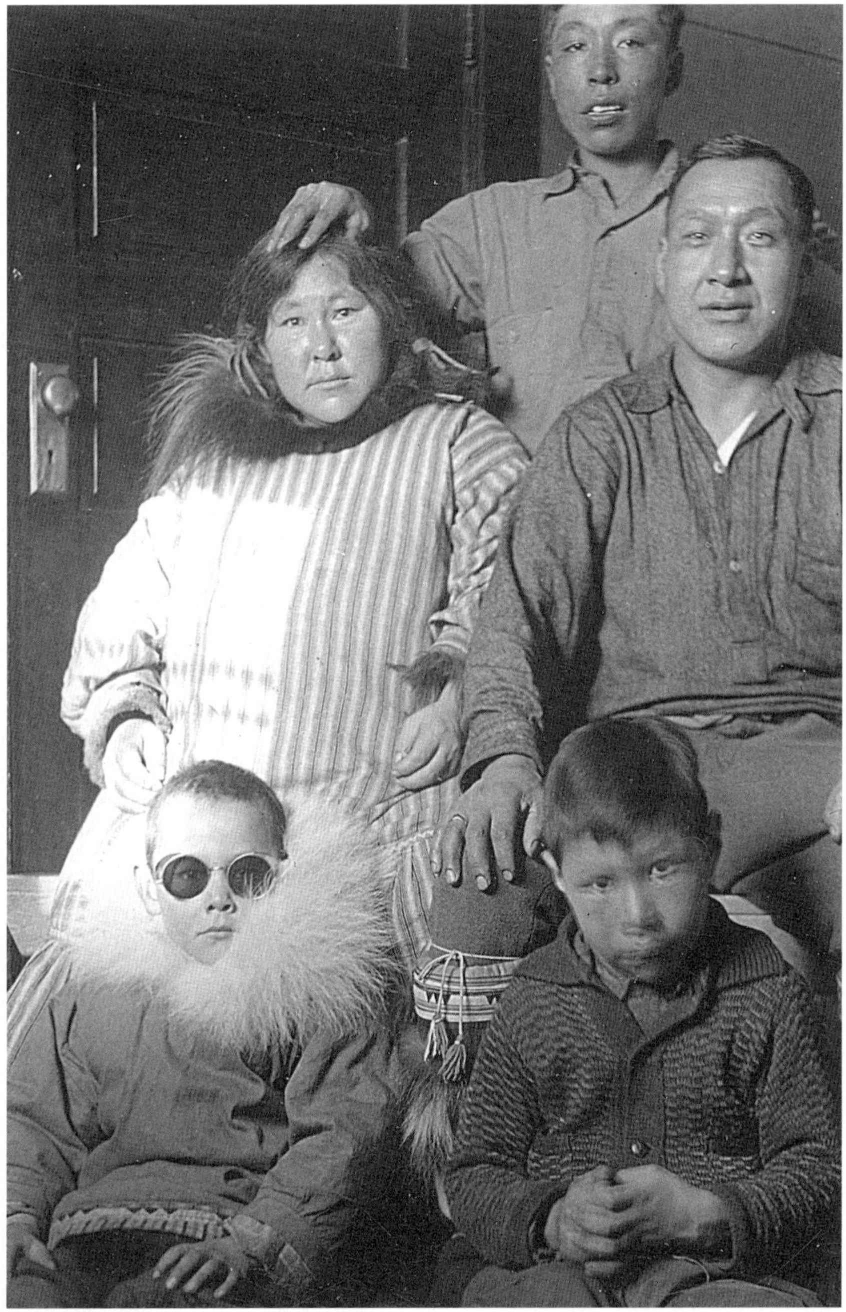

Molly and Tommy Tingmeak (Goose) with their three sons, Roy (behind his parents), Wallace and Jack in November 1936. Roy drowned the following summer, Jack was shot in the face a few years later but survived. Molly contracted TB and died of a heart attack in Edmonton. Tommy, much respected in his community, died at age 62 in 1964.

At Coppermine there was no more information on the Paulatuck trip. Instead, we were to return to Resolution with four Inuit children who were destined for the Anglican mission at Hay River. Apparently some family crisis had left them with no immediate family to care for them, and the Anglican minister at Coppermine, the Reverend Webster—"Webby" to the locals—had made arrangements for this move.

It was nearly noon before the fog cleared the next morning, but our excited little passengers were on hand well ahead of time and anxious for their first airplane ride. There were two boys, about 8 or 9, one girl a couple of years younger and one girl perhaps 12 or 13. They spent most of their time with their noses pressed to the windows although there was little to see until we reached the Bear Lake area, then the sight of the massive, rocky hills and the tree-covered valleys lying between them caused much excitement and comment. A whole new world lay before them! Because of our delayed start we had to cancel our plans of pushing on to Rae that day, but we enjoyed a comfortable night at Cameron Bay, where Webby had made arrangements for D'arcy Arden's wife (herself part Native) to care for our brood.

The next day our passengers were on hand early, all ready to go, but we had further weather problems—heavy overcast followed by a strong wind—and we were finally forced to cancel the operation. Rudy and I had lunch, then I collected up the kids from Mrs. Arden's house and took them for a long walk. Though Cameron Bay is only a narrow opening in the rocky hills perhaps a half-mile in length and is a dark and gloomy canyon in the depths of winter, it was not unattractive in the warmth and daylight of that mid-November afternoon, and it was thoroughly enjoyed by our little passengers. They marvelled at the size of trees that we looked on as scrub timber and were fascinated by their first view of the local wildlife—squirrels, whisky-jacks and ravens.

Poor weather the next day meant that we got only as far as Rae, where Mrs. Dodman took care of our charges besides providing excellent meals for Rudy and me. We had hopes of reaching Resolution the following day, but uncertain weather forced yet another late departure. However, coming down the North Arm toward Gros Cap we could see a combination of low cloud and extensive fog patches ahead. We made a cautious start across the lake, dodging fog banks but still maintaining a few hundred feet of altitude, but as we neared the halfway point, the fog patches joined together

Our four orphans preparing to board CF-ATZ at Coppermine, late November 1936. The Anglican church had made arrangements for them to be cared for at the Hay River mission.

and Rudy wisely decided to turn back. The weather improved as we neared shore again so Rudy turned east. There were islands in this eastern portion of the lake—not that they were of any actual benefit to us as a landing place as they were rugged and timber-covered—but their presence meant there was less open water here. We flew east for about 15 minutes but the low fog ceiling continued and the channels between the islands were all fog-filled. Rudy shook his head. "Well, I guess we'll have to give it up for the day. The light's starting to fail." With that we turned north, heading for the mining camp at Yellowknife.

It was late when we landed. Since I had the aircraft to care for, Rudy volunteered to take the kids up to the cookshack to see what sleeping arrangements could be made for them. Webby had given us some caribou hides with the hair still on them for use as sleeping covers/mattresses for the youngsters, and when I arrived an hour or so later, I found our kids on the floor in a corner, tumbling about on their caribou skins. Rudy was sitting at an extra table the cook had provided, updating his log books. As none of us had eaten since early morning, we were a hungry crew, but the cook, a quiet, elderly man, had made a batch of doughnuts and, after some cautious sampling, the youngsters decided they were edible. Knowing that these largely igloo-raised children were unfamiliar with our food, I then visited with the cook to see what was on the menu. I knew the roast caribou would be devoured instantly, but they would balk at the vegetables. The cook suggested rice as an alternate and this we agreed on. He explained that the miners would be in for their dinner at 5:30 and suggested that we should have our dinner after they had eaten.

Normally there was a mine manager at this site, but that gentleman had just missed the last northbound flight before freeze-up. The crew was therefore operating under the direction of the foreman—a chap who showed little interest in our activities. In spite of the earlier doughnuts, Rudy and I and the children were all very hungry, and when our turn came, the food quickly disappeared. The young ones, unaccustomed to "table tools," ate with their hands, but the older girl—whom we had nicknamed "Susie"—managed her fork quite well. We had decided that jam sandwiches might be an easier dessert for them to eat than the excellent pie that the rest of us enjoyed, but Susie cast glances at our pie, and upon being offered a piece she made short work of it. I then obtained a damp cloth and a towel from the cook and cleaned up the younger ones' grubby hands and faces. Susie, however, took the cloths from me and did her own cleaning. With dinner behind us, Rudy and I each had a book to read while the kids played a game that Susie must have brought along—apparently her sole possession—hidden in her *ahtegi*. The game consisted of two pieces of bone joined by a piece of sinew or heavy thread. One piece of bone was square with a small hole in the centre, the other slim with a pointed upper end. To play the game, the pointed section was held in the right hand and the square piece tossed into the air. The objective of the game was to insert the pointed end into the hole of the square piece as it tumbled through the air. There was much smothered laughter, but I never did see a successful attempt. Our sleeping arrangements were better than average as the cook, who appeared to have a certain amount of authority around the camp, had a couple of mattresses brought over from the bunkhouse for Rudy and me. Since we were quite accustomed to sleeping on "the planks" (the floor), this was utter luxury. We were all sleepy after a long day in the cold and the head-nodding started early. In the darkness after we turned off the Coleman lamps, there was some squirming and giggling from the caribou skins but the children were soon asleep, and Rudy and I followed quickly.

The miners had finished their breakfast by the time the cook presented scrambled eggs and sausages for our flock and this offering disappeared in moments. As the local weather looked "flyable," I started the engine-heating while Rudy went to the radio shack to check the Resolution weather. I was still at work on the aircraft when Rudy came down with all the kids trailing behind him. "Resolution's got heavy snow," he reported. "But there was a wire from Jim Darwish [the trader at Fort Rae]. He wants us to bring him the supplies that were stranded here at freeze-up."

Having overheard some of the miners' remarks regarding Susie, I said "Rudy, we may not get back tonight and Susie wouldn't be safe here by herself."

Rudy considered this in silence for a few moments, then said, "Yeah, you're right. So here's what we'll do—you stay here with the kids and I'll go by myself. If I don't make it back tonight, I'll be okay. I can drain the oil and do the heating in the morning." He then arranged for the freight to be brought down, we loaded it, and he was soon on his way.

It was nearly noon by then, so the kids and I went up to see what our friend, the cook, could provide in the way of lunch. Following this I took our flock down to the bay for another of our long walks. Ptarmigan were plentiful and the boys spent their time stalking them and trying to down them by throwing chunks of ice. The odd wrestling match developed between the boys, occasionally exposing a bare rump. This was due to the clever design of the caribou-hide pants worn by small Inuit boys. A slot in the back, which was normally covered by an overlapping piece of hide, automatically opened when they squatted when nature made its call.

Darkness was falling by the time we returned and it became obvious that Rudy was spending the night at Rae. The cook welcomed us back to the cook-shack. Quite intrigued by these little visitors who had brought a small ray of sunshine into his otherwise dreary life, he had prepared a meat dish for them that could be eaten quite readily by hand. The miners were having their dinners as well—and again I noticed the many glances in Susie's direction. The cook was also aware of this, and I noticed a slightly heated exchange between him and one of the miners, but the evening passed pleasantly enough. I chatted with the cook for a while and the young people played their game of "spear the bone." After the cook departed, I made a try at reading, but my eyes were too heavy. I turned off the lights and we were soon asleep.

The weather had cleared overnight, so in the morning I rounded up our gang—they with their caribou hides, I with my kit bag and sleeping bag—and assembled them down near the piled gasoline barrels, where the kids started some sort of a tag game. The boys were tussling and rolling in the snow when Susie called to them in some excitement. They immediately scrambled to their feet and stood looking off to the north. After a few moments they began to point and to exclaim "*Ting-meak! ting-meak!*" Aeroplane! Aeroplane! It was another few moments before I heard the drone of the Wasp engine, then ATZ came into view, flying low over the bay. Rudy landed in our old ski tracks and taxied up to where we were gathered. Not knowing whether the flight would continue, I held up one of the underski poles. Rudy shook his head and shut off the motor.

"How did it go?" I enquired as he climbed down from the cockpit.

"No problems at all," he responded. "Jim gave me a hand with the oil and we topped up the fuel. The weather's good south so pile in and let's go!" It took but moments to load our gear, I cranked the inertia starter, and we were on our way.

The weather was good—better than any we'd seen on this trip—and we were soon southbound with 800 feet of altitude beneath our skis. Our lake crossing was almost a pleasure. At Resolution we stopped only long enough to unload some bales of fur and then we were on our way to Hay River Post, slightly less than 100 miles to the west. We had an unexpected passenger on this leg of the trip, "Shorty" Rolfe, one of the RCCS operators at Resolution. Since this was to be a brief return trip, he had asked if he might come with us. As the Signals boys at all of the northern stations were most helpful to us and always concerned for our welfare when we had weather problems, we were delighted to have him along.

At Hay River the Anglican Church people, somehow aware of their arriving visitors, were assembled in a group to meet us. As we wanted to get back before dark, we chatted only briefly with them, explaining what little we knew about their guests, then it was time to go. It was with some regret that we said goodbye to our homeless little charges. The younger ones had puzzled expressions on their faces, not comprehending that this was to be their new home. But having observed the white man's handshake routine, all of them lined up for this when the request was made—though they obviously didn't understand why. Susie, however, seemed to be aware of the plans. She spoke to the others briefly, and all of the proffered hands were shaken. Then Susie looked at both Rudy and me for a moment, said a few words in her own tongue, and turned to go. One of the Anglican sisters led the little group away. They turned for a last look before rounding a corner and disappearing from our sight. Rudy, Shorty and I stood in silence for a few moments. All had similar thoughts, I'm sure, about these four homeless youngsters, taken from the only life that they had known to live with strangers who knew nothing of their language and habits. Afterwards Rudy and I often spoke of this parting and wished that we had taken the time to enquire further about "our kids" and to learn something of the church's plans for their future. Much later we were relieved to learn that they had been sent to Aklavik on the first boat the following summer. The Anglican Church operated a hospital and mission there so the kids would still be cared for but be closer to people of their own race.

Our return trip to Resolution was uneventful. We taxied in and shut down the motor for the night. Normally Rudy would have stayed to assist with the refuelling, but Shorty volunteered instead. Later he accompanied me to Bob's lodging house to catch up on local news. We immediately noticed the absence of Bonny and the crew of the *Fort James* and learned that winter flying had officially started. One of our aircraft had been to Resolution in our absence to deliver a load of mail and express items and had taken them south on the return flight. But there was more. The Paulatuck trip was imminent and would be made by Matt Berry. "Rudy," I said, "I want to take that trip with Matt. I'm going to wire Don to see if I can arrange it."

The following day, Tuesday, December 1, we were again grounded by 30- to 40-mph winds and blowing snow, but that evening Shorty came over from the station with a message. We were to proceed to McMurray the next day without any intermediate stops. This was unusual as normally we picked up mail and passengers on southbound flights, but we were happy to comply. Assisted by a good tailwind, we reached McMurray in mid-afternoon.

Two or three of our aircraft were there, loaded with mail for the north, and we were welcomed back by their crews and our base staff. Then just as I finished installing the engine cover on ATZ, Don Goodwin, our chief mechanic, walked over. "You'd better transfer your tool box to ARI, Rex. You'll be going north with her in the morning."

14 Journey to Paulatuk

This story is dedicated to the memory of Matt Berry,
a great pilot, a fine gentleman, and a good friend.

Darkness had fallen early on that winter evening at Fort Chipewyan, the last of the daylight being hastened away by the heavy overcast. The frozen shoreline of the lake was deserted except for a lone aircraft—Canadian Airways Junkers W.34, CF-ARI. Out of deference to the usually brisk winds, the wing covers had been tied more securely than usual. Poles were under the skis, the oil had been drained and stored for the night in the heating shack, the blow pots were tucked under the engine cover—everything in readiness for morning. Matt Berry and I—the crew of ARI—had made our way to the unpainted frame building nearby. The handmade sign outside declared it was a restaurant. Its proprietor was Dan Mah, at that time the farthest north Asian person in the restaurant trade, a fine fellow in every sense of the word and highly regarded by all who knew him. Dan had converted the unfinished second storey of his establishment into sleeping quarters for itinerant travellers and installed the added luxury of mattresses on the floor. On the main floor the small area that served as his dining room was illuminated by a Coleman gasoline-burning lamp suspended by a hook from the ceiling, and the white light shining from the window silhouetted a pair of prowling husky dogs, drawn by the smell of cooking and hopeful of a handout.

We sat at one of the small wooden tables. Our meal completed, we had pushed our plates away and were enjoying a second round of hot coffee as I leaned back in my chair and looked at Matt across the table. He was at that time past middle age, and lines of perpetual good humour creased his craggy face. He was the oldest and most experienced of our pilots while I was the youngest of our air engineers. He broke the comfortable silence to ask, "What made you come on this trip, Rex? You must have been ready for a few days off by now, I should think."

He was right, of course. I had just spent the freeze-up period with Rudy Heuss freighting supplies to Coppermine and had only got back to Fort McMurray the day before. "Well, the truth is," I told Matt, "I always wanted to have a look at that country along the Arctic coast east of Aklavik, and this looked like one of the few chances that might come my way."

"You haven't seen it before?"

"No. I'm familiar with the Coronation Gulf area as far east as Cambridge Bay, but I've never seen the coast west of Bernard Harbour or east of Aklavik."

"I've flown the Hudson Bay area and Coronation Gulf as far east as Gjoa Haven," Matt said, "but I've never seen that stretch of coast between Aklavik and Coppermine. How did you know I was going?"

"We heard it on the radio when Rudy and I were in Resolution on our way back to McMurray. I wired Don to ask if I could go." (Don Goodwin was our chief mechanic.)

Matt nodded. "When I asked Wop if I could take the trip, he said, 'Sure. I was on the point of asking if you'd go.'"

The date of this conversation was December 3, 1936, and Matt and I were northbound in ARI for Aklavik and thence to Paulatuk, a remote Catholic mission on the Arctic coast, some 400 miles east of Aklavik. Bishop Fallaize and his party, travelling in their well-known schooner, *Our Lady of Lourdes*, had been attempting to reach Aklavik before freeze-up, but the schooner had been trapped by early, heavy ice at Pearce Point, some 300 miles west of Coppermine. This was in no way unusual, ice and weather having always been integral elements of any story dealing with travel in the Arctic, but 1936 was a particularly bad year. Abandoning the ship, the party had walked the remaining 60-odd miles to their mission at Paulatuk, a grim and nearly fatal journey, the details of which we did not learn until later. Fortunately, the mission was equipped with a power plant and a small radio transmitter/receiver, and with this they were able to advise Aklavik of their plight and request an aircraft be sent to pick them up.

The mission at Paulatuk at the mouth of the Hornady River on Darnley Bay in December 1936. It was built at this location because of its proximity to the Hornady River coal seam and because the natives gathered at the river mouth for char fishing each fall.

In my journal for Friday, December 4, I noted low cloud and poor visibility all day. We made it as far as Fort Smith, but we had to wait there for some improvement in the weather. "Finally got away in the afternoon," I wrote that night, "but bucked a stiff wind all the way and only got as far as Fort Resolution." On this trip we were taking the most direct route to Aklavik to conserve precious time for the Paulatuk trip, so the next day we flew from Resolution to Rae—temperature -40°F but fortunately no wind—refuelled and flew to Fort Norman. "Weather perfect all day," I wrote in my journal. That night the RCCS radio operators had two radiograms for us. The first was from Bishop Fallaize at Paulatuk.

MATT BERRY—FT. NORMAN. RECEIVED MESSAGE FROM MAY CAL ASKING TO MARK LANDING RUNWAY ALSO PUT SOME SMOKE SIGNALS WILL DO ALL REQUESTED WITH PLEASURE AND HOPE YOU HAVE SUCCESSFUL TRIP STOP LANDING IS ON COAST IN A GOOD HARBOUR ABOUT FOUR MILES BY TWO MILES STOP BEST REGARDS—FALLAIZE.

The second was an informal and unsigned message, also from Paulatuk, concerning landing locations, surface conditions and fuel.

THE MISSION IS AT THE BOTTOM OF DARNLEY BAY ABOUT 5 MILES SOUTHWEST OF HORNADY RIVER AND NOT AT LETTY HARBOR STOP THERE IS A GOOD LANDING HERE IN HARBOUR IN FRONT OF HOUSE AT LEAST TWO MILES WIDE AND THREE LONG STOP WILL MARK PLACE WITH SACKS STOP COME HERE FIRST AND THEN PICK UP GAS AT LETTY STOP GOOD LANDING THE WHOLE WEST SIDE OF DARNLEY ROUGH ICE ON EAST SIDE.

A summer view of the radio station buildings at Aklavik outlined against the bright northern sky. It was this station's operators who provided the crew of Junkers CF-ARI's with weather reports on their trip to Paulatuk.

For our information the Aklavik radio operator had added, "The mission at Letty is out of grub and wants the mission at Aklavik to send some in with Matt."

A third message was delivered in the morning just before our departure.

MATT/VEX [FORT NORMAN]—MISSION WANTS ONLY FISH NETS 50 LBS LARD AND BEANS FROM VEF [AKLAVIK] OR VEX STOP WANT AS MUCH FLOUR RICE OATS AS YOU CAN CARRY FROM LETTY TO PAULATUK STOP RUNWAY PAULATUK IS ON COAST ABOUT FIVE MILES SOUTHWEST OF MOUTH OF HORNADY EASY TO REACH ONCE YOU MAKE LANGTON BAY STOP FOLLOW FOOTHILLS OF MELVILLE MTNS STOP IN EMERGENCY LAND EAST SIDE DARNLEY BAY WEST SIDE ROUGH STOP THEY ADVISE U PICK UP COUPLE OF THEM TO SHOW WAY TO LETTY AND HELP LOAD GRUB AS NO ONE THERE NOW AKL/6.

In both the second and third messages the critical food situation was mentioned and this would later prove to be an item of major concern for us. But we puzzled over the conflicting information in these last two—the second said that the rough ice was on the east side of Darnley Bay, the third said it was on the west side. As a landing in rough ice would probably demolish our aircraft—and incidentally just might bend the occupants a bit—we asked that Aklavik confirm this information one way or the other.

We left Fort Norman at first light—10:00 a.m.—on Sunday, December 6, heading for Fort Good Hope. There we faced a fairly common situation—a layer of ice fog from the Ramparts Rapids about five miles above the settlement. This, for some strange reason, always seemed to migrate downstream, and because of the contribution of fractured ice from upstream, the river in front of the post always froze in a mass of rough ice. The townspeople would then select the most suitable site and flatten or remove the rough ice as much as possible in order to provide a landing runway for us. These strips were invariably narrow and surrounded by rough ice on all sides—and today was no exception. We made three landing approaches but were unable to get lined up on the runway because of the fog. We finally landed behind Manitou Island, the large island on the west side of the river, and taxied back to the landing strip. All this was time-consuming, and by the time we finished refuelling, it was too late to go farther, Good Hope being only fractionally south of the Arctic Circle and the hours of useable daylight there scanty.

The temperature was -56°F the next morning and frost had formed on the ski bottoms, even though I had poles under them, and at full throttle we still couldn't taxi. I got out and put the poles back under the skis, then with full throttle and lots of pushing and pulling on the tail, we were able to move a foot or so at a time. By repeating this operation a couple of times, we were able to scrape the frost off the ski bottoms and were finally able to taxi back to our landing place behind the island as the heavy fog and poor light made takeoff too risky on the marked runway. We had planned a landing at Thunder River for fuel but couldn't due to fog, and refuelled at Arctic Red River instead, then bypassed McPherson as we had barely enough light left to reach Aklavik.

The following day at Aklavik was overcast with poor visibility—definitely not the kind of a day for a trip along the Arctic Coast—but we welcomed the delay because it gave us time to re-check our spares and emergency equipment. Matt always carried his own rifle—a .30 Remington pump gun—and because he was most expert in its use, I knew if we had an extended forced landing we would never starve as long as there was game in the area. He also carried his own eiderdown sleeping robe in a specially made packsack instead of the factory-provided bag. This was to enable him to carry it easily if he had a long hike from a disabled aircraft. I had also discarded the standard bag on mine and substituted an envelope-style cover of sail silk with built-in shoulder straps. This protected the robe from dirt and moisture, and it could be rolled up and ready to travel in less than a minute. Matt was not a snowshoe enthusiast and therefore relied upon standard-issue, factory-made ones, but I travelled with my own personal snowshoes, these being a pair of the long, graceful Loucheux-made shoes from Fort McPherson, complete with lamp-wick bindings that were fitted to my mukluks. I also carried the snow knife that Tommy Goose had given me on my last trip to Coppermine.

With our equipment check completed, we tried to find out more about the best route to Paulatuk. No surveys, aerial or otherwise, had been made of the area, but with the help of Sergeant Frank Riddell of the RCCS and the use of marine charts, we were able to hand-draw a map of the coast, adding notes on landmarks and reference points that Frank had obtained from Natives and trappers. When one of the younger Signals operators, "Red" Scharfe, asked if he could go along for the trip, Matt agreed, a fortunate decision as Red proved to be a willing helper, and his cheerful good humour was a ray of sunshine to everyone.

It was while we were making our final preparations for the trip that we at last discovered the reason for the conflicting statements concerning the location of the rough ice in Darnley Bay. This bay, we learned, was about 25 miles wide from east to west, and the mission was located just east of a point that projected from the south shore of the bay. There was, therefore, a second and smaller bay immediately in front of the mission. The message about smooth ice on the west side had reference to this small bay. We also learned that the Inuit word "paulatuk" referred to a small seam of coal about 25 miles up the Hornady River that had been known and utilized by the Inuit for many years. Apparently it has a high oil content, producing volumes of sooty smoke when ignited; according to local legend, it was an elderly Native lady, stepping from her caribou-skin tent and observing this for the first time, who commented, "Paulatuk," which means something like "Sure smoky stuff!" Paulatuk was also the Inuit name for the actual location of the mission.

As I made my way to the aircraft in the early morning hours of December 9 to commence heating the engine, the stars were clear overhead, giving promise of good visibility. The temperature was -55°F, which was also encouraging in a sense. While the low temperatures made all phases of winter flying more difficult and unpleasant, they were usually an indication of a few days of clear weather, and that was just what we needed. The heating operation had been underway for some time when, above the roar of the torches, I heard voices and Red opened the engine cover to check on my progress. The propeller now moved freely—far different from the rigid state of an hour earlier when, had the blade been in the horizontal position, I could have chinned myself on it. I extinguished the blow pots, put them out to cool, Red handed up the pails of oil, and a few minutes later we were ready to remove the engine cover. Because our air-cooled engine, once uncovered, would rapidly lose heat and had to be started within minutes after the cover was removed, I had to work at top speed. Standing above and behind the motor, I lifted the heavy cover and dropped it over the side, following it down to fold and stow it, along with the torches, oil pails, and our other pieces of overnight equipment. With all of our gear and Red safely on board, I closed the cabin door, scrambled back up the slippery right wing root, and commenced cranking. Matt, in the cockpit with the engine primed, was ready and waiting. With no load on board the Junkers hopped into the frosty air after only a short run, and we were on our way.

In early December at these latitudes the sun is in hibernation along with the bears. Aklavik sits at about 68 degrees 12 minutes north latitude and roughly 120 miles north of the Arctic Circle. The southern horizon, however, was bright with reflected light as we gained altitude and headed northeast. A half hour of flying put the myriad channels of the Mackenzie River delta behind us together with some slightly higher ground that lay to the east of the river. Although the air was clear, forward visibility was reduced by the millions of frost crystals that filled the air, a situation caused by the invasion of the polar air masses by warm air from aloft. The crystals falling through the cold air below reduce visibility over a wide range of altitudes.

From the point where we left the delta, we followed the northern limit of tree growth as it slanted to the northeast. These trees were stunted spruce, growing in irregular, snow-covered clumps. The light, however, was strong enough to create the suggestion of a shadow beside them, providing a line of contrast that we appreciated. Our first landmark was a fair-sized body of water (actually ice), Sitidgi Lake, fairly regular in shape and about 15 miles in length, and we followed it north until we picked up the first of the Husky Lakes. (During the 1930s in the Western Arctic the word "husky" was generally applied to the Inuit—though not in a derogatory sense. When this went out of fashion, these bodies of water were renamed the Eskimo Lakes,

The Husky lakes are a labyrinth of water bodies, all irregular in shape, and surrounded by hundreds of tundra polygons.

and in the future they will probably become the Inuit Lakes!) These four lakes are highly irregular in shape with many deep bays, long arms, and islands, and looking down on them, Matt remarked, "This would be a great place to get lost in poor visibility." Below us, and stretching off to the south, lay hundreds of tiny lakes, also known as tundra polygons.

After flying for roughly one and a half hours we came upon a series of long, narrow channels, running nearly at right angles to our course. This caused us some concern for a few minutes, but then beyond them we saw what appeared to be a large bay. After watching it take shape for a few minutes, I called over to Matt, "Would that be Husky Inlet?" He turned with a half-grin. "It had better be," he said. (Husky Inlet is now known as Liverpool Bay.)

With breakfast more than five hours behind us, we had a hasty, tasty lunch of cold roast reindeer meat between robust slices of homemade bread, courtesy of the cook at the Signals station. And before some readers decide that reindeer is a typographical error here, let me say that it's not. A reindeer herd had been purchased in Alaska by the Canadian government and driven to the Mackenzie delta, a journey of considerable difficulty that took nearly three years. The herders were Laplanders, and during the drive they were accompanied by their wives, children and dogs. To the amazement of the local Inuit, the Lapps also used some of the reindeer as draft animals, harnessing them to pull sleighs. The government's expectation was that the Canadian Inuit would abandon their nomadic lifestyle and settle down to herding the reindeer in the same manner as the Alaskan Eskimos. Our Canadian Inuit had other ideas, however, so the herd became a government-managed source of year-round fresh meat for the RCMP, the RCCS, and the hospital, as well as, I believe, the Catholic and Anglican missions. As the Junkers aircraft had no access between the cabin and the cockpit, we were out of touch with Red but assumed that he, back in the cabin, would be eating his lunch when we ate. Red was a hearty eater, however, and a later check disclosed that his lunch had been devoured much earlier, and ours might have been in peril if they had been accessible to him.

We now swung east across an area interlaced with tundra polygons, and then through the dim light we were able to make out the mouth of the Horton River. Beyond that, in the blue-white haze to the east, was Franklin Bay. Below us and to the south the Smoking Hills lay along the coastline. While the word "smoking" was applied to these hills, the columns that arose were actually fumes created by a chemical reaction between acids and the carboniferous layers near the surface. This phenomenon, though observed and recorded by early explorers, has only received scientific investigation in recent years and may not yet be fully understood.

Like Matt, I stared out through the windshield and the right side window as we swung south and then east to follow the coastline. From this point to the west side of Parry Peninsula is roughly 35 miles and would have been a simple and desirable shortcut to Paulatuk in conditions of good light but was certainly not to be contemplated in the waning light of a December afternoon. The coastline south of the Horton River then east across the base of Franklin and Darnley bays, while known as the Smoking Hills and then the Melville Hills, is actually the broken east and north faces of a 1,000-foot-high plateau. In the Horton River area it slopes quite steeply to the sea coast but is withdrawn from the coast and less pronounced where it becomes the Melville Hills. Fortunately for us, it is well defined from the air and leads in the direction of Paulatuk.

It was past noon, and we were flying away from the sun, so we were losing daylight as we travelled. Our immediate concern became surface visibility;

The Smoking Hills

The Smoking Hills are mentioned in the journals of a number of Arctic explorers. On September 4, 1850, Captain Robert McLure of HMS *Investigator*, eastbound from the Pacific in the search for the lost Franklin party, sent a party ashore to investigate the strange occurrence that gave the hills their name. Langton Bay, just to the south of the Smoking Hills, was chosen by Vilhjalmur Stefansson for his winter quarters on his second Arctic expedition. The year was 1909, and Stefansson wrote, "We got there, however, all safe September 11 after a good deal of hard rowing in a rough sea against adverse winds."

Another early traveller who was intrigued by the smoke and steam that erupted from those snow-covered hills was Knud Rasmussen, the Danish polar explorer and ethnologist and one of the greatest of the early explorers, who came this way on his fifth Thule expedition, an epic three-year journey. In *Across Arctic North America*, published in 1927, he wrote, "On the 15th of March [1923] we reached Horton River. Next day we camped for a spell to take some pictures, though we could stay only a few hours. We had reached the Smoking Mountains."

finding our destination would be pointless if we couldn't see to land. If the surface was obscured by a bank of fog or low-lying cloud, a landing would be impossible. However, even in clear weather a strong wind could create ground drift, clouds of blowing snow that can extend hundreds of feet into the air, completely blanking off any view of the surface. As a result, we stared down, trying to pick up the outline of a pressure ridge or some indication of a shoreline. But as the light began to fade, so also did the visibility, and it became necessary to reduce altitude so that we could remain in contact with the surface. It was only at that point that we realized that a strong southeast wind had come up, causing ground drift, and the drifting snow made it even more difficult to see the surface. So it was with some relief that we again picked up a definite indication of coastline when we reached the western edge of Darnley Bay. Shortly after this Matt pointed ahead and said, "There's the mission."

Recalling the radio advice that there would be a landing strip marked,

Matt Berry and "Red" Scarfe with the four Inuit children who were marooned with the priests at the Catholic mission at Paulatuk.

The schooner *Our Lady of Lourdes* had become trapped in the pack ice off Pearce Point, 300 miles west of Coppermine, NWT, in October 1936. The crew and passengers walked 60 miles to the mission at Paulatuk.

we peered down, searching for the markers, but without success. Matt swung to the right in order to keep the mission building within his view, then turned again to face into the wind. Because of the ground drift, we did not have a clear view of the ice surface but, remembering the message about the location of smooth ice, Matt landed parallel to the shoreline just north of the mission building. The clatter of the skis on the small, hard drifts was a comforting sound, and as we taxied in, we realized that we had actually landed on the marked-out strip. The coal sacks were there all right, but they had been laid flat on the ice and were partially obscured by drifting snow. No time was lost in putting our aerial steed to bed for the night and retiring to the mission and a warm welcome from Bishop Fallaize, Father Bename and Father L'Helgouach. There was much excitement also among the four Native children—two boys perhaps 4 or 5, and two girls, 9 or 10. These children, incidentally, were a constant ray of sunshine in the days ahead, when the adults were becoming increasingly concerned over the deteriorating situation.

During the evening we learned of the hardships that the party had endured in their lengthy march from Pearce Point, 60 miles to the northeast. *Our Lady of Lourdes*, westbound from Coppermine to Aklavik with Father Bename as skipper, had encountered heavy ice conditions as they travelled along the coast west of Dolphin and Union Strait. When they reached Pearce Point, it was obvious that they could go no farther. The pack of heavy, old ice was solid and unmoving. There were no open leads and the temperature was falling steadily. Their only hope was to reach Paulatuk before their meagre food supply was exhausted, although they knew that the trip would be doubly hazardous at this time of year because there was neither the quantity nor the quality of snow necessary for igloo-building. Fortunately, they had a supply of caribou skins, which they utilized for sleeping mats and covers and for shelter in lieu of an igloo. Without these, it is probable that the entire party would have perished. Carrying such supplies as they had, their daily progress was painfully slow as it was dictated by the walking speed of the two small boys. With little more than half of the distance behind them, they consumed the last of their food. This was nearly the end of the trail for them but their prayers were answered: they found a dead seal that had been washed up onto the beach during the past summer. Though long dead, it was their salvation. They made their caribou skins into a shelter and camped

Father Bename, his skin burned to a Native hue, on a seal-hunting expedition. Like most of the Catholic fathers in the Arctic, he had learned to live off the land.

beside the dead seal for two days while they rested and salvaged as much of the precious blubber as they could. Then somewhat rejuvenated, they resumed their slow and painful journey. It must have been with a feeling of profound relief that they finally crossed the Hornady River and realized that the mission lay just beyond. Later, when their prayers of thanksgiving were offered up, I wonder if a small query might not have crossed their minds—that perhaps the Great Provider could have selected a seal that was slightly less ripe? Father Bename was most emphatic concerning the antiquity of the seal; with considerable feeling in his distinctively Gallic voice, he stated, "And I tell you, sir, that seal was rot–ten!"

The nearest gasoline cache was at the abandoned HBC post at Letty Harbour, 40-odd miles to the north. Our original plan had been to leave with the party the next morning, refuel at Letty, and proceed directly to Aklavik. But it was now apparent that the Paulatuk mission was seriously short of food, coal for heating the building, and dog feed. Could we possibly stay an extra day to bring back a load of supplies from the closed-down Hudson's Bay post? And at the same time could we pick up two of their people, Father Griffin and Brother Kraut, who were still at the mission there? Although it was urgent that we depart for Aklavik before the weather changed and before the days became shorter, refusing them was out of the question.

The typically neat Hudson's Bay post at Letty Harbour beside the Catholic mission building, the first with its trademark flag pole, the second with its cross.

Thursday, December 10, was a beautiful day, weather-wise, and one that we would think of frequently in the weeks to follow. It was clear and calm with a temperature of -25°F. We were hopeful that we would still have time that day after our return from Letty to make the trip to Aklavik, and plans were made accordingly. Father Bename was to accompany us to Letty to speed up the loading, while the rest of the party would be packed and ready to leave as soon as we returned. As there was no wind, we warmed up the motor, turned, and took off toward the north, flying at low altitude. The light and the visibility were both good so there was no need to follow the shoreline, and we cut directly across to the west side of Darnley Bay. As we flew north, we noticed a gradual change in the terrain; instead of the low and flattened ridges to the south, the surface of Parry Peninsula rose in rocky hills, perhaps 200 to 300 feet in elevation, infinitely more visible than the country around Paulatuk. Flying across a shallow bay, we could see the point where Letty Harbour was located, but we were near at hand before we spotted a sizeable schooner, and then the few buildings. Most prominent was the typically neat Hudson's Bay post sitting on a rocky knoll; nearby was the small mission building. Before each was the trademark of their endeavours—a tall cross at the mission and a flagpole in front of the Bay post on which the HBC flag would be flown on all important occasions. To many Natives in the north it was better known and far more important than our national flag. As one Inuit said in later years when being questioned on his

CF-ARI at Letty Harbour with Father Griffin and Brother Kraut loading supplies from the "closed down" Hudson's Bay store.

knowledge of the last war, "There was a big war between the Bay and the Germans. The Bay won."

Looking down on this lonely spot and the two small buildings, I could not help but think how symbolic they were of the Canadian frontier. For 300 years these two diverse enterprises, one dealing in souls and the other in furs, had pushed to the west and the north beyond the farthest reaches of civilization in Canada. Only the RCMP, in most cases the companion to both, did not have an outpost at Letty. Instead, the winter RCMP presence along the Coast consisted of a dog team patrol from Cambridge Bay to Aklavik and return. The summer patrol was carried out by the RCMP schooner *St. Roch*, based at Cambridge Bay.

As we did a short circuit to check landing conditions, we saw two figures running from the mission, and as we taxied up, Father Griffin and Brother Kraut were there to meet us. These two, being completely out of touch with their comrades, were surprised and delighted to see us. When *Our Lady* had not arrived to pick them up, all they could do was expect the worst and hope for the best. While Matt and the others carried the supplies down to the aircraft and loaded them, Red and I located the barrels of fuel, dug them out of the snow, and rolled them to the aircraft. I carried out the refuelling with Red manning the pump. It required 105 gallons to fill the tanks, which meant that they still held about 15 gallons when we arrived at Letty. We would certainly have preferred a more generous reserve of fuel, but we had known before leaving Aklavik that we would be close to our maximum range. We could have chosen to carry a 45-gallon barrel of fuel in the cabin, landed and refuelled en route, but the risks involved in such a venture far outweighed the comfort of a larger fuel reserve. Instead, we had carried a 10-gallon container with us from Aklavik to be used only in the event of a fuel-short emergency landing. As it finally developed, this 10 gallons of fuel would become the difference between an airborne arrival at Aklavik and a lengthy hike.

During the return flight from Letty we could see that the visibility to the south and west had become obscured. This observation was confirmed by a noon weather report from Aklavik, advising that they had low clouds and poor visibility. We would not be leaving Paulatuk that day after all, and in the afternoon Red and I went out to re-establish the runway markers. The coal sacks had been laid flat with snow blocks placed along their edges to keep them from blowing away, but the wind had drifted snow over them so that they were almost invisible from a distance. To rectify this, we cut snow blocks that would just fill a coal sack and set these up vertically with the bases imbedded in the snow—a line of Newcastle *inukshuks*.

That evening Matt and I had a quiet, private talk about our less-than-desirable fuel reserves. As we would now be leaving for Aklavik with less than full tanks, there was much wistful, wishful thinking and discussion. If we had waited for the Aklavik weather report before leaving that morning, we would have taken the time to load a barrel of fuel into the cabin at Letty. On the other hand, if we had waited and the Aklavik weather had been good, we would then have missed our departure deadline. So ended December 10.

Stars were visible the following morning as with great optimism I started to heat the motor. But before I finished the job, a 35-mile-per-hour wind had developed, blowing snow across the bay and ripping the cover from the engine, and I had to suspend the heating operation in order to build a snow-block windbreak, with a mental "thank you" to Tommy Goose for my snow knife. This shelter would be knocked down and rebuilt a number of times before our final departure. Daylight, such as it was, had arrived, but the sky must have been overcast as the light was extremely dim. With poor light, snow, and blowing snow, the mission was barely visible from the aircraft though the distance was no more than 100 yards.

That evening we enquired about the plans of Fathers Bename and Griffin. They were not going back with us, and even with the supplies we had brought

The author in front of the snow-block windbreak which was built and rebuilt to protect CF-ARI from at Paulatuk's blowing snow and 35-mile-an-hour winds.

from Letty, the fuel and food situation was far too meagre to last them through the winter. Their plan, we were told, was to wait at Paulatuk until they received word of our safe arrival at Aklavik. Then they would close down the mission for the winter and proceed to an area around Cape Parry, north of Letty and about 60 miles from here. They knew that a number of Inuit families would be wintering there where seals were plentiful, and they would spend the balance of the winter in the igloos with them.

In case we received a favourable weather report from Aklavik, I had to start heating ARI early in the morning, hoping for sufficient visibility for flying by the time daylight arrived. Wind and ground drift would not necessarily prevent us from flying, but if these were accompanied by an overcast sky, then flying would be impossible. Unfortunately, in the early morning darkness it was difficult to determine what sort of visibility we could expect—if any—that day. So it was that on Saturday, December 12, when Aklavik reported good weather, I heated the motor, but it turned out to be a waste of time. Daylight brought another day of wind, snow and zero visibility. It was also a waste of the precious fuel for our blow pots. Their normal diet was unleaded naptha gasoline, and I had brought a small reserve supply of it from Aklavik. If we ran out, we would have to use aviation fuel, but it contained tetraethyl lead—an ingredient the blow pots would only burn under protest and, once it was burned, made much cleaning of jets necessary.

Fathers Bename and Griffin left that morning for Tessuriak Lake, west of Darnley Bay, to set nets for dog feed—the poor beasts were gaunt from lack of food. We knew it would be a tough trip for all of them, men and dogs alike, as they faced a stiff wind, and they would probably have no igloo for shelter that night. Later the Bishop produced a deck of playing cards, suggesting that he and Matt should certainly be able to beat Red and I at four-handed crib. We accepted the challenge and the battle raged and seesawed through most of the day and evening.

Optimism prevailed as we had our usual early breakfast on Sunday, December 13. Aklavik reported good weather, and ours looked favourable—warm, with no wind or snow. While we heated the engine, the others packed their belongings and loaded them into the aircraft in readiness for departure. Then we waited for daylight, all the while trying to convince one another that the light was improving. Finally, the weather man decided things for us; the overcast sky developed into a heavy snowstorm that lasted all day. Red and I considered going for a walk to break the monotony but gave this idea up as being too risky; we couldn't see from one *inukshuk* to the next. We didn't see much of the bishop during the afternoon and concluded that he was requesting a little Divine Guidance for our party, an activity that we endorsed most heartily. After all, if a seal could be produced, then one clear day should be only a minor miracle. The fathers arrived back that night after a slow, hard trip. They had caught a few fish and left the net set under the ice to be rechecked in a few days. They had used the sleigh for shelter the previous night, with canvas pulled over it to form a windbreak.

Monday, December 14, looked like a going-home day. Once again there was a good report from Aklavik, and the pre-dawn sky at Paulatuk was clear with visible stars. Heating and loading were carried out, the hot oil was added, and our passengers climbed aboard. Then we waited. Slowly the light strengthened, and finally Matt decided there was enough visibility for takeoff. I'm sure that there was a quiet feeling of jubilation in all of our airborne hearts that morning. As we turned to the west, Fathers Bename and Griffin stood in front of the mission, waving farewell to us, no doubt with the same feelings of relief that we had. Matt rocked the wings in reply and we settled into a slow climb, all the while scraping frost off the windows and staring ahead in an attempt to pick up the coastline of Darnley Bay. We had taken off at 10:15 and had flown for 10 minutes or so when we realized that the light, instead of strengthening, was beginning to fade. There was still some reflected light on the horizon to the south, but it was becoming increasingly difficult to see the surface below us. On my side of the aircraft with the view to the north, it was an opaque world with the expanse of ice and snow merging with the sky, unbroken by object or horizon. I glanced quickly at Matt, hoping that he was having more luck on his side of the aircraft. The seacoast was to the south, to the left of the aircraft, and though it was flat and featureless country, I thought that there might be some object visible—a slab of ice upended against the shoreline, an exposed ridge of gravelled coast , perhaps. Matt returned my glance and shook his head in silence.

I concentrated my gaze downwards through the side window and caught the odd glimpse of the surface—a protruding chunk of ice here, a small pressure ridge there. Another 10 minutes had passed when suddenly I realized that for the past couple of minutes I had seen nothing. I looked at Matt.

He gave a despairing shake of his head and said, "I can't see a damned thing." We both knew then that we were in serious trouble.

With infinite skill he executed a slow turn to the left, using the southern horizon as a reference point. Knowing there were no hills ahead of us, he reduced altitude to something below 100 feet, a point where visual reference was possible, then he concentrated on maintaining our course and keeping the aircraft in level flight. Blind flying instruments, had they been installed, would have been useless because those old aircraft were rarely provided with electrical systems and interior lighting, and our cockpit was in total darkness by this time. I checked my watch—Paulatuk should be 15 minutes ahead, somewhere in the endless whiteness of snow and sky. As flying the aircraft and maintaining visual contact with the ground required every bit of his concentration, Matt called out, "Watch for the mission." The minutes ticked by as I stared into the gloom ahead. I did not dare take my eyes from the windshield to check my watch again, but I had a panicky feeling that our ETA had already passed. My eyes ached from staring into the white and shadowless void before us. A brief downward glance provided little encouragement—I could see nothing below, and I wondered how Matt was able to prevent his visual contact from deteriorating into physical contact. Other thoughts, equally sober, crossed my mind. The mission was one lone building and we could easily have passed by without seeing it even if we were on course. Lacking any visual reference to the surface, I had no sense of speed or altitude, nothing to mark the passage of time or of distance covered. The strength and quality of the light was diminishing by the minute, and I knew that under these conditions Matt could not continue much longer. If we had missed the mission, his only option would be to throttle back and attempt a landing, not knowing whether we were over sea ice or tundra, rough or smooth, with only the slight hope of last-minute evasive or corrective action to avoid the worst of it. Then ahead and to the right appeared a shadow—at first dimly seen—then a dark object floating in the whiteness. I blinked and stared, hoping that my eyes were not playing tricks on me. A moment later a great feeling of relief filled the cockpit as I pointed ahead. "Matt! There's the mission!"

By this time we were in whiteout conditions at their worst. With no light there were no shadows. We knew the surface was there but it was invisible. We had only our *inukshuks* and the distant view of the mission building to guide us. Flying under such conditions, we might easily have stalled and crashed or flown straight into the ice. But Matt's judgement and skill were superb. We touched down smoothly beside our runway markers.

We had lunch—bannock, beans and tea—while we discussed the activities of the morning, and the tension gradually dissipated. Red and I then returned to the aircraft to drain the oil, rebuild the protective snow wall for the engine cover, and add the 10 gallons of reserve fuel. It was 11:00 when we landed so we had consumed a further 45 minutes of the gasoline that we needed to reach Aklavik. Matt and I had no further discussions about the fuel situation. We both knew that our tanks would probably be empty and we would be faced with a forced landing before we reached the Mackenzie River delta. Although Red made no mention of it, he must also have been aware of how critical the situation was. He had helped me refuel at Letty and knew how much remained at that point. We didn't tell the others as there was no point in adding to their worries.

The next morning the weather looked promising at Paulatuk, but we were unable to contact Aklavik for a weather report. By noon it had cleared up beautifully, and I'm sure the same thought crossed all minds—perhaps we should take our chances on Aklavik's weather—but we were too low on fuel to chance another aborted flight. Matt, Red and I went for a good long walk that afternoon; we enjoyed the exercise and it lifted our spirits.

We had been at Paulatuk for six days and eating well enough during that time on basic food stuffs—porridge, beans, bannock and tea. Most of this was from the supplies that we had brought back from Letty, so without that provisioning trip we would certainly have been on short rations. The mission also had some caribou meat that had been killed during the summer and stored on ice in a rock shelter, but while the stones may have kept the varmints at bay, they had done little to preserve the meat. The brother, who was also the cook, boiled some of it up every day or so but it didn't go down too well. It was definitely ripe, though not in the same category as Father Bename's seal.

There were a few books at the mission, but most were in French. However, Matt had brought a couple of books with him and shared them with Red. I had brought Nansen's *Farthest North*—two volumes of dry reading that would last me a long time. In the meantime our crib tournament continued each day and was our best entertainment.

Wednesday, December 16, was another dismal, discouraging day. Wind and snow all day with zero visibility. Our coal supply was getting low, and Fathers Bename and Griffin left that morning to dig some from a small outcrop up the Hornady River. It was a one-day journey from the mission, they would spend one day digging coal and return on the third day. This would be a hard trip for the poor dogs, too, as the snow in the river bottom would be soft, making the pulling hard.

Thursday was quite calm but heavily overcast. We went for a walk in the afternoon but there was no light and no shadows. It was impossible to see the snow surface or to see sizeable chunks of ice. In my journal that night I noted that we were averaging about 20 crib games a day with breaks in between.

On Friday, another day of heavy overcast and no visibility, the fathers returned with five sacks of coal. The dogs were almost exhausted, and the fathers were doubtful that the animals would have enough strength to make another trip for coal. They decided to rest the next day, then make the trip back to Tessuriak for fish. If they had a good catch, the fathers assured us, and the dogs had a few days' rest, they would start to regain their strength. Much wishful if-ing, I thought. All this time we were fully aware that our situation was steadily worsening, with food, fuel and dog feed all being depleted and no way to improve the situation. We considered using the next clear day at Paulatuk to make another trip to Letty for fuel and food.

However, on Saturday morning, Paulatuk weather looked good and Aklavik came up with a promising report. We heated up ARI and loaded our people, though not without a general feeling of pessimism as Monday's events were still fresh in our memories. We were airborne at 10:15, but with our meagre fuel supply in mind, Matt operated the motor at reduced speed (1,700 rpms instead of the normal 1,800) with the carburetor mixture control in the maximum lean position—that is, one notch richer than the point where the motor would start to complain. Although the light was not bright, we had sufficient visibility to follow the coast and the hills without difficulty until we reached Horton River. Once we turned away from the coast and started in a southwesterly direction, we expected to have clear sailing all the way to Aklavik, but as soon as we crossed over into the flat and featureless country around Husky Inlet, we were in trouble again. An overcast had developed and the

CF-ARI at Paulatuk on December 10, 1936, having made the 400-mile journey from Aklavik the previous day. The plane was weather-bound at Paulatuk for another 10 days.

light was fading. In addition, intermittent fog patches occurred, making it almost impossible to maintain contact with the surface. By this time we were down close to the snow, flying over what appeared to be a lake, so Matt decided to land while it was still possible. The light by now was so dim that we were unable to check the ground drift for wind direction, but there was little we could have done about it in any case. A low-level manoeuvre in near-whiteout conditions could have fatal consequences. We hit the surface with a fierce jolt and then were airborne again. I was sure that we had left the undercarriage behind us and that the next touchdown would be on the belly of the aircraft. Matt swore (rare for him), applied engine power again, and nursed the aircraft down a second time. After that first impact I had braced myself, expecting the worst. We hit the surface and bounced a second time, but the bounces gradually decreased in size and intensity, though collectively they added up to the roughest landing that I had ever experienced. As we slowed to a halt with blowing snow coming from behind us, Matt exclaimed,

"No wonder it was so rough—we landed downwind!" It turned out that we had landed with a wind of approximately 25 miles per hour in the wrong place—behind us instead of in front.

With the poles under the skis, the oil drained, and the engine cover on, we set about preparing a shelter for the night. Spreading the wing covers to their full width and joining them together, we extended the canvas as a curtain behind the skis and undercarriage, then forward to the engine cover where the ends were joined. After banking snow against the bottom of the covers to keep them in place against the driving wind, we used pieces of rope and wire to tie the upper edges of the covers up against the wings and fuselage and achieved a roomy and protective shelter. We set up our tent inside of this, and it became our cookshack and mess hall. With our Coleman stove in operation, we took rice, rolled oats, and bully beef from our emergency rations, cooking them together to form a half-soup half-stew meal. As we had to share the utensils, we took turns eating. The eaters stayed inside the tent where there was a bit of warmth, while the waiters hopped around inside the shelter, exercising to keep warm. But food never tasted better.

Sleeping accommodations were our next concern. We placed Brother Kraut and the four children in the tent and the Bishop and Father L'Helgouach under the engine cover, the extra layer of canvas that surrounded them giving at least the illusion of warmth. Matt, Red and I occupied the cabin of the aircraft, the coldest and most uncomfortable location of all. Fortunately, by the time we turned in for the night, the wind had dropped, though as usual the temperature was skidding downhill, registering -30°F on our last check.

Our takeoff time that morning had been 10:15 and our landing time 12:30. Taking into account the fuel used on our practice run on December 14, I calculated we had about one hour's fuel left in the tanks. Although we were still far from being out of trouble, at least we were inland and off the coast, and a couple of hours closer to Aklavik. By this time the priests left at Paulatuk would have notified Aklavik of our departure, and if we did not appear within a couple of days, they would know that we were in trouble and a search would be organized. If we could reach the treeline before our fuel was exhausted, our situation would improve considerably, and once on the delta, our downed aircraft would not be too hard to find. Of course, this was some more iffy thinking on my part, but our percentages had already improved greatly, I decided, as I dropped off to sleep. I'm sure that Matt had been going through the same mental process.

While the Junkers was a truly great aircraft and the best of the early bush planes, the cabin was never designed as sleeping quarters. The floor was actually a continuation of the wing surface and it was impossible to find a smooth or level place on which to lie. We envied our passengers, lying on soft, level snow with their caribou skin mattresses and covers. Because of the cold and our uncomfortable sleeping accommodations, we all woke periodically during the night, and sometime toward morning while changing our sleeping positions—and waking one another in the process—we exchanged some uncomplimentary remarks concerning the aircraft's designers. But it was then that we realized there appeared to be genuine daylight coming in through the cabin windows. Investigating, we discovered that the sky was clear and bright with the surface visibility, even at that early hour, better than anything we had seen since leaving Aklavik.

The temperature was -46°F but there was no wind. Everyone was up in short order and, with the blow pots operating under the engine cover and some heat escaping into our enclosure, it became relatively comfortable. Starting up the Coleman stove, we had a small but tasty snack of hardtack and hot chocolate. As we were now using the last of our unleaded fuel in the blow pots and had need to conserve both fuel and heat, we placed some of the caribou skins on top of the engine cover as added insulation. With the heating well underway, I left the blow pots in Red's care for a few minutes and went out to investigate our landing field of the night before. From the point where we had first touched—bounced?—down, it was about a half-mile to the next contact point—a sizeable bounce. I could also see that the previous gale had been from the southeast, leaving snowdrifts with sharp faces toward the northwest, and we had landed against these drifts with a stiff wind behind us. With a renewed respect for the excellence of the design and construction of the Junkers aircraft, I returned and carried out a thorough inspection of the undercarriage, amazed that it was still intact.

With the heating completed and all of our gear and people safely stowed, we had another bruising takeoff. Then we turned our nose—and our thoughts—toward Aklavik. To further conserve fuel, we reduced the motor's operating speed to 1,600 rpms and adjusted the carburetor to the leanest possible mixture setting. Although the light was good, we encountered the same haze and frost situation as on our northbound trip, making horizontal visibility very limited. We now realized that our landing place the previous night must have been somewhere to the south of Husky Inlet because today, flying in a southwesterly direction, we saw nothing of the Husky Lakes. As the light grew stronger, we were able to maintain good contact with the surface, but having no landmarks to follow here, Matt used the compass to maintain our course, knowing that if we continued to the southwest, we would eventually strike the Mackenzie River delta.

As we droned on, I calculated that we must have had about 100 gallons of fuel on board at the time we left Paulatuk, leaving us with a bit less than 30 gallons . We had only an approximate idea of our present location, but I felt that we had not wandered and would still be fairly close to being on course. Therefore, with normal fuel consumption, we could expect to run out of fuel 25 or 30 miles short of Aklavik. There were, however, a couple of factors that might offset this. To begin with, we had been running at reduced power and with the carburetor adjusted to the maximum lean condition. This should have saved us a few gallons. Our final ace in the hole was a supply of extra fuel carried in a small auxiliary tank just forward of the cockpit. This fuel container, known as the gravity tank, had been incorporated into early Junkers designs because of problems with the engine-driven fuel pumps, which had a nasty habit of failing during critical manoeuvres. It had, therefore, become standard practice to use the fuel from the gravity tank during takeoff. While the fuel pump problems had long been corrected, we at CAL still followed the practice of keeping this tank full, and I knew that those few extra gallons could be important to us on this occasion.

Ahead of us the visibility improved dramatically and a few minutes later we were in clear weather. The sky above was blue and far ahead a dark line of timber indicated the Mackenzie River delta. Our shortage of fuel—and impending forced landing—were forgotten for a moment. Matt's smile was like a sunrise as he waved his hand in the direction of the trees and exclaimed, "Isn't that a beautiful sight!" Our admiration of the landscape was brief, however. Our most immediate concern was the location of Aklavik, somewhere ahead amid the myriad channels and lakes that form the delta.

Our normal approach to Aklavik was from the south, down the mile-wide channel of the Mackenzie, with a routine stop at Arctic Red River on the edge of the delta. From there we usually flew west to Fort McPherson on the

Peel River and finally northward down the Peel Channel to Aklavik. Approaching the 4,000-odd square miles of the delta from the northeast, however, was quite another matter. There were no landmarks that we recognized, and our fuel supply would not allow us to go exploring. Our only hope was to maintain our course, keep a sharp watch, and trust to luck. We had been flying for well over an hour and our airborne condition might terminate at any moment. In anticipation, I kept a close watch on the fuel pressure gauge, ready to open the gravity tank selector at the first indication of falling fuel pressure. I could see that Matt was paying close attention to the terrain immediately before us, searching for a suitable forced landing site, and I took similar action on my side. Then, during one of my brief glances through the side window, I happened to look beyond, and there, over the wing tip to the northwest, rose a cluster of smoke columns in the -50°F air. Aklavik at last!

Finding Aklavik was one thing. Getting there might be a different matter. It was still about 15 miles distant. Matt executed a cautious turn to the right, using extreme care so as not to disturb the remaining few gallons of fuel in the tanks. A shallow turn might cause the fuel in the left wing tanks to flee to the outer end of the tank. An overly steep turn might have a similar effect on the fuel in the right tank. The net result would have been the same in either case: momentary fuel starvation and loss of power with very little altitude below us for recovery action. Our progress during those last few minutes was agonizingly slow. The oxygen consumption in the cockpit during this period was minimal; we were both holding our breath. Finally, the river channel was in front of us and we were down and taxiing toward the settlement. Not wishing to be accused of grandstanding by running out of fuel 100 yards before our destination, I selected the gravity tank "on" and the mains "off," and we taxied to a stop in front of our welcoming committee—the entire population less dogs. Matt shut off the engine and we sat for a few moments in unbelieving silence. Finally he turned with a broad grin on his face, and we shook hands. "Some trip!" he said.

This would have been the time for welcoming speeches and group photos, but events moved too quickly. By the time I had covered the engine and retrieved my camera, our passengers had been whisked away to the mission. We retired to the Signal Corps station then to a warm welcome and more food than we could possibly eat—though we tried. Later I returned to the aircraft, and Red gave me a hand refuelling. When the tanks were finally filled, we had emptied two 45-gallon barrels completely, and a dipstick showed us that we had taken all but 19 gallons from a third barrel. We had, therefore, loaded 116 gallons into ARI, which meant that the fuel remaining after the flight from Paulatuk was about four gallons—the equivalent of approximately eight minutes flying time.

Later that evening Matt and I lay stretched out on top of our sleeping robes on the metal cots in the room we shared at the RCCS station. The building was quiet after the excitement of the afternoon. Clean, warm, well-fed, with the worries of the past 10 days behind us, we relaxed and enjoyed the comfort. Few words were spoken as both of us mentally relived our experiences, but presently we heard footsteps, and Frank Riddell appeared in the doorway. He was keenly interested in all details of our trip and we discussed these at length. Being a most knowledgeable and proficient northern traveller, he had a better appreciation than most of the experiences and conditions that we described. At our account of the mission people's walk from Pearce Point, he slowly shook his head in silent admiration of their courage and fortitude. Finally he rose to leave, then stood in silence for a few moments. He studied each of us in turn, then said, "You know, I was getting worried about you guys." Matt turned to look at me for a long moment, then his craggy face broke into a grin as he turned back to Frank. "Well, Frank, we were, too!" he said.

My journal entry for that Sunday, December 20, begins, *"Finally, the Bishop must have made contact with Those On High because amazingly this diary entry is being made at Aklavik."*

The next day, December 21, the shortest day of the year, we were southbound again, planning to make Fort Norman that night. One of our passengers on that trip was Bishop Fallaize, on his way to Fort Smith after his Paulatuk adventures. For a change of ecclesiastical flavour we also had on board Mrs. Webster, the wife of one of the high-ranking Anglicans in the Arctic. As these two religious groups very carefully ignored the presence of one another, the journey would doubtless have been rather strained had it not been for the moderating influence of Mr. and Mrs. Copland, Hudson's Bay people, going outside on furlough. In later years, after spending most of his working days in the Arctic, Mr. Copland wrote a book describing his northern experiences. He called it *Coplalook*, meaning Big Copland, the name the Inuit had bestowed upon him.

The author drains the oil from CF-ARI after returning to Aklavik from the Paulatuk mission, December 20, 1936. *Photo: Matt Berry*

A happy group assembles at the Signals station in Fort Norman after the successful Paulatuk rescue. "Snoot" Ross is second from the left, Rex Terpening is seated centre front, Frank Rapp is second from right, and pilot Matt Berry is at the far right.

Our problems on this trip, however, were not yet over. The temperature at Aklavik was -55°F that morning and, just as Matt and I had experienced at Camsell River a year earlier, there was granular snow that rolled in front of the skis. Here, however, there was one improvement over Camsell—the snow was not as deep, so I got out and shovelled two paths down to bare ice then did some tail pushing until we had the skis onto the ice. At that point Matt throttled back so I could return the shovel to the cabin and climb back up to the cockpit. Full throttle again gave us enough speed to keep moving after we reached the snow. We had a mail pickup at Arctic Red River and ran into the same conditions again—deep, granular snow with a -50°F temperature. This time we couldn't taxi after landing, and I tried the tail-pushing operation for as long as I could stand it, but we moved only a few feet. We shut down the engine and did our mail exchange, then it was out with the shovel and a repeat of the Aklavik experience. It took full throttle again to get us moving, and the takeoff was slow but we made it. All of this involved some extra work and cost us some precious time that meant we made it only as far as Fort Good Hope that night.

15 A mid-winter tale

"Better pack up your gear and get your tools ready, Rex! BAU is down with a washed-out undercarriage on some little lake outside Yellowknife." The speaker was Bert Field, chief mechanic for Canadian Airways at Edmonton, and the date was January 12, 1938. I had been assigned to a base job in Edmonton just a few weeks earlier and for the first time in my career with the company no longer took part in regular operations.

Bert's news was disturbing because BAU was a fairly new Norseman, and "washed-out undercarriage" could mean serious structural damage. All of the Norseman aircraft were well put together—Bob Noordyun, the Norseman's designer, didn't just tack the undercarriage onto the outside of the fuselage as aircraft manufacturers had done before him. The structures that formed the foundations for his shock struts were sturdy extensions of the fuselage, and I could not visualize a landing with impact of sufficient magnitude to remove them. Naturally, I couldn't help but wonder whether we'd heard the whole story.

Putting these less-than-cheerful thoughts from my mind, I checked over my tool kit to make sure that everything I would need was present and accounted for. I took the added precaution of including a dozen top quality 32-tooth hacksaw blades. The chrome-moly tubing from which the Norseman was made seemed to eat hacksaw blades. Then after touching up my own assortment of cold chisels on the grinding wheel, I raided other tool boxes to increase my supply. I could not imagine any sort of a steel-tube repair operation without them; their prolonged and serious application would be needed to remove the old weld material as well as the failed structural members.

The next morning I was on my way north with Harry Winny, overnighting at Fort Chipewyan and on to Fort Smith the following day. According to my diary entries, poor flying weather held me at Smith until January 17, but I took advantage of the delay to wire ahead for a dog team, winter camping gear and salvage equipment. Then to further hasten my departure from Yellowknife for the bush, I went over to Smith's Hudson's Bay store and purchased a camp stove and pipes, axe, steel-framed bow saw, ice chisel, camp utensils, candles, rabbit snare wire, and basic grub supplies—a slab of bacon, flour, baking powder, tinned butter, tinned jam and honey, beans, macaroni, and dried vegetables.

While still at Smith, I asked Yellowknife for the names of the unfortunate BAU's crew, particularly the engineer, because I would need a partner for this repair job and assumed that BAU's engineer would be the logical party. I was informed that this had been Ted Bowles and that he was standing by, ready to accompany me. Ted was one of those even-tempered, cheerful individuals who seldom complained about anything—a first-rate companion for a session of winter camping in the bush. To demonstrate the full extent of his accommodation and forbearance, after our adventure was over, he even claimed to have relished my cooking.

The next day we joined forces at Yellowknife and I learned the details of the mishap. The pilot had been Don Lawson, one of the company's "mossbacks" from the Pacific Coast, happy to be flying and earning his three-cents-a-mile bonus but unhappy about our climate. He had been landing BAU on a smallish lake a few miles northeast of Yellowknife, a lake that, so it developed, was not quite long enough for their particular flight. (To Don's chagrin, we christened it Lawson Lake.) BAU's progress had been interrupted by the very solidly frozen low bank at the end of the lake. Don, Ted, and their two prospector passengers had made their way across an intervening ridge to a neighbouring chain of lakes, which by great good fortune were on the main route of the tractor-trains that operated each winter between Yellowknife and the CM&S camp at Gordon Lake.

As the main concern of the crew and passengers had been getting back to Yellowknife, they hadn't spent much time examining BAU's damage, but from Ted's report of his brief inspection I understood that we had a very

Dog team driver Willie Wylie had been instrumental in building and operating the Wildcat Cafe, a Yellowknife landmark.

unhealthy aircraft on our hands. Both sides of the heavy structure that provided the attachment points for the undercarriage had almost certainly been damaged. The propeller was bent, and since Ted reported that the motor was resting solidly on the hard, frozen ground, there was a strong possibility that there was damage to the engine mount. Obviously, the duration of this salvage job would be measured in weeks rather than days. However, there were certain positive benefits to the accident site: its proximity to Yellowknife (a matter of 12 miles) and the tractor-train service (though the finer points of its schedule would constantly elude us.) The only minor flaw in the location was the well-timbered, snow-covered, rocky ridge that separated the site of the downed aircraft from the tractor-train road.

The equipment required to salvage aircraft, either from the bush or after an ice break-through, is always heavy-duty stuff. Fortunately, there was an abundance of such equipment at bases where mining operations existed, and the mining people were invariably most helpful if we were in trouble and generous with the loan of equipment. On this occasion, CM&S provided us with a chain hoist, a couple of logging chains, some lengths of heavy rope, and an extra axe. This last item might appear to have been overkill, but this was January and we would be entirely dependent upon wood for fuel. Broken axes make for cold camps. For the immediate transportation of our camping equipment, we were fortunate in being able to hire an old friend from the Fort Chipewyan area, Willie Wylie. A totally reliable individual and experienced northerner, he had a fine team of dogs. (Willie had also been instrumental in building and operating the Wildcat Cafe, a Yellowknife landmark that has been preserved in the old town. A replica of it has now been constructed in the wonderful Museum of Civilization in Ottawa.)

We would also need to set up a communications system between our camp and Yellowknife to report our day-to-day progress but more importantly to let company headquarters in Winnipeg know the extent of the damage and thus set the repair wheels in motion at the Norseman factory in Montreal. Leaving Ted and Willie to sort out our equipment and divide it into separate loads, I paid a quick visit to our company's radio station to arrange a schedule with Cliff Brindley, our operator there. It was decided that we would contact one another between 7:00 and 8:00 each evening; Cliff would then relay our messages to and from Edmonton and Winnipeg. Cliff would also relay our orders for food supplies. (Thanks to his efforts and to Pete Racine, pioneer operator of the first restaurant and bunkhouse on Latham Island at Yellowknife, Ted and I were destined to fare well.)

BAU's radio was to be our camp radio. Although CAL's aircraft were not equipped with radios that would allow voice contact with ground stations, each of them did carry a small, dry-cell-battery-powered emergency unit with continuous wave (CW) capability. These radios required knowledge of Morse code and the ability to operate a hand key, and fortunately I knew how to do both, though my sending speed was probably in the 25-word-per-minute range, my receiving speed half of that. (Professional operators using semi-automatic keys known as "bugs" could send and receive at four or five times that.) As far as the unit itself was concerned, the only slight drawback was that the output of dry batteries diminishes as temperatures drop into the below-zero range. Because the batteries for our unit had to be stored in our unheated tent, at times their output would prove marginal.

As we assembled our gear for departure, the only missing item was one of considerable importance: a tent. The mining corporation at Gordon Lake

The author takes a rest from breaking trail over the portage to Lawson Lake where Norseman CF-BAU awaits repairs. January 18, 1938.

Engineer Ted Bowles carries an armful of repair equipment as he heads for camp on Lawson Lake.

had agreed to supply one and promised to send it over on one of our aircraft. But this was a promise for the future, and since our tent requirements would become very real in just a few hours, we were rather reluctant to take to the timber without one. Willie, however, volunteered to stay behind to wait for its arrival and assured us that he would not leave Yellowknife without it.

That night I made my first diary entry from Lawson Lake.

> ***Tuesday, January 18:*** *Ted and I left Yellowknife at 12:35. Tractor road well-packed so made good time but needed snowshoes on that evil ridge. Trail drifted over. Willie caught up with us at portage. Had to break new trail so forced to leave most of load by tractor trail. Arrived about 5:30, set up tent and tin stove, found dry wood, had supper ready*

by 7:30. Willie stayed overnight to give a hand setting up camp. Turns out tent never arrived from Gordon Lake so he borrowed this one from a friend. Had a quick look at BAU, but it was too dark to determine extent of damage. Weather pleasant: -20°F and no wind.

The next morning we went back over the portage for the balance of our load plus the heavier items that the tractor train was to have dropped off when they went through, but we found they had forgotten some of our equipment, including my tool box. It took two trips to our campsite to bring the load they'd left for us. Later Harry Winny landed with the mining corporation tent so we set it up in place of the borrowed one, which Willie took back with him. We cut wood, sawed a hole in the ice to get water, and set up the radio antenna. That night we tried to reach Cliff but couldn't make contact, probably because the batteries were too cold. "*Weather staying mild,*" I wrote in my diary, "*-5°F, overcast, no wind.*"

We reached Cliff by radio on Thursday morning, but with Winnipeg getting anxious, he had already dispatched a dog team to get a list of necessary parts from us. We removed the fairings from both sides of BAU that morning and stripped the fabric off to discover that five tubes and the shock leg socket would need replacing on the left side, two tubes and the shock leg socket on the right. As expected, the bottom half of the engine mount had been overstressed and the mounting lug had collapsed in one place.

Cliff's dog team arrived about 1:00 p.m., bringing bread, bacon and candles from Pete Racine; we had actually been okay for bacon and candles but the bread was a great treat. I made a wire out for Tommy Siers, our maintenance superintendent at Winnipeg, with a copy for Bert and sent it back with the dog team driver. By the time darkness fell about 5:30, Ted and I had managed to get a tripod up and the chain block rigged. That night, using poles and spruce boughs, we made up two bunks, a big improvement over the previous night's sleeping accommodations.

Friday, January 21: *Daylight about 8:45. Cut and squared logs for blocking. Raised aircraft with chain hoist, then collapsed left shock strut by jacking under ski. Wired torque scissors to prevent it extending. Jacked up right side and chain hoist. Had to remove engine cowl and one induction pipe to get engine sling in place. Removed ski pedestal by drifting*

Norseman CF-BAU on the shore of Lawson Lake. The broken stub of the right shock leg was imbedded a foot into the frozen ground, but the skis had suffered only superficial damage. January 18, 1938.

The shock leg socket on the left side of Norseman CF-BAU. The upper fore and aft member has been torn away and the lower member compressed.

out steel bushing—very tight. Cleaned ski bottom (frost and dirt) and lowered shock strut stub into axle groove. Aircraft ready to go down onto ice tomorrow. Went over to tractor trail after supper to put up more markers. Worked Cliff at 7 but signals poor. He was unable to work McMurray all day. Weather clear. Temperature dropped to -20°F but cloudy and warm tonight.

Though BAU had been ready to go down onto the ice the next day, she didn't go without a struggle. We tried pulling her with the block and tackle, but she wouldn't budge. Then we took one ski off and cleaned the frost and ice from its bottom with a torch. Because the tail ski was down in the hole, we had to remove its fairing and jack the tail up to get it out, then fill the hole with snow and dump water on it to make ice. We also packed snow behind the main skis and iced it as well, but that aircraft still would not move. Finally, we had to take the chain block off the tripod and use it to do the job—slow, hard work—but we got her down onto the ice at 5:00 p.m. and quit for the day as we were both kind of beat. Ted then went over the portage to see if the tractor had dropped off the rest of our tools and equipment as we would be ready to take the engine out in a few days. When he came back empty-handed, I radioed Cliff to ask him to check on their whereabouts. That night I made a big batch of macaroni and cheese, enough for dinner and for meals all the next day.

It had snowed all day Saturday while we worked on BAU, and on Sunday we had to shovel runways for the skis before we dug stirrups into the ice for the chain block anchors. We then pulled the aircraft back and gave it a quarter turn. Our next job was to cut down a big tree, square it and cut it into lengths for blocking. Then to aid in the jacking and levelling operation, we removed the bottom fairing. Around 3:30 we thought we heard a tractor engine and found they had at last left my tool box, a heater, ropes and pipes, but not the empty gas can or the length of chain we had asked for. We carried the tool box as far as the edge of the lake, then went back to bring the other items over. I had arranged to radio Cliff at 11:30 that morning but had been too busy, and when I tried that evening I couldn't raise him. However, I did send Bert a wire, asking him to ship float struts for BAU as they would be handy in positioning the shock leg sockets. On those early Norseman aircraft the float struts were positioned by a lug welded

The author's cook shack, sleeping quarters and radio station for his 5-week stay on Lawson Lake. At -50° F a tent is not the warmest accommodation.

onto the outside of the shock leg socket. The angle of this socket when it was welded to the structure was therefore critical.

In my diary for January 23, I noted: *Caught a rabbit this morning and had him fried for supper. Weather -25°F this morning, -15°F at noon, -40°F tonight.*

> *In the morning when we heard tractors, we hurried over to meet them and discovered they had brought the remaining missing equipment at last. We collected my tool box from the edge of the lake and carried it back slung between two poles—an interesting exercise in balance and coordination between two men on snowshoes on a rough trail. It was almost noon before we reached camp, and Ted went back to get the logging chain and the gas while I made dinner. That afternoon we cut open the wing to inspect the spar at its strut attachment point and check the diagonal tie rods for equal tension, and finding them okay, we sewed up the holes in the fabric again. We finished the day by jacking up the*

The author using an axe to square trees which were then sawn into short lengths to make a crib to support the fuselage.

aircraft to begin the levelling process and building a log crib under it, then knocked off to cut firewood.

Monday, January 24: *Mixed up a bannock tonight and have batch of beans soaking to cook tomorrow. Weather warming up, -45°F this morning, -30°F noon, -10°F tonight.*

Over the next two days we cut trees, blocked and levelled. On Tuesday we levelled the aircraft laterally—slow work—then cut ice stirrups so we could tie it down to prevent movement if a wind came up. Next we jacked up the tail to level the aircraft fore and aft but ran out of blocking. While we were busy with this manoeuvre, we also discovered that the tail fork was cracked, though we concluded that it must have been that way for some time. North Sawle passed over us a couple of times that day in AQW, flying low to see how we were doing. On Wednesday we made more blocking and jacked the tail up higher, but it was still not enough to get it level, and we realized that by the time we did get it level, our crib was going to be completely unstable. The only answer was to lower the front end by removing the shock struts. This meant dismantling the tripod and re-erecting it over the engine, embedding the tripod ends in the ice, and once again putting up that heavy old chain block. Looking over the damaged tubing that day, I realized that there was sufficient room to attach external splice tubes, and that night I worked Cliff again and wired for splicing sleeves and a new tail fork.

> **Wednesday, January 26:** *Lots of ptarmigan around but no gun.* [Though a gun was a regular part of all CAL aircraft's equipment, we hadn't found one in BAU.] *Macaroni and cheese, hot biscuits and rice pudding for supper tonight. Ted claims he's putting on weight with my good cooking.*

> **Thursday, January 27:** *Hoisted aircraft, removed damaged shock struts, then lowered it until laterally level and re-installed cribbing. Shock strut sockets now just clear of ice. Jacked up tail again until fore and aft level and installed aft crib. North* [Sawle] *circled over this p.m. and landed across portage. Scampered over and met him and Jack Dame walking over. Brought us bread, cake, pie, and magazines—boy, just like Christmas! Lent us their* Game-Getter. [This was the small, over-and-under firearm, .22 calibre above and .410 shotgun below, that was normally carried in each aircraft along with the emergency rations.] *Late in evening North flew over again and dropped more supplies and mail, first we'd had and very welcome. Tomorrow will start building canvas shelter around aircraft. Got three ptarmigan with Game-Getter tonight. Today's temps: -30°F a.m., -10°F noon, -15°F night.*

On Friday, a cold day with a strong wind, we used our two tarps, each about 20 by 24 feet, to fashion a shelter around BAU, wrapping one around the tripod and the other over the top of the nose, then stretching the wing covers under the belly. We put one airtight heater on each side, installing stovepipes and tin guards in case the pipes happened to get hot enough to burn the canvas. We now had three stoves to feed, but dry wood was getting scarce, and we spent Saturday cutting down four trees and carrying two of them back to camp. There was plenty of birch around but it was all green, though we did split some of it into fine pieces and mixed it with the dry spruce. On Sunday we discovered some dry wood across the portage, spent all morning (temperature -48°F) cutting it, and all afternoon (-26°F) carrying it back to camp. By this time we had been in camp 12 days.

> **Monday, January 31:** *Tried out stoves this morning to see how much heat they generate. Let them go out before noon to conserve wood. Started removing motor this p.m. Exhausts, carb and scoops off. North pulled a sneaky landing across the portage today—didn't hear him at all. He, Jack Dame and Al Pierce* [our agent] *walked over to surprise us. Very decent chaps, I must say. Brought bread, cake, pie and mail, so we feasted tonight. Weather nice today: am -35°F, noon -20°F, night -35°F.*

But the cold was starting to get to us. It was not so bad when we were moving around and working hard, but standing on the ice to work on the motor was pretty cool work. On Tuesday morning, February 1, we lit the two heaters so that we had a degree of warmth while we removed the exhaust pipes, gas lines and shrouds, slacked off the four top engine bearer bolts, and removed the lower five. When we quit for the day, there was only the starter to come off before we could remove the motor. A young Native lad stopped by that afternoon. He had been out caribou hunting, saw our trail and came over to see what was happening. That evening I made a meat pie—ptarmigan and dried vegetables, but there was more pie than meat as the crust rose more than I expected.

> **Wednesday, February 2:** *Ted removed starter a.m. I stripped fabric from left side stub leg, loosened and raised floorboard to provide welding clearance. Be a shame to burn our bird after working so hard to retrieve her! No word on parts. Ted will go to town in a.m. so finished letter writing. Warm today, -30°F, -15°F, -15°F.*

Early the next morning I contacted Cliff but he still had nothing to report on the parts situation. I walked Ted across the portage, carrying his sleeping bag for him that far. On my return to camp I saw caribou tracks on the lake but couldn't locate the animals, which was probably just as well

Norseman CF-BAU, with its makeshift hangar completed and stoves installed, ready to be repaired.

as the Game-Getter was really too light for the job. In the afternoon I constructed a workbench in the shelter and mounted our vise on it. That night the signals were bad, and I couldn't raise Cliff to let him know that Ted was on his way in, but comforted myself that he would be okay as the trail was good and the weather warm: a.m. -16°F, noon -14°F, p.m. -14°F.

On Friday there was a wire from Bert to say that he was coming north with the parts, and I assumed he would bring Jim Dick along to do the welding. I finished installing the vise, inserted a piece of tin under one of the stoves (the ice was beginning to melt and we certainly didn't need wet moccasins), and then cut down a big birch tree, sawed it into stove lengths and split it—slow work with frozen wood. Around 4:30 p.m. I tramped across the portage to meet Ted, but when he didn't show up, I returned to camp and got supper underway. He turned up around 6:00 accompanied by a hearty appetite from his walk. That night I wired Al Pierce to arrange for an extra tent and stove for our incoming repair crew as well as a cook so we could spend all our time working on the aircraft. *Weather cooling off tonight: a.m. -1°F, noon -10°F, night -30°F.*

On Saturday, February 5, our 18th day in camp, we learned that the repair parts and crew had left McMurray that morning aboard Rudy Heuss's aircraft. They made it as far as Resolution that day and landed on the lake beside us at 2:30 on Monday afternoon. As I expected, Bert had brought Jim Dick—expert welder and fixer of aircraft—and had hired Jack Carey of Yellowknife to cook for us. Their load included a second tent, a cookstove, lots of grub, and ample repair parts. Winnipeg had actually sent the complete engine mount plus both the left and right stub undercarriage assemblies and shock struts, which was more than we needed. The only negative thing now was that the weather had turned really cold the last two days, and it hit -52°F that night.

> **Tuesday, February 8:** *Real cold this a.m.—quite a shock for our visitors! As Robert Service says, "It was 50 below, and crouched in the snow. . . ." Though in our case it was 55 below! Started stoves first thing but 10:00 before we could work. Intended to salvage tubing from old stubs to make splicing sleeves, but new tubing larger—1¾" and 2¾". Original tubing 1¼" and 2¼". Cut away left side damaged tubing but slow job ahead to chisel away old welds. Repeat on right side. Hoped to replace just damaged section of engine mount ring, but Winnipeg sent the whole thing, so lots of hacksawing and chiselling needed on mount. Nobody got much sleep in last night's cold so we're all going to sleep in the cook tent tonight and take two-hour shifts keeping the stove going. Temperature: a.m. -55°F, p.m. -46°F.*

> **Wednesday, February 9:** *Made good headway. Worked 10 hours solid. Quit at 9 tonight. Jim finished left side chiselling and new stub ready to weld in but will first have to remove the wing strut attachment bolt and support wing. Took motor out this p.m. and cut mounting ring away from support tubes. No radio tonight—all static and no signals. Weather: a.m. -48°F, noon -27°F, p.m. -30°F.*

> **Thursday, February 10:** *Slow and frustrating day. Blueprints measurements don't agree with actual aircraft measurements. Checked and*

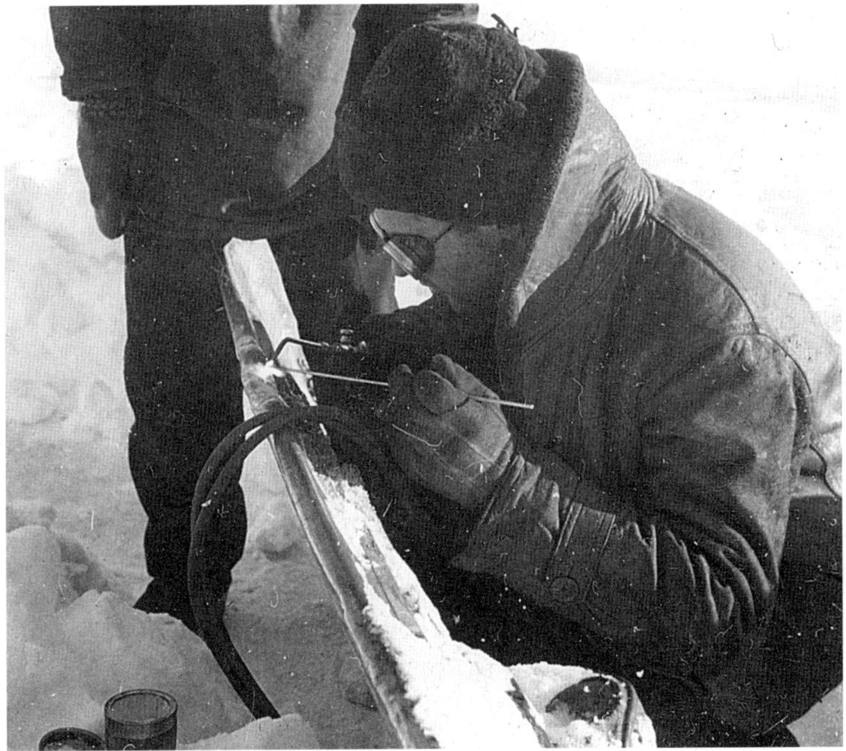

Welder Jim Dick brazes the torn brass on one of CF-BAU's ski bottoms.

measured then finally concluded blueprint applies to earlier model Norseman. Was going to wire Winnipeg for additional measurements and levelling points but radio signals out so decided to forge ahead. Bert and Jim working on stub and blueprint—I spent day on motor mount. Temperature: a.m. -50°F, noon -40°F, p.m. -40°F.

Friday, February 11: *Good day. I fitted ring—all plumb and square. Jim welded it this p.m. and welded left stub tonight. Should get motor back in tomorrow. Bert cutting away old welds right side. Ted and I cut wood this p.m. (Cook was supposed to cut wood but has other ideas.) Radio signals still out. Cold again today: a.m. -48°F, noon -27°F, p.m. -54°F.*

Saturday, February 12: *Put motor in. All bolts lined up perfectly, starter, carb and all plumbing in and connected. Jim fitting left-side fairing frame. Most of old welds chiselled away. Didn't work tonight as* *everyone thoroughly chilled and real tired—partly from lack of sleep. Jim and Ted both coming down with colds. Worked Cliff tonight, ordered grub. Weather still cold: a.m. -50°F, noon -30°F, p.m. -30°F.*

Sunday, February 13: *Oil lines, gas lines, shrouds, hot spot and part of exhaust on. Ted started covering left stub with fabric—a slow, barehanded job. Bert and Jim working on right stub. Fitting and alignment completed today and welding finished tonight. Radio signals still out. Heard a couple of aircraft today but couldn't see them—probably not ours. Temperature: a.m. -50°F, noon -24°F.*

Monday, February 14: *Grub running low. Worked on engine installation all day, Jim fitting right-side fairings, Ted sewing and doping, Bert repairing skis. Took radio batteries out of box, heated them up, re-installed them and now in touch with Cliff again. Grub arrived by dog team this p.m., also mail, very welcome. Weather moderated a bit: a.m. -46°F, noon -20°F, p.m. -24°F.*

Tuesday, February 15: *Finished motor this a.m. and cowlings on. Ted finished fabric on right side. Bert and Jim finished ski repairs. This p.m. raised aircraft with chain hoist and put shock struts on. Fitted okay except attaching bolt holes needed some filing. Hung aircraft in engine sling, pulled right side down far enough to get left ski on, then jacked up right side and installed right ski. Installing engine fairings tonight. Worked Cliff tonight and no word on replacement tail fork. Will have to repair old one. Warm today: a.m. -35°F.*

Wednesday, February 16: *Shock leg fairings don't fit too well—exasperating and time-consuming. Installed main exhaust stack, hooked up cockpit and cabin heaters, removed engine sling and installed top inlet cylinder baffle. Repaired tail fork. Fortunately, Jim had foresight to bring assortment of 4130 plate and tubing.* [4130 was the technical designation for chrome-molybdenum steel, the principal ingredient of the steel tube fuselages of the Norseman and most other aircraft of that era.] *Applied a sheet of .125 steel plate across top of fork and welded it in place—stronger than new. Dog team brought*

Norseman CF-BAU repaired and ready to fly again.

The author after five weeks of camping on Lake Lawson.

Ted Bowles after five weeks of camping on Lake Lawson.

new propeller this a.m. Installed it, pumped up shock struts, packed up tools and equipment, took shelter down. About ready to go. Worked Cliff tonight. Says pilot will be over at 10 a.m. to fly aircraft out. Warm today: a.m. -35°F, noon -12°F, p.m. -15°F. 29 days in camp.

The dog team arrived at 8:30 the following morning and we gave him a load to take across the portage. I went over to meet the pilot and bring him back with me—a new man in the district, Delamere, but Del for short. Then just when we were all ready to start the engine, I noticed a gas leak, and we had to remove the cowling again to locate it. Turned out it was just a piece of bonding under a rubber hose connection. Del took off in BAU while we were still breaking camp. Afterwards we walked across the portage for the last time. Rudy Heuss was waiting for us in a CAL Fairchild 71, and we loaded all of our loose gear into the cabin, climbed aboard ourselves, and in a few minutes were in Yellowknife. There we transferred our gear to BAU before going up to Pete Racine's for dinner. He welcomed us back and we thanked him mightily for all of the goodies he had sent over. He told us dinner was "on the house" and we could order anything we wanted. As it turned out, there were only three items on the menu and two of them were caribou. (Not to disparage Pete's offering, but caribou—particularly lean, winter-killed caribou—was not considered the greatest of culinary treats.) I made out a final weather report for Lawson Lake for February 17, 1938: a.m. -15°F, noon -10°F, p.m. -15°F. With that we were southbound, looking forward to an overnight at Fort Smith at the only hotel in the Territories, a hot bath and the removal of a batch of evil, itchy whiskers. *(As a postscript to this story, I'd like to say that Ted Bowles is still in the circuit to this day, and we manage an annual meeting to review and relive the events of January and February 1938.)*

16 A change in flight plans

After I was assigned to a base job in Edmonton at the beginning of January 1938, I saw little of day-to-day flight operations, other than the Norseman repair job on Lawson Lake and a trip to Cambridge Bay a month or so later. But in September of that year we were short-handed—maintenance-wise—and I became the temporary base engineer at Yellowknife. It was an extremely busy period. Mining exploration was in full swing, and there was a huge backlog of freight to be moved before freeze-up.

The company had a sizeable dock at Yellowknife, and as this was where we loaded all our aircraft and serviced them between trips, we had one standing rule: so as not to interfere with our morning loading and departure routines, no visiting aircraft was allowed to remain at our dock overnight. Well, one overcast day in mid-September a Waco cabin biplane belonging to a mining firm that was one of our good customers arrived and tied up at our dock. Late afternoon came and it was still there, and our company agent approached me to ask if we might bend the rules a little and allow the Waco to stay the night. Knowing that this would cause some delay in the morning, I was reluctant but finally agreed, on the understanding that he would depart early and not hold up our operations.

Morning came and we engineers went down to the dock early to warm up the engines of the three CAL aircraft tied up along the shoreline, only to discover that the unwelcome Waco was still at the dock, occupying valuable and much-needed space. Finally the pilot (who shall remain nameless) appeared and made hasty preparations for departure, tossing his bag into the cabin, then climbing into the cockpit. Our visitor then primed his Waco's Jacobs engine and turned on the ignition, forgetting that, with the colder autumn weather and overnight frosts, he would first have to rotate the engine two or three times by hand to break the oil film in the cylinders. Apparently, he remembered this at last and climbed down again from the cockpit.

I was watching this operation from along the beach, becoming more and more exasperated with the delay. I saw him stand on the right-hand float and turn the prop to a near vertical position. He then moved to the left float and I watched while he reached across to pull the lower prop blade toward him. Fortunately, he couldn't quite reach the blade. I say "fortunately" because it turned out that it was only the fact that he couldn't reach it that saved his life; he had not switched off the ignition when he climbed out of the cockpit, and he was now standing squarely in front of the propeller.

At the time, however, all I could see was that this operation was going nowhere, and I called out, "Hold on a minute, Mac! I'll give you a hand." With that I walked over and hopped down onto the right-hand float. Though unaware that the ignition was still on, I was always wary of props, and that was why, when I reached out, I used my left hand so my body was kept clear of it. Reaching well forward, I touched the blade. I have no recollection of actually moving it; I only remember applying pressure to it.

Moments later, when I became conscious, I was standing on the lake bottom in eight feet of frigid water! Revived by its iciness, I was immediately aware of three facts: my left side from the shoulder down was numb and paralyzed, my head was throbbing and my ears were ringing. I glanced down and noted to my surprise that my left hand and arm were still there and apparently in their normal locations. Then I remember thinking that it didn't much matter because my skull must have been shattered and I probably would be conscious for only a moment or two. However, when it dawned on me that there was no blood in front of my eyes, I reached up and touched my skull with my right hand. To my utter amazement my skull seemed to be intact! (I still have a vivid recollection of this act.)

My next realization was that, not being gill-equipped, I was literally out of my element. Obviously a return to the surface was in order. Staying close to the dock structure seemed like a wise precaution since that nasty Jacobs engine might still be running and ready to take another bite out of me.

Grasping the logs of the dock with my right hand, I pulled myself to the surface where three anxious faces greeted me—CAL pilot North Sawle, his engineer, George Wilson, and the pilot of the Waco. I was promptly fished from the water and flown to the hospital at the Con Mine, where a doctor named Stanton cared for me. Because of my heavy clothing and the fact that I had been off balance, the blow to my shoulder had not broken the skin, though it was apparent that some bone damage had occurred. This appeared to be minor at the time but it would later result in partial arm disability. My head, aside from a massive goose egg, was as good as ever or—as a slightly sarcastic friend observed—no worse than it had been.

As most members of the aviation fraternity will tell you, in encounters of this kind the propeller usually comes out the clear winner. (Yes, I know! It was my own stupid fault! I should have ensured that the switches were off!) But there were a couple of aspects to this incident that puzzled me and still do. First, a person falling into the water would not normally sink to the bottom immediately. I can only assume that my downward journey was accelerated by the prop. The other point relates to the length of time I was underwater. I had a very clear recollection of the thoughts that went through my mind. These seemed almost leisurely—I had no sense of panic. I was submerged for an appreciable length of time, and yet I realized later there had been no water in my lungs. I can only assume that the blow from the prop had briefly paralyzed my breathing apparatus and cancelled the normal automatic breathing function.

This incident slightly rearranged my career. As I was off work for a few weeks, I took a trip to Winnipeg to visit my old buddy Frank Kelly who had recently joined Trans Canada Airlines. And with a view to gaining more experience and writing my aircraft overhaul exams, I also wanted to see our Canadian Airways Brandon Avenue overhaul shops. Subsequently, I declined a TCA offer with thanks, but I did accept an offer of a transfer to our main shops and reported there in early January 1939.

During the 18-odd months that I remained there, I worked with shop foreman Albert Hutt, an expert in all mechanical matters, on the installation of an oil dilution system—the first ever in Canada—on one of our Junkers aircraft. This was a revolutionary concept of cold-weather starting for engines without pre-heating them and without draining the oil. It had been proposed earlier but we experts had always claimed it was impossible.

Fortunately, Albert's wiser head was in charge of this operation, and he soon convinced me that the concept was valid. After completing the modifications, we transferred the Junkers to the Winnipeg airport where three weeks of testing, modifying the various components, and developing a procedure ironed the bugs out of the system. On February 21, 1939, with an overnight temperature of -40°F, we were finally able to successfully cold-start a Wasp engine without applying heat and without draining and reheating the oil. For having recognized the potential of this system to the aviation industry, our highly respected superintendent of maintenance (and Aviation Hall of Fame recipient) Tommy Siers was awarded a well-deserved McKee Trophy.

There were other exciting experiences for me during this period. I was involved in the crash investigation and partial salvage of Junkers AQV in the Sioux Lookout area, a weather-induced accident with no loss of life. The crash of Junkers ARI in heavy timber in the McMurray area didn't have as fortunate an outcome. There was loss of life even though it had happened in clear weather—an accident that should not have happened. Again we were able to partially salvage the aircraft. Then between November 27 and December 20, 1939, with pilots Bill Catton and "Holly" Hollingsworth, I went on a lengthy emergency flight to Repulse Bay—66 degrees 32 minutes north latitude, just north of the Arctic Circle. As in the trip to Paulatuk, this happened at the darkest part of the winter with near blizzard conditions. It was the longest such flight in the history of the company to that time.

In the midst of all this activity I managed to take a four-week course in aerial mapping photography at CAL's survey division in Montreal. But with WWII now underway, CAL began operating a number of British Commonwealth Air Training Program (BCATP) schools for the government, and I was assigned the job of crew chief at #2 AOS Edmonton, followed by a year as maintenance superintendent at #7 AOS at Portage la Prairie. However, while the salaries and working conditions were excellent, I found the activity—or lack of it—to be monotonous, and in the spring of 1942 I arranged a transfer back to airline operations in Edmonton. That spring was a hectic and difficult time for all of us working for the airline. Canadian Pacific had just taken control of all "bush operations," their worthy goal being to amalgamate the personnel and equipment of a half-dozen companies and from this nucleus develop a modern air transport company. As well, with the war on, many of our experienced pilots and engineers, the pioneers of the 1930s, had been siphoned off into the air force. As a result, we had some personnel who, while holding the necessary licences and having the mandatory technical abilities, still lacked some of the qualities essential for the peculiar requirements of a bush operation. The odd pilot, for instance, while technically well-qualified and apparently experienced, seemed to lack the sound judgement and built-in compass that was so much a part of a good bush pilot.

I spent four years in airline operations in Edmonton before making my escape from this melee in 1946. My next four years were in Regina as chief mechanic of our Saskatchewan district, operating first with Lockheed Lodestar equipment and then with DC3s. In 1950 I went to Whitehorse as chief mechanic, Yukon district, and in 1952 was transferred to Vancouver, then CPA's headquarters, as maintenance superintendent, BC/Yukon district.

This was a period of dramatic change for all the airlines of the world, but particularly so for our company. The demands of the war had at last persuaded the federal government of the need for year-round transportation, especially for the mining industry in the north, and they had begun building airports and associated facilities. At the same time, within CPAir it was decided that as far as that company was concerned, the bush flying that had been a way of life for so many of us was at an end. Smaller companies were invited to take over these important transportation services, though now with far better equipment and facilities than had been our lot in the '30s.

With the conclusion of WWII, the well-established major carriers of the world—KLM, Air France, PanAm—had resumed service along their original routes, and they began concentrating on the introduction of the new aircraft types then coming into use, including the first of the jets. In CPAir's case, however, with no background other than our bush flying experience, we had to make enormous strides to catch up and become competitive. There were new routes to develop, a major maintenance and overhaul base to establish, field maintenance stations to staff and equip, and new personnel to be hired and trained in every department.

As growth continued within our airline, my areas of responsibility expanded accordingly. My position became that of manager, line maintenance, and by the time I retired in 1978 my office was responsible for the line maintenance activities at all our domestic and international bases—Europe,

Central/South America and Pacific/Orient. In common with many of the pilots with whom I had flown in the north, I had in my working lifetime spanned the technology from the rough-hewn aircraft of the bush flying years to the most advanced of modern airliners. But reviewing my 45-odd years in aviation, I would say that the '30s placed the greatest responsibilities on all of us as individuals. Those were the years when the equipment was untried, the facilities primitive, the terrain unmapped and mostly uninhabited, and we were largely dependent upon our own resources and efforts for the well-being of ourselves and our trusting passengers. The margins separating us from misfortune were often slim and those misfortunes frequently held the potential for disaster.

After my retirement and while I was engaged in the first of my writing efforts, I began to appreciate more fully the value of my colleagues' contributions to aviation in Canada, particularly that of Albert Hutt. After a review of the required procedures for nomination to the Aviation Hall of Fame, I prepared the papers to nominate him, obtained the support of seconders, and submitted the forms. To the collective pleasure of all those in the industry who knew him, Albert was inducted into the Hall of Fame with a citation that read: "A pioneer in the field of aircraft maintenance and engineering at a time when there was only his knowledge and integrity for guidance, his lifetime of excellence provided an example for all who followed, thus benefiting the Canadian aviation industry." Since then I have nominated two more worthy individuals to the Hall of Fame and am hopeful that they will receive similar treatment. In November 1991 I was awarded a Pioneer in Aviation Award from the Western Canadian Aviation Museum, and then in March 1997, I too was inducted into Canada's Aviation Hall of Fame.

Happily retired since 1978, I've had time to think about the extent of my good fortune. Blessed with good health, supported by a loving wife, enjoying the company and friendship of sons, daughters and grandchildren, I could not hope for or expect anything more. Coupled with this has been the comradeship of a couple of generations of friends who have also spent a lifetime working in aviation. Obviously I've had the best life has to offer.

Glossary

Aircraft: Used in either the singular or plural form to indicate one or more aircraft.

Beyond limits: In modern aviation, limits have been established by government regulatory bodies to cover most phases of flying. In bush flying the limits were self-imposed and varied from one individual to the next.

Blow pot: A gasoline-burning heater used to heat the motors in winter. Also known as a torch or a fire pot.

Booster magneto: A small, hand-powered magneto installed in the cockpits of the early aircraft. The engineer would bring the inertia starter up to the proper speed by use of the hand crank, and then the pilot would engage the starter and at the same time spin the handle of the booster magneto. This produced high voltage current that was fed to the main magnetos for distribution to the engine.

Bulldog: A biting fly about the size of a wasp that was common throughout the north. Also known as the horsefly.

Chipewyan skiff: A dory-type of craft developed by the early boat-builders at Fort Chipewyan. About 18 feet long, they were patterned after the York boats used throughout the north by the HBC fur brigades. However, the skiffs were much smaller than the York boats and had square sterns to accommodate outboard motors. Seaworthy, easily handled, and capable of carrying great loads, no finer boat exists in its class.

Choker: A method of cross-tying a rope lashing to increase the tension.

Cut line: Also known as "slash lines." Where ground surveys had taken place, straight boundaries, such as provincial borders, were indicated by lines slashed through the surrounding timber. These were an excellent aid to aerial navigation but unfortunately were non-existent in the NWT.

Cutting the throttle: The act of closing the throttle to reduce engine power output.

Deck: The "deck" might be snow, ice, trees or water. If a pilot was "down on the deck," he was flying at far less than his desired altitude.

Deck load: A term that was applied to float operations in summer. Any cargo that was too large or ungainly to fit into the cabin was lashed to the deck of the floats, and thus became "deck load."

DoT: Department of Transport—the federal government agency that controlled civil aviation. It is now the Ministry of Transport.

Down: Generally refers to flying weather—a low cloud ceiling, blizzard conditions, heavy rain. The phrase "the weather was down" would be applied to such situations.

Floats: Flotation devices made of aluminum alloy sheets and installed on the aircraft for summer operations. Each float had a flotation capacity equal to the maximum loaded weight of the aircraft.

Ground drift: Clouds of snow, driven by high winds, frequently encountered on the Arctic Coast or on large lakes. These clouds of drifting snow could obscure the terrain to such an extent that the surface (snow or ice) would be totally obscured.

Inertia starter: Inertia starters were commonly used by the early aircraft as a weight-saving measure. Electric starters required the support of generators and batteries, which were heavy and therefore cut down on the payload of the aircraft. With the inertia starter, a hand crank was applied, driving a small, heavy flywheel up to a speed of about 12–15,000 revolutions per minute. This energy, applied through a set of reduction gears, would turn the aircraft engine/propeller about three revolutions.

Inukshuk: A distinctive Inuit monument constructed of loose stones to look roughly like a man and serving as trail guides, cache markers or river crossing indicators. They were also used in quantity to aid in driving caribou toward a river ford or similar such killing spot.

Lobstick: A tree in the timber country of the north that has been pruned, leaving only a few branches in a distinctive pattern near the top. These served as trail guides, cache markers, river crossing indicators and memorials to people or events.

Making ice: The freezing process, as applied to lakes and rivers, particularly in early winter. If a cold snap developed, the expression would be something like "The temperature's dropping. It'll sure make ice tonight!"

North canoe: The standard freighting canoe of the Hudson's Bay Company prior to the use of the York boats. It was made of birch bark and about 35 feet in length.

On the step: The floats or pontoons that provided the summer footgear for our aircraft had a "break" or step on the hull bottom, dividing the float bottom into two separate planing surfaces, one forward, one aft. With sufficient speed the floats would ride or "plane" (from "hydroplane") on these surfaces, reducing the area in contact with the water. The reduced friction would allow the aircraft to increase to takeoff speed. An aircraft was "on the step" when riding on these two surfaces.

Outside: If you were leaving the north, you were "going outside."

Photographic day: For map-making purposes, aerial photography required cloudless conditions. Thus, any day that was cloudless for an extended period was known as a "photographic day."

Primer: A small, plunger-type pump installed in the cockpits of all early aircraft. These delivered small portions of gasoline under considerable pressure to some or all of the cylinders. Usually four or five applications of the primer would provide enough fuel for an engine start.

The raspberries: A slang expression from the bush flying days of the north. If you overshot your landing, or had a forced landing in "the bush," you were "down in the raspberries."

Running ice: In northern rivers, the beginning of freeze-up is indicated by small "pans" of ice drifting with the current. These increase in size and quantity as the freezing process continues. The river is then said to be "running ice."

Steamboating: If an aircraft was following a river during bad weather, it was customary to fly at tree-top level or "steamboat" along the river to get maximum visibility.

Stirrups: To anchor a rope to an ice surface, two eight-inch-deep cavities were cut into the ice about eight inches apart. A hole was then made from the bottom of each cavity to join them, and a rope end was passed through and knotted. They were used on the Arctic Coast to tie aircraft down because of the strong winds; also used as an anchor point for a hoist or tripod.

Stoneboat: A crude type of sleigh with small logs as runners and a deck of similar material, drawn by a team of horses or oxen, first used during frontier farming days to aid in clearing loose stones from fields before cultivating.

Torch gas: Unleaded gasoline for use in the blow pots.

Windmilling: Following an engine failure in flight, the forward speed of the aircraft acts upon the propeller blade surfaces, causing the propeller/engine rotation to continue.

York boat: Originally built at York Factory, the main supply depot of the Hudson's Bay Company. Staunch and seaworthy, they had three times the capacity of the canoes that they replaced.

Index